FAITH THROUGH THE PRISM OF PSYCHOLOGY

Faith Through the Prism of Psychology introduces readers to the structure and function of the inherent ability of our Self to invest objects with reality – existentialization (EXON). The author moves away from traditional ideas of existence and faith, arguing that it is an inherent ability of an individual mind to invest entities (both objective and subjective) with reality.

The book treats faith as a psychological ability of the mind to upgrade the existential statuses of imaginary entities, such as ghosts or gods; the working of faith is operationalized and analyzed in empirical psychological studies. It presents a new model of investing objects with existence, with such structural elements as the belief in object permanence (BOP), magic/ordinary distinguisher (MOD), magic/trick distinguisher (MTD), imaginary/perceived distinguisher (IPD), BOP defense mechanism (BOP/DM) and realities distinguisher (RD).

It will be essential reading for anyone interested in existence from psychology, philosophy, art, theology or psychotherapy backgrounds.

Eugene Subbotsky is Reader Emeritus at Lancaster University, UK. He is a BPS Charted Psychologist who has conducted research on moral development, metaphysical reasoning, magical thinking and consciousness.

FAITH THROUGH THE PRISM OF PSYCHOLOGY

A New Framework for Existentialism

Eugene Subbotsky

LONDON AND NEW YORK

Cover image: © Getty Images

First published 2022
by Routledge
2 Park Square, Milton Park, Abingdon, Oxon OX14 4RN

and by Routledge
605 Third Avenue, New York, NY 10158

Routledge is an imprint of the Taylor & Francis Group, an informa business

© 2022 Eugene Subbotsky

The right of Eugene Subbotsky to be identified as author of this work has been asserted by him in accordance with sections 77 and 78 of the Copyright, Designs and Patents Act 1988.

All rights reserved. No part of this book may be reprinted or reproduced or utilised in any form or by any electronic, mechanical, or other means, now known or hereafter invented, including photocopying and recording, or in any information storage or retrieval system, without permission in writing from the publishers.

Trademark notice: Product or corporate names may be trademarks or registered trademarks, and are used only for identification and explanation without intent to infringe.

British Library Cataloguing-in-Publication Data
A catalogue record for this book is available from the British Library

Library of Congress Cataloging-in-Publication Data
A catalog record has been requested for this book

ISBN: 978-1-032-11358-6 (hbk)
ISBN: 978-1-032-11357-9 (pbk)
ISBN: 978-1-003-21952-1 (ebk)

DOI: 10.4324/9781003219521

Typeset in Bembo
by MPS Limited, Dehradun

Printed in the United Kingdom
by Henry Ling Limited

CONTENTS

1 Facts we perceive, maxims we trust: Introduction   1

   1.1 Catching the uncatchable 1
   1.2 Multiple faces of existence 2
   1.3 Faith and existence 3
   1.4 The light beam of existence 4
   1.5 What we will learn: Synopsis, comparison and novelty 5
   1.6 Brief glossary 8
   List of abbreviations 9
   References 9

2 The meaning of existence   11

   2.1 Reality and illusion: What does it mean to exist? 11
   2.2 Statuses of existence 20
   2.3 Upgrading existence: Cucumbers, mermaids and Gods 21
   2.4 Emotional dimension of EXON 25
   2.5 Detecting existence in physics 28
   2.6 Conclusion: Basic and high levels of EXON 30
   References 33

3 Now it's there, now it isn't: EXON on perceived objects   35

   3.1 Existence and psychology: A sketch of history 35
   3.2 Shaping existence: BLEXON in children 37
   3.3 Tools of BLEXON: Magical versus ordinary entities 38
   3.4 Tools of BLEXON: Magic versus tricks 43

3.5 Driving licence versus own hand: HLEXON on perceived objects 50
References 51

4 Cat with a fish's tail: BLEXON on imaginary objects   53

4.1 Perceived versus imaginary: What is the difference? 53
4.2 Rabbit out of the box: Permanence of perceived and imaginary physical entities 57
4.3 Green rabbits versus flying dogs: Permanence of fantastical entities 59
4.4 An offer from the witch: Upgrading magical suggestion 64
4.5 Simulating the witch: Is an ordinary suggestion as effective as a magical one? 67
4.6 BLEXON on imaginary objects in the developmental perspective: Conclusion 69
References 71

5 Generating God   72

5.1 Does God exist? Upgrading the idea of God by external assistance 72
5.2 Upgrading the logical proof of God's existence 74
5.3 Jumping out of the mind: Children's response to the ontological argument 76
5.4 Upgrading God's existence: Adults' response to the ontological argument 78
5.5 Upgrading God's existence: Psychological HLEXON in adults 80
5.6 The HLEXON dilemma: Am I a creator or a product of God? 84
References 85

6 Faking existence   88

6.1 There is, and there isn't 88
6.2 Two kinds of magic: Unravelling the confusion 88
6.3 Imitating existence 89
6.4 Upgrading the impossible as a booster of the mind: Summary 93
References 95

7 Adjusting reality: Protecting beliefs through memory failures   96

   7.1 Belief in object permanence: The challenge 96
   7.2 Belief in object permanence: The protection 96
   References 102

8 Separating realities: The structure of EXON   104

   8.1 The realities distinguisher 104
   8.2 Magical thinking as a corrupted RD 107
   8.3 Distortions of the mind: Suspending the RD by a person with a healthy brain 110
   8.4 Hallucinations: Suspending the RD by a person with disturbed psyche 113
   8.5 Hallucinations: Suspended RD in the cultural-historical context 119
   8.6 Witchcraft: Suspending the RD by the belief in magic 120
   8.7 The voices of gods: Illusion or reality? 121
   8.8 Conclusion: The price for being conscious 122
   References 123

9 Existentializing the Self   125

   9.1 Can one's existence be a dream? Cognitive EXON on the Self 125
   9.2 The emotional tension of personal existence 131
   9.3 Self-isolation as a challenge to the 'normal Self' 132
   References 136

10 Uses of the impossible   137

    10.1 Something from nothing: Practical functions of impossible entities 137
    10.2 Impossible entities as promoters of creative imagination 138
    10.3 Impossible entities as facilitators of fantasy/reality distinction 142
    10.4 Impossible entities as inhibitors of negative BLEXON 144
    10.5 Impossible entities and education: Conclusion 146
    References 148

11 Crossing the edge: Summary   151

    11.1 Facing the void 151

11.2 Existence, faith and psychology 152
11.3 Who might benefit from this knowledge 153
References 154

Faith as an effort of will: Epilogue   *155*
Index   *159*

1
FACTS WE PERCEIVE, MAXIMS WE TRUST: INTRODUCTION

1.1 Catching the uncatchable

Existence. Is there a simpler and at the same time a vaguer term in our language?

In fact, all we can think and speak of, see and hear, feel and experience exist, but everything exists in its own way. There exists even something existence of which we deny; indeed, by saying that a flying elephant does not exist, we nevertheless have this elephant in our imagination, and therefore, make it existing.

It seems that many issues in life and in thinking bounce into the problem of defining what 'existence' really means. The great physicist Albert Einstein gave much of his creative efforts to the problem of finding the so-called unified field theory, in which it would be possible to combine gravitational and electromagnetic fields. Many times it seemed to him that he caught the elusive solution yet each time it turned out that this solution didn't match physical reality [1]. This means that the solution existed only on paper, in the form of mathematical formulas, but either it was not possible to test the solution's correctness in physical experiments, or the test led to results that refuted the theory. So, did Einstein's unified field theory exist or did it not? Of course, in some way it did, but its existence was partial, incomplete and unreliable. It still exists as a part of physics' history. In contrast, another Einstein's theory, which predicted that gravity bends light rays, was supported by subsequent observations of the position of stars near the sun during a solar eclipse [2], and such confirmation moved the prediction from the status of a hypothesis to the status of a mainstream scientific theory. In other words, the same theory that previously existed only in the imagination of a scientist, began to exist as a description of physical reality confirmed by experience.

Such 'leaps' in the status of existence we constantly observe not only in science but also in life. For instance, we might think that our bank account still has money in it, but when we try to pay in a store we find that the account is empty. This

DOI: 10.4324/9781003219521-1

disappointing discovery moves our belief in our financial credibility from the status of reality to the status of a delusion. Note that the belief in credibility did not cease to exist and will remain in our memory; all what happened to this belief after we had discovered it was wrong was that it became less important and ceased to guide our practical actions. Sometimes the opposite conversion occurs: What we have long believed to be a fallacy, suddenly turns out to be true. For example, some smokers don't believe that smoking leads to lung diseases, but when they got ill themselves the smokers change their attitude to the doctors' warnings and quit smoking. In this case, the doctors' statement about the link between smoking and lung diseases has not changed; what changed was the 'weight' of this statement on the invisible 'scale of existence' in the smoker's mind.

Sometimes we like to play hide and seek game with existence. Thus, going to the performance of a magician, we mentally anticipate the pleasure of such a game. After all, we know that such events as the emergence of a rabbit in the magician's empty hat or the resurrection of a girl who had just been cut in half by the magician's saw could never happen. But for some reason, it gives us pleasure to watch that such non-existing events are really happening. Why? Maybe because non-existing things do indeed exist in our head, in the form of the imagination. For instance, in a dream we can see a rabbit suddenly appearing from thin air, and in most cases it does not surprise us. Unlike a dream, the real world can be a rather dull place, and seeing the impossible thing happening 'for real' on the magician's stage may make this place a little more exciting.

So, what does this simple and at the same time mysterious verb 'exist' really mean? In this book, we will examine what the concept of existence means, and in what forms or 'statuses' our thoughts, images, and perceptions exist; we will investigate how we can transform existing things into illusions, and vice versa, how, with the help of faith, we can literally 'convert' non-existing things into existing ones.

1.2 Multiple faces of existence

Some philosophers say that the most important question of all times is 'Why there is something rather than nothing?' In this book, we assume that there is a question even more fundamental, namely 'What does it mean – to be?'

Indeed, when we say that something exists or doesn't exist, we implicitly assume that the verb 'to be' is clear to us, but is it? Certainly, when we say that 'nothing' exists, it exists in a different way than does 'something'. The 'something' we experience through our senses or understand via logical proofs, whereas the 'nothing' we can only name and keep in mind as a thought. On a smaller scale, we also know that there are things that exist only for a fleeting moment (e.g., a short sound or a doughnut made of smoke), whereas other things exist for centuries (e.g., buildings) or billions of years (e.g., planets and galaxies); some objects exist only for us (e.g., a night dream), whereas other we share with other people (e.g., a perceived physical object or a theory); some objects exist with the high degree of certainty (e.g., a toothache we are experiencing), whereas the existence of others requires the assistance of faith (e.g., ghosts and gods); some perceived relations between objects exist 'really and truly' (e.g., that a building is bigger than our palm), and others are illusions (e.g., our palm looking bigger than the building situated on a distance from us); some entities exist as sheer thoughts (e.g., the ideas of 'roundness' or 'triangleness'), whereas others, in order to be there, require assistance of perception (e.g., a circle or a triangle); some objects exist as observable entities (e.g., a tree in our garden), whereas others can only be inferred from observation over other objects (e.g., 'dark matter' or some elementary particles in physics).

There are multiple other ways for things to exist. Many people and even some scientists think that the verb 'existence' is a commonly accepted notion, while in reality it isn't. This potentially inexhaustible semantical content of the verb 'exist' creates multiple confusions and misunderstandings in our reasoning about the world. There are scientists that claim that God doesn't exist, but they wouldn't deny the existence of the concept of God. Likewise, believers in God hold a different view on the existence of God, but they too need to clarify the meaning they invest in the expression 'there is god'. Physical scientists don't believe in miracles while superstitious adults do, but who of them do we have to trust? Might it be the case that, due to the different meanings of the verb 'exist', both parties are right? Perhaps, in order to upgrade a certain object from the status of 'not existing' to the status of 'existing', all we need to do is to apply to this object the verb 'exist' with a different semantical and psychological filling?

1.3 Faith and existence

Whenever we think about something or do something, we always have some grounds for thinking about or doing this. We think about going to bed because we are tired, we eat because we are hungry, we write a message to a friend because we need to communicate, and so on. Our perception, memory, imagination and sensations are conditioned by certain things as well: we perceive a tree because there is such a thing in the world, we memorize a person's name because we see a person in front of us, we are imagining a horse because we are reading a novel in which a character is riding a horse...There is only one psychological faculty that is not conditioned by anything, and this faculty is faith. So, what is faith?

In his work 'De Carne Christi' (Of the Flesh of Christ) the early Christian author Tertullian (155–240 AD), wrote, "It is certain because it is impossible" – the phrase that later transmuted into the famous "I believe because it is absurd" [3]. What Tertullian had in mind was the belief in God's existence, but in essence this statement is true about any kind of faith. Indeed, if there were evidence of God's existence, the belief in God would not be necessary. But so is true regarding any belief. Although we often say, "I believe in what I see with my own eyes", we don't really need to believe in something we have available in our perceptual experience. For instance, knowledge about the law of gravitation is supported by our perception of weight, which provides us with evidence convincing enough to render the belief unnecessary. If someone is in doubt, the doubt would fast dissipate as soon as the person jumped from a chair and tried to fly in the air. *Belief* is different from *knowledge*. For knowledge, we need to *manipulate with perceptions* that we receive from the world out there. In contrast, for the belief, we need to imagine something that we can't possibly have in perception and *invest this something with existence* by the sheer effort of will. Simply put, our knowledge is conditioned by the external world, but our faith (belief) is being generated by our own Self. What it also means is that knowledge deals with things that already exist, whereas faith literally makes things appear from nothing. In other words, *faith is a manufacturer of existence.*

"And what about faith absorbed from social environment? – I hear the reader's question. – Indeed, children believe in God because their parents tell them that believing in God is the right thing to do. Isn't this kind of faith conditioned?" Yes, faith can be influenced by the environment, but this doesn't make faith an effect of an external cause. Even if your faith is influenced, it is still your faith. Not only gods and other invisible entities have to be believed into in order to exist but ordinary things around us as well. Our belief in science is a product of faith as well. Most people believe in the laws of nature not because they discovered them independently, but because their social environment told them that these laws exist.

Everyone, even the most sceptical person, has to believe in something. But what do scientists believe in? They may not believe in God, but they have to believe in their own consciousness. "I am thinking, therefore I exist" – this Cartesian maxim is the credo of scepticism, yet it demonstrates the faith in personal consciousness. Taking from this, sceptics have to believe in their perceptions of things other than themselves. If I exist, then the perceived object (e.g., the Moon I am seeing in the sky) is a part of my mind, and therefore it exists. And even if I wrongly take the Moon on the horizon for a streetlight, the wrong perception is nevertheless there. As a result, all scientific truths, even logical and mathematical ones, ascend to the basic faith of the sceptical mind – the faith in existence of personal Self.

1.4 The light beam of existence

"All roads lead to Rome" says a medieval proverb. In a similar vein, anything that exists is connected with our Self by an invisible thread. For a thing to exist, we need to be conscious of this thing as existing, and the first thing that we are conscious of is our own Self; therefrom comes the famous "I am thinking therefore I exist". It follows from this that the only thing that *exists absolutely* is our own Self. Our Self is the torch that brings forth the 'light of existence'. All things around us – this computer in front of me, the table the computer is on, the tree in the window, the bird on the tree – all of them exist only because my Self throws the light of existence on them. And the light of existence is my consciousness. Like a powerful projector, my Self (mind) illuminates the universe around me with the beam of my consciousness. Buildings and landscapes, people and animals – all what we call the universe, from the smallest quantum objects to the largest galaxies, are there because I am aware of them. After all, what is the universe if not a collection of three things: the images on my sensual organs, the texts and formulas on the paper in front of me, and the thoughts and dreams that occasionally come to my mind? *I, my own Self, both conscious and subconscious, is a necessary condition for existence of the universe.*

Sometimes we say that our perception reflects things, but this is not the case. Perception is not like a passive reflection in the mirror, it is even not like an active reflection by a scanner; in fact, it is not a reflection at all. Perception is creation, in which external stimuli (e.g., images on retina of our eyes or vibration of air at our ears) play only a certain part. Somehow our mind has a subliminal, perhaps magical, link to the 'things-as-they-are' (the Kantian 'Ding an sich'), and it is this miraculous link that, in connection with the external stimulation, allows our mind to convert external stimuli into colours, shapes and sounds. So, it is with full right that we may treat perception as creation.

The light of my Self not only illuminates things out there but also produces novel things. Languages, art, science – everything based on symbolic structures is brought to existence by the magnificent projector of my mind. In this book, we will call this projector *'existentialization'*, or *EXON* for short. Literally speaking, EXON is *bringing things to existence by being aware of them*. By definition, EXON is a basic process and cannot be reduced to other, simpler processes. Our sensation, perception, memory, thinking, volition and other psychological processes are based on EXON, but not the other way around. Nevertheless, as we will see later in this book, EXON has a structure and can be analyzed. But why do we need to study EXON?

The answer is – in order to understand and control. Understanding and taking under control are ultimate goals for studying, and studying EXON is no exception. In essence, all studying is a manipulation with consciousness. Early people noticed that round-shaped logs could roll down the hill and began to use such logs for rolling heavy objects on them. Eventually, they invented a wheel. Further, they noticed that red ochre leaves traces on the hard surfaces and invented drawing and then a symbol. Ancients noticed that when they plunge their bodies into water their bodies begin to feel lighter – and they discovered the Archimedes' law. Similarly, for a little baby to adjust the milk bottle the baby first needs to notice that the milk bottle turned to him or her with its bottom end has the nipple end at the opposite side; in the beginning, the baby becomes turning the bottle around only when a fraction of the nipple is within the baby's view, and only later he or she learns to do the same even when the nipple is completely out of view [4]. Understanding is a way to the ability of control.

Understanding EXON is the goal of this book.

1.5 What we will learn: Synopsis, comparison and novelty

In this book, we will describe the structure and functions of the inherent faculty of our mind to *invest objects with reality through being aware of them* – existentialization

(EXON). Psychological structure and functioning of EXON will be discussed and illustrated with psychological experiments. We will discuss the meaning of the concept 'existence' in detail (Chapter 2). We will see how the 'light of existence' illuminates external, perceived entities, and what components of EXON participate in this process (Chapter 3). Next, we will analyze how our Self invests existence into imagined physical objects and into fantastical entities that have no counterparts in the perceived physical world (Chapter 4). We will consider how EXON works on such unusual imagined entity as the almighty and omnipotent God (Chapter 5). We will see how EXON can be tricked by stage magicians via faking existence (Chapter 6), and how our Self 'learns' to make up for such trickery by developing special protective defence mechanisms (Chapter 7). We will discover how, as a result of this development, reality is divided into two separate realms – the realm of ordinary and superordinary reality (Chapter 8). We will examine how EXON can be 'turned on itself', and how this 'backfiring' of EXON can narrow down or expand the limits of our Self (Chapter 9). Finally, we will show that EXON can be influenced with the help of special 'psychological tools' – the Impossible Entities (IE); as a result of such influence, we can improve people's creative imagination, thinking and memory (Chapter 10). In the conclusive Chapter 11, the problems raised in the book are briefly reviewed in the context of more general philosophical and social issues, and practical applications are discussed.

Thus far, the concept of existence has been mainly managed by existentialist philosophers and psychologists. Among popular books on the topic, there are texts such as Kirk Schneider's 'The Psychology of Existence' [5], Rollo May's 'Man's Search for Himself' [6] and 'The Discovery of Being' [7], Irvin D. Yalom's 'Existential Psychotherapy' [8], Carl Rogers' 'A Way of Being' [9] and similar books that ascend to the works by J.P Sartre, Soren Kierkegaard, Karl Jaspers, Sigmund Freud and other existentially oriented thinkers. These fundamental texts illuminated many aspects of individual human existence. Nevertheless, they share a common feature – these are clinically oriented texts, centred on issues of psychiatry and psychotherapy. In these books, the concept of existence is understood in a broad philosophical sense and directly projected onto specific psychological domains, such as self-awareness, communication and the meaning of life.

The focus of this book is entirely different: The concept of existence is taken not as a general notion, but as an inherent faculty of an individual mind to invest entities (both objective and subjective) with reality. This unique faculty (which in this book is referred to as existentialization\EXON) is conceptualized as the main function of the mind, which exists along with, and in connection with, other psychological functions, such as sensation, perception, imagination, volition and memory. It is for the first time, that EXON is operationalised and subjected to rigorous experimental analysis. As a result, psychology of existence stopped being just a theoretical framework for psychotherapy and philosophy of religion and became a subject for empirical studies; at the same time, the mind, instead of being an umbrella term for other psychological faculties, found its specific faculty (EXON), with structure (the domains of reality) and function (existence attribution) of its own. Empirical studies of EXON became a separate psychological domain, similar to such traditionally studied domains as psychology of sensation, perception and memory.

Experimental studies reviewed in this book distinguished and analyzed the structural components of this fundamental psychological process. Individual and historical development of EXON were traced, and the ways of controlling EXON by special psychological manipulations (e.g., suggestion or demonstration of apparent violation of physical laws) were examined. Practical applications of the knowledge about EXON in various areas (science, art, psychotherapy, politics, commerce and education) were also discussed.

A particular form of EXON is *faith*. Traditionally, faith has been understood in the theological context, as a religious belief [10]. However, the American theologian James W. Fowler proposed that faith is a universal human ability that is involved in any human action, with religious faith being only a special kind of this ability [11]. It is this view of faith that is adopted in this book. But whereas Fowler only gives the alleged developmental description of stages of faith, similar to the stages of cognitive development described by Jean Piaget [4], experiments reviewed in this book examined *psychological mechanisms of faith as a special form of EXON*. The integral components of faith\EXON are distinguished, such as the belief in object permanence (BOP), magic\ordinary distinguisher (MOD), magic \trick distinguisher (MTD), and others. All these components are operationalized and illustrated with experimental research.

Altogether, the following new points will be advanced in this book:

1. Traditionally, the concept of existence was adopted by psychologists from existentialist philosophy and used in connection with clinical psychology and psychotherapy.

In contrast, in this book the concept of existence will be taken not as a general notion, but as an inherent faculty of an individual mind to invest entities (both objective and subjective) with reality through awareness (EXON).

2. The most popular concept of the mind adopted in psychology treats the mind as an umbrella term for sensations, perception, thinking, memory and other psychological faculties.

In contrast, in this book the mind will find a faculty of its own – EXON, which has its specific structure (the domains of reality) and function (existence attribution). Empirical studies of the mind will become a separate psychological domain, similar to such traditionally studied domains as psychology of sensation, perception and memory.

3. Traditionally, faith was understood in the theological context, as a religious belief. Even when faith was understood more broadly, as a universal human ability to invest life with meaning, it was only described 'from the third

8 Facts we perceive, maxims we trust

person point of view', by distinguishing states similar to stages of children's cognitive development.

In contrast, in this book faith will be treated as a psychological ability of the mind to upgrade or downgrade existential statuses of imaginary entities, such as ghosts or gods. The work of faith will be operationalized and analyzed by empirical psychological studies.

4. A new model of investing objects with existence through awareness (EXON) is proposed, with such structural elements as the belief in object permanence (BOP), magic\ordinary distinguisher (MOD), magic\trick distinguisher (MTD), imaginary/perceived distinguisher (IPD), BOP defence mechanism (BOP/DM) and realities distinguisher (RD). All these components and their relationships with each other will be operationalized and illustrated with experimental research.
5. For the first time, existential statuses of objects (absolute, strong, incomplete and weak) will be distinguished and applied to describe various phenomena in science, religion and psychology. The ways that our Self can upgrade or downgrade an entity's existential status will also be described and illustrated by psychological experiments.
6. Manipulations with EXON in the domains of social communication, politics, economy and education will be discussed.

1.6 Brief glossary

1. *The object of faith* – any entity within the mind: Concept (god, soul, miracle, atom and electron), statement ('this box contains pencils', 'dogs hate cats') or image (a mermaid, a dream of becoming rich).
2. *Existential status of an entity* (absolute, strong, incomplete, and weak): the degree of entity's reality in a person's mind, as measured by the entity's ability to (a) conform to the rules of EXON and (b) influence the person's behaviour.
3. *Existentialization (EXON for short)* – a person's ability to invest an entity with an existential status through awareness.
4. *Quality of EXON*: positive (upgrading) vs negative (downgrading).
5. *Types of positive EXON*: Internal (via personal effort of will or self-suggestion) and external (via perception or suggestion).
6. *Faith*: the internal positive EXON.
7. *Personally significant imaginary entity* : A person's future life, future lives of those close to the individual, the future of personally significant environments (e.g., a house, a homeland, the planet), and other imagined events closely related to an individual's health and well-being.
8. Possible entity: En entity that can exist as a perceived phenomenon, which conforms to the known laws of nature and can't be influenced by the observer's direct mental effort.

List of abbreviations

BLEXON	basic level of existentialization
BONP	belief in object non-permanence
BOP	belief in object permanence
CSESE	cognitively strong emotionally strong entity (entities)
CSEWE	cognitively strong emotionally weak entity (entities)
CWESE	cognitively weak emotionally strong entity (entities)
EXON	existentialization
EXUP	existential upgrade
HLEXON	high level of existentialization
IE	incomplete entity (entities): an entity or entities with incomplete existential status
IMPE	impossible entity (entities)
IPD	imagined/perceived distinguisher
MOD	magic/ordinary distinguisher
MTD	magic/trick distinguisher
NPE	non-permanent entity (entities) (an entity or entities that violates the OP demands)
OP	object permanence
OR	ordinary reality
PE	possible entity
PME	permanent entity (entities): (an entity or entities that conforms to the OP demands)
PNE	personally not-significant entity (entities)
PNIME	personally not-significant imaginary entity (entities)
PSE	personally significant entity (entities)
PSIME	personally significant imaginary entity (entities)
RC	rational construction
RD	realities distinguisher
SE	strong entity (entities): an entity or entities with strong existential status
SOR	superordinary reality
SUI	state of upgraded impossible
WE	weak entity (entities): an entity or entities with weak existential status

Those who are curious about how Nothingness turns into Being and how Being plunges into the depths of Nothingness – this book is for you.
Welcome to 'Existence Workshop'!

References

[1] Berkovitch, E. (2020). Tragedia Einsteina, ili schastliviy Sizif. *Nauka I zhizn'*, 1, 40–48.
[2] Siegfried, T. (2015). Einstein's genius changed science's perception of gravity. *Science News*. https://www.sciencenews.org/article/einsteins-genius-changed-sciences-perception-gravity

[3] Harrison, P. (2017). "I Believe Because it is Absurd": The enlightenment invention of Tertullian's Credo. *Church History*, 86, 2, 339–364.
[4] Piaget, J. (1954). *The construction of reality in the child*. Routledge and Kegan Paul. Ltd.
[5] Schneider, K (2012). *The psychology of Existence*. McGraw Hill.
[6] May, R. (2012). *Man's search for himself*. W.W. Norton & Co.
[7] May, R. (2012). *The discovery of being*. W.W. Norton & Co.
[8] Irvin D. & Yalom, I. D. (1980). *Existential psychotherapy*. Basic Books.
[9] Carl Rogers, C. (1980). *A way of being*. Houghton Mifflin.
[10] Astley J. (2009). The psychology of faith development. In: de Souza M., Francis L.J., O'Higgins-Norman J., Scott D. (eds), *International handbooks of religion and education*, vol 3. Springer. 10.1007/978-1-4020-9018-9_13
[11] Fowler, J. W. (1995). *Stages of faith: The psychology of human development and the quest for meaning*. Bravo Ltd.

2
THE MEANING OF EXISTENCE

2.1 Reality and illusion: What does it mean to exist?

In the perspective of EXON theory, we can understand existence only on the basis of our own experience. For a person to exist is to be aware of his or her own existence. When we are asleep without dreams or in the state of general anaesthetics, we don't ask whether we exist or not and learn about our existence retrospectively when we recover our waking state and remember the nearest past; alternatively, we are told about our existence in the unconscious state by someone (e.g., a doctor) who had observed us in the state of unconsciousness. As for inanimate objects, for them to exist means 'to exist for us'. Those things we don't know about and cannot think about don't really exist.

Indeed, is there anything beyond the eggshell of the mind? Or are even such fundamental concepts as God or absolute truth the prisoners of my mind? When we are talking about whether God or absolute truth exist, what we really mean is the concept of absolute existence. But what is absolute existence? By definition, a thing exists absolutely if it is unrelated to any other thing, including me and my mind. But the expression 'something (e.g., God or truth) has absolute existence' is inherently contradictive, because I generate this expression, therefore, it is conditioned by my mind. From this, it follows that the existence of any object beside my own Self is always relative and not absolute. Not a single thing can exist absolutely and independently from the subject who is talking (thinking) about existence. Even the concept of Nothing obtains existence (and sometimes even takes a variety of forms) only when we direct our consciousness onto the idea of Nothingness [1]. When we discount a thought or a perceived object from the status of *reality* down to the status of an *illusion*, the thought or the perceived object doesn't cease to exist, but only changes its existential status, becomes, so to speak, 'less important' for us. So, it appears that God and truth – all exist within our

DOI: 10.4324/9781003219521-2

mind. But their existential statuses can vary. So, what statuses does our EXON attribute to different entities?

Entities that we accept as most certainly 'real' are subjective experiences we perceive. Philosophes call such subjective experiences *phenomena*.

As we argued in previous publications, in order to meet the definition of a phenomenon, our subjective experience has to meet four basic criteria, with the first of them being *identity*. Identity means that the subjective experience has some features that make the phenomenon a unique entity so that this particular experience is distinct from other experiences. Accordingly, each phenomenon conserves its identity and is not influenced by other phenomena for as long as it exists in our mind. Like other fundamental criteria, identity can only be registered in degrees. Thus, it is impossible to find two identical persons, but two atoms of hydrogen are almost identical, yet still have a unique property that makes them different from each other – their location in space/time.

Linked to identity is the requirement of *permanence*. This property requires that a subjective experience maintains its identity throughout a certain period of time and cannot instantly change into another subjective experience. One more general requirement is *locality*. To be counted as a phenomenon a subjective experience needs to possess a certain amount of solidity, which prevents the phenomena from merging with each other. According to this property, a solid object (e.g., a bullet) cannot permeate another solid object (e.g., a human body) without causing destruction in it. The implication of locality property accepted in modern physics is that one object can act on another object only via one of the four known physical forces (gravitation, electromagnetic field, strong and weak nuclear forces), because be it otherwise, the two objects would merge into one. Finally, the last general requirement for a phenomenon is *inclusion*. According to this property, every phenomenon is included in some preceding phenomena, emerges from its predecessors and having lived for a certain amount of time, turns into some other phenomena.

Although phenomena are subjective experiences, they are, nevertheless, independent from the sheer effort of our mind. We can change the perceived size of a building by approaching towards it, but we cannot make it disappear or change shape by solely thinking of it or wishing this to happen. This means that besides the effort of our conscious Self to perceive this object there is something behind the object that makes a certain contribution into the entity we perceive. Immanuel Kant called this 'something' a *'thing-in-itself'*. We are unable to perceive the thing-in-itself, but the thing-in-itself makes a contribution into objects that we perceive, and it is this contribution that makes perceived entities largely independent of our conscious Self, but only to an extent. Because we can only get access to these entities by converting them into our *subjective experiences* (qualia), things-in-themselves are 'translated' into the 'language of the mind'. In other words, phenomena result from the merger of two opposite factors: The impact of things-in-themselves, and the fabric of the subjective screen of our Self that converts the impact of things-in-themselves into perceived entities (Figure 2.1). Looking a little ahead, it is important

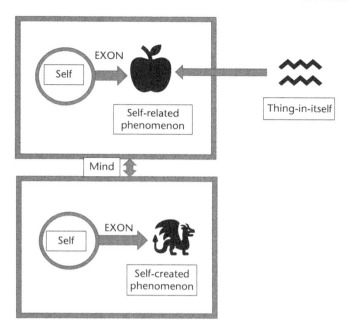

FIGURE 2.1 The relations between Self, Things-in-themselves, Self-related and Self-created phenomena, and EXON

to note here that the link between a phenomenon and the thing-in-itself is not a causal but representational; the phenomenon represents the thing-in-itself like a track in the detector screen represents an invisible quantum particle that had left the track, but the track even remotely doesn't look like the particle or have the particle's physical properties.

Because phenomena of this kind are *only partially created by our Self*, let us call such phenomena *Self-related*. Self-related phenomena we usually call 'matter' or 'real things'. One can say that our Self attributes existence to these phenomena by illuminating things-in-themselves by its beam of EXON, which is a spontaneous involuntary process. It is impossible to tell whether things-in-themselves existed 'before' they are being illuminated by EXON or emerge at the very moment of the illumination; all we can say is that phenomena which are connected with things-in-themselves cannot appear or disappear on a whim of our will.

A typical error scientists make when describing Self-related phenomena is assuming that physical objects or the laws of nature are independent from an observer. What is missing in this assumption is the understanding that the observer - our Self (mind) - is not a homogeneous entity but includes various modes of subjectivity, such as perception, memory, thinking, imagination and voluntary action. A typical physical object or a law of nature are indeed independent from a voluntary effort of our mind, but they are dependent from our perception and memory. Indeed, I cannot create or destroy a galaxy or a law of nature by a single effort of my mind, but if I don't have any subjective experience of the galaxy or the law of nature via perception, thinking or imagination, or completely lose my memories about them, they don't exist or cease to exist in my personal universe, and as a consequence, in the physical universe as well (see [2] for more on the connection between personal and physical universes). For the Self-related phenomena to exist they must be illuminated by the beam of EXON.

Apart from meeting formal requirements for phenomena (identity, permanence, locality and inclusion), Self-related phenomena possess three additional properties. One of these properties – *independence from the conscious efforts of the mind* - has already been mentioned. Another property is *intersubjectivity*: the Self-related object (e.g., an apple on the table in front of our eyes) is experienced not only by my Self but by other people as well. Finally, the third property of Self-related phenomena is *intermodality*, which means that a phenomenon can be experienced by all accessible senses at one time. For example, if I see an i-phone lying on the table and ringing, I can also take the i-phone in my hands, feel its weight, consistency and temperature. Based on these properties, EXON attributes to Self-related phenomena the property of *externality* – the ability to exist *individually outside our mind*. Usually, we call this attribution *the belief that the objects are there*.

Self-related phenomena can be contrasted with *Self-created experiences* – those that are a sheer product of our mind. Unlike Self-related phenomena, *Self-created experiences* don't have a support of things-in-themselves, and don't have to meet the requirements and properties listed for the Self-related phenomena. Nevertheless, when Self-created *experiences* meet some of the requirements for Self-related phenomena, they become Self-created *entities*. Unlike a pure Self-created experience (e.g., mood), Self-created entities meet the requirements such as identity and locality. For example, I can imagine a fantastical animal by conflating parts of existing animals (e.g., a mermaid), or producing an alien animal that has nothing to do with any of the animals on earth; finally, I can wipe the creature out of my mind by switching to thinking about something entirely different. My fantasies and night dreams mostly contain this kind of Self-created entity (see Figure 2.1).

A special sub-class of Self-created entities are *representing phenomena* – phenomena that represent, or symbolically stand for, Self-related phenomena: symbols and signs, including spoken and written languages, digital codes, numbers, theories, schemes, pictures and mathematical equations. For example, an apple that we are eating at the moment is a Self-related phenomenon – a 'real thing' that 'presents itself'; in contrast, a picture, a name or a photograph of the apple is a representing phenomenon. A book about birds represents real birds, but the book itself can be represented in the form of a summary, which is a 'representation of a representation'. Some of these representing phenomena, such as photographic images, proper names, schemes and blueprints of individual objects and processes, represent individual phenomena - this particular person, this particular tree or this particular mountain. Other representing phenomena represent general concepts via words, schemes or descriptions. For example, the feline family can be represented by the spoken or written word 'cats'.

A sub-class of representing phenomena are *simulating phenomena*. Simulating phenomena are Self-related phenomena artificially converted into Self-created ones. For example, simulating phenomena are fictional stories and virtual reality (e.g., movies or computer simulations), which do not represent real events but simulate them. Art is a version of EXON that specializes into such conversion. In classic art, ordinary Self-related phenomena are simulated in paintings and sculptures, and in modern art mundane everyday phenomenal objects are invested with the meaning of representing phenomena. Examples of classic art simulations are ancient Greek sculptures and Madonna's of the Renaissance paintings, and examples of modern art can be Marcel Dushamp's readymade sculpture 'Fontaine' (a urinal presented in a museum as a piece of art) or paintings by Andy Warhol 'Campbells' Soup Cans'. Fiction books, theatre performances and movies belong to this subclass as well. To prevent the viewer from taking created events for real ones, authors of movies and books specially mention that the events portrayed in the presentation have been made up and do not represent real events.

One more subclass of Self-created entities are *hallucinatory phenomena*. Usually, hallucinations are defined as deceptive phenomena, which seem real but don't really exist [3]. This means that hallucinatory phenomena, despite they are created by our imagination, wrongly assume the status of Self-related phenomena: They meet the criteria of identity and independence from the mind but do not meet the other criteria. In other words, a hallucinatory phenomenon (e.g., an animal in front of us) cannot be changed by the effort of our mind, but this phenomenon cannot be touched (or disappears when touched) and is not experienced by other people. Finally, *illusory phenomena* (e.g., a perceptual illusion) is another kind of Self-created entity, which, unlike hallucinatory phenomena, meets the criteria of permanence, locality and intermodality. The types of subjective experiences as a function of requirements and properties for phenomena are summarised in Table 2.1.

Because Self-related phenomena do not depend on our voluntary efforts, they are significantly more stable and permanent than Self-created entities. Still, even Self-related phenomena have a considerable degree of instability: We are unable to perceive a physical object twice from exactly the same position, and the objects' shapes constantly change. For example, my house takes different shapes depending on whether I am outside or inside the house. In order to take the unstable and ever-changing nature of phenomena under control, we create *rational constructions* (RC), by applying certain standard procedures (comparisons, measurements and symbolic designation) to a bunch of related phenomena. RC include scientific concepts, schemes, blueprints and other symbolic representations of phenomena. Whereas Self-related phenomena exist because our conscious Self, teamed with things-in-themself, makes them exist via perception, RC are created by our thinking. For example, we can observe multiple pictures of various breeds of cats by just googling the words 'cats images', yet all these diverse creatures share the same RC (feline), which accumulates all our knowledge about this kind of animal: their shape, origin, biological structure and behaviour.

16 The meaning of existence

TABLE 2.1 Relations between *Type of subjective experience* and *Criteria and Properties* of Self-related phenomena

Type of subjective experience Criteria and properties	Self-related Phenomena	Mood	Mental image	Representing phenomena	Simulating phenomena	Hallucinatory phenomena	Illusory phenomena
Identity	v			v	v	v	v
Permanence	v		v	v	v	v	v
Locality	v		v	v	v	v	
Inclusion	v						
Mind-independence	v	v			v	v	v
Intermodality	v						
Intersubjectivity	v			v	v		v

Finally, our Self creates a *mental image* of a Self-related phenomenon, which is a sheer mental entity. Mental images include Self-created entities, but also images that are supported by corresponding phenomena and/or RC. For example, we can see a butterfly sitting on a flower (phenomenon), we have the sum of knowledge about this kind of insect accumulated by biological science (RC), and we can imagine a butterfly sitting on a flower after the butterfly is gone (mental image). As a result, entities can be presented in our mind in three different *modes* – as a phenomenon, RC and mental images (see Figure 2.2).

The relation between the phenomenon and its mental image is hierarchical. The phenomenon has an existential advantage over the image, because every phenomenon can be presented as an image (i.e., imagined, photographed or filmed). On the other hand, not every image can be given a matching phenomenon, since the class of mental images includes fantastical Self-created entities (see Figure 2.3).

The relation between mental image and its matching RC is hierarchical too, with the RC having an existential primacy over the image. Indeed, every RC can be converted into some kind of image, but not every image can be provided with a matching rational construction. For example, a mathematical equation, such as a famous $E = mc^2$, can be converted into an image, such as a nuclear blast or a nuclear power station. On the other hand, models of a perpetual motion machine can be imagined, however, an RC of such a machine cannot be built, for building such an RC is prohibited by the fundamental physical law of energy conservation (Figure 2.4).

Finally, the relation between a phenomenon and its RCs is not hierarchical. Not every phenomenon can be provided with some kind of RC. Thus, the

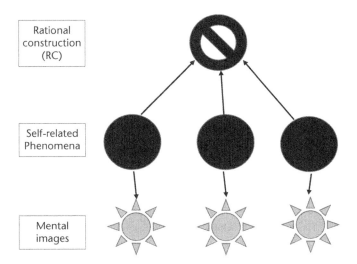

FIGURE 2.2 The relations between Self-related phenomena, their Mental images and their Rational construction (RC).

18 The meaning of existence

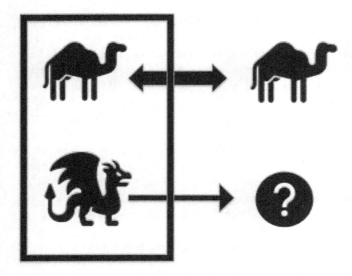

FIGURE 2.3 The relation between Mental images (left) and their related Phenomena (right): Some Mental images don't have related phenomena, but all Phenomena can be represented as Mental images

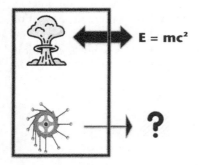

FIGURE 2.4 Figure 2.4 The relation between Mental images (left) and their related RC (right): Some Mental images don't have related RC, but all RC can be represented as Mental images

phenomenon of a voluntary movement or the effect of a thought on the EEG of the brain cannot be rationally explained. Unidentified flying objects (UFO) don't have rational explanations as well. Similarly, not every RC is a result of comparison between related phenomena. For example, the RC for infinity can be shown an equation $\sum_{n=1}^{\infty}$) and a mental image ∞, but not as a phenomenon accessible to our senses (see Figure 2.5).

The relations between mental images, mental images that have matching phenomena, mental images that have matching RC and mental images that have matching phenomena and RC are shown in Figure 2.6. In the following chapters,

The meaning of existence   19

FIGURE 2.5 The relations between Phenomena (top) and their related RC (bottom): Some Phenomena don't have related RC, and vice versa, some RC don't have related Phenomena

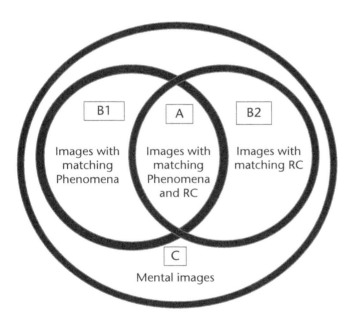

FIGURE 2.6 The relations between Mental images (C), Images with matching Phenomena (B1), Images with matching RC (B2), and Images with matching Phenomena and RC (A)

by physical entities (objects) entities (objects) will be understood that are included in Section A, whereas entities (objects) covered by Sections C, B1 and B2 will be referred to as mental entities (objects). Although RC, like an image or a phenomenon, is a mental construction as well, it is a result of a complex effort of measurements, comparisons and logical thinking, which, in combination with raw phenomena and images, solidifies into *science generated objects*. Whereas psychology mostly operates with phenomena and images, physical sciences deal with science-generated objects.

Now we are equipped enough in order to have a closer look at the statuses of existence.

2.2 Statuses of existence

As argued above, there are three modes an entity can be present in my mind: *a phenomenon* (a perceptual image of the computer which I am typing this text on), *a mental image* (the computer that remains in my memory when I close my eyes), and *an RC* (my knowledge of what a computer is, how it functions and how it emerged). Depending on availability of these modes, and on their combination, an entity can be attributed *an existential status in my mind*. An entity's existential status is linked to *the degree to which my Self participates in the creation of and maintaining the entity*. On a most general scale, there can be *zero, minimal, moderate, strong and maximal degree* of my Self's involvement in the entity's existential status.

As Descartes famously argued, the question whether I exist is circular, which simply confirms the old Greek's idea that *thinking and existence are the same*. Because my existence and my Self are one and the same thing, I don't have to make any efforts for my Self to exist. In formal terms, this means that my conscious Self's input into maintaining its existence is *zero*. From this, it follows that my Self has the highest *absolute existential status*, whereas all other entities have to 'borrow' their existence from my Self.

Next in the hierarchy is the *strong existential status,* which is attributed by my Self to entities that are present as phenomena, mental images and rational constructions, and *all the three forms match* (Figure 2.6, section A). Usually, we call such entities *physical objects*. Thus, I am seeing a computer I am typing this text on (phenomenon), can have it in my visual memory (mental image) and know what a computer is (RC). Similarly, a scientific theory (RC) which is supported by empirical observation of phenomena has a strong existential status as well. For example, Einstein's theory of the mass/energy equivalence can be presented as an RC (e.g., the equation $E = mc^2$), supported by the phenomenon of radioactive decay (e.g., by looking at the display of a Geiger counter), and converted into a mental image (e.g., an image of the mushroom cloud that appears after the explosion of an atomic bomb) [4]. The degree to which my voluntary effort is involved in maintaining the existence of an entity with a strong existential status is *minimal*. The only difference between absolute and strong existential statuses is that regarding an object with the strong existential status my Self still has to decide whether that object exists as true reality and is not an illusion or a hallucination.

Further, let us say that an entity has *incomplete existential status* if the entity lacks one or two of the modes (Figure 2.6, sections B1 and B2). Thus, we can have a memory of our late relatives (mental image), and know who they were (RC), but can no longer see them in flesh (a phenomenon). Some real phenomena can be represented as mental images but don't have corresponding rational constructions. For example, we don't have a rational explanation for a voluntary movement – how our intention to move our hand, which is an action that doesn't exist in space, moves our hand, which is an object that occupies physical space. In psychology, psi-phenomenon is occasionally supported by experiments, but it doesn't conform to the demand of complete replicability, and its RC can't be built [5]. Unidentified flying objects (UFO) come under this class of unexplained phenomena as well. Other entities such as the Big Bang [6], quantum entanglement [7] and the concepts of dark matter and dark energy in cosmology [8] [9] exist in the modes of RC and mental symbolic images, but don't have matching phenomena. Unproven theories and abstract logical systems (e.g., possible worlds in modal logic [10]) also can be listed in the domain of entities with incomplete existential status.

In creating and maintaining such entities my Self is involved to a *moderate degree*: It requires more effort from my Self to maintain such entities in my mind, because my Self doesn't have a support from phenomena or objects-in-themselves, or/and has to constantly overcome the logical contradictions between various modes of existence. Nevertheless, an entity with incomplete existential status has some support in memory (e.g., a memory of a late person) or is indirectly linked to Self-related phenomena (e.g., traces of the Big Bang or dark energy in the existing physical universe). The unproven scientific theory or an abstract logical world has some support in the possibility for these systems to find a phenomenalistic representation in the future.

The *weak existential status* can be attributed to entities that are present in our imagination as pure created forms (Figure 2.6, section C). Such forms are represented symbolically as mental images or representing phenomena (e.g., pictures or movie characters) but they don't have corresponding phenomena and rational constructions. Fantastical entities, such as mermaids and ghosts, can be described or drawn, but there is no evidence that they could ever be observed and science doesn't have knowledge about such creatures. Internally contradictive logical systems and impossible images (e.g., the perpetual motion machine) belong to this domain as well. When we speak about weak objects, we usually say that such objects don't exist, or that their existence is impossible (see, for example, an 'impossible triangle' [11]). Maintaining such entities in our mind requires a *strong degree* of conscious effort of our Self since such entities lack any support in other forms of representation. Indeed, a rational construction is made via comparing and measuring phenomena, and how can you do such procedures for a ghost or a fairy?

However, things become more complicated when we speak of an existential status of special entities. One of such special entities is the entity we call God.

2.3 Upgrading existence: Cucumbers, mermaids and Gods

What did Rene Descartes mean when he wrote that God exists necessarily outside my imagination because God is perfect and being perfect includes existence? In terms of the EXON theory, what he meant was that God, despite being present in our minds only as an RC (a concept of an entity which possesses all possible virtues: omnipotence, omnipresence, etc.) has nevertheless a strong existential status. When I am thinking of any *contingent entity* (e.g., a cucumber or a mermaid), this object can have or don't have a strong existential status, depending on whether I can (a cucumber) or cannot (a mermaid) find a bunch of corresponding phenomena for it and create the object's RC on the basis of these phenomena. But when it goes about my thinking about God, this logic fails, since God's RC by definition contains God's mental image and God's phenomenon within itself. But how can that be?

Indeed, in a contingent entity the entity's RC (concept) is always derivative of the entity's phenomena. For example, a cucumber's RC comes from us studying the appearance, taste and genetic origins of the perceived vegetable, and a mermaid's mental image is created by our mind via a combination of parts of different mental images (i.e., of a girl and a fish). However, in the case of the *perfect entity* – God – the relations between RC and phenomenon are *reversed*. For God, its RC inherently contains God's ability to exist outside of my mind (as a phenomenon) and inside my mind (as a mental image). But because the concept of God is still an entity within my mind, this is a logically *impossible entity*, because God must exist outside my mind while being my mind's creation. In order to think about an entity which is logically impossible, a person has to make a special effort of EXON – the effort of faith.

"Hold on – a reader might say – but god is not the only entity which I cannot perceive. And how about objects that existed but disappeared before I was born? Or about the part of physical universe that exists today, but which is beyond my 'event horizon' – a region in spacetime beyond which events cannot affect an outside observer [12]?"

Indeed, if we admit that the world existed before the conscious observer (time) and beyond the event horizon (space), we have to part with the very idea of the mind/world unity; instead, my mind becomes an event in the temporal chain of events, such as the Big Bang, the formation of Earth, the emergence of life, the raise of the humankind, the history of my country, my family and my own birth. The alternative is, that all the history before my mind and cosmos beyond the event horizon is a construction of my mind.

But what for does my mind need this monumental 'scaffolding' in the form of history? Obviously, it needs history in order to make sense of itself, to extend itself in time (backwards and forwards) and space (beyond the edge of the observable cosmos). Indeed, according to Kant, time, space and causality are not entities that are external to my mind, rather they are 'a-priori' forms in which the world is given to my Self. Being *a-priory* (i.e., prior to experience) means that these forms are inherent to my mind, whereas what we usually call physical space and time are rational constructions built on the basis of phenomena illuminated by our EXON. But if this is true, then it is only natural (and necessary) that I do not limit myself with the intervals of time and space of my closest environment but want to extend this interval forwards into the hypothetical future and backwards into the hypothetical past. Similarly, I am not happy to just observe the chaotic interplay of phenomena in my mind but want to put them in order, through the cause-effect relations. Like space, time and causality, the need for the extension is given to me 'a-priori'.

Now, we can see that the entities like the concept of God and the concepts of 'the world before me' and 'the world beyond my horizon' have something in common: They are necessary (because the mind is built in such a way that these ideas are a constituent part of the mind, like wings are a constituent part of a bird) and unobservable. This means that these entities are sheer products of my mind and do not correspond to any perceived phenomena. In philosophy, entities like that are called *transcendental objects*. Some of the transcendental objects (e.g., mermaids, dragons or angels) remain solely imaginary, but others I upgrade to the status of really existing entities by making a special effort, and this effort is *the effort of faith*. The effort of faith is therefore literally 'pumping existence into an imaginary thing", or the effort of *existence upgrade* (*EXUP* for short).

So, by creating history and cosmos beyond my horizon I commit the acts of EXUP. Another object for EXUP is the mind of other living entities, such as a bat, an elephant or a person. Indeed, minds of other living creatures are transcendental entities: they are as inaccessible to my senses as the world before me or beyond my horizon, and yet I have to live among and communicate with these entities. In order to be able to do this, I begin to believe that other entities have minds similar to my own, and although I cannot perceive their minds, they nevertheless have a strong existential status – they 'really exist'.

It is important to bear in mind that EXUP of transcendental entities doesn't mean that I am able to control these entities. We know that even in our immediate perceived environment most of our internal (the works of our organism or our thinking and dreams) and external (the perceived world of inanimate and animated objects) reality is independent of our conscious efforts, and so are transcendental entities and events. Transcendental entities are created by our imagination and existentially upgraded by faith, and yet they are independent of our voluntary efforts, in the sense that we cannot control transcendental entities on our whim.

To summarise, we established that psychologically for something to exist means to be present in my mind, but the entities vary in terms of the degree of such presence: Some of them (e.g., houses and trees) are present in my mind in all of the possible three modes (i.e., perception, imagination and thinking), others (e.g., mermaids and ghosts) exist only in my imagination, still others are upgraded from purely conceptual (God) or imaginary (the world in the past or in the future, other living entities' minds) to really existing entities (see Figure 2.7).

The question arises *how is it possible that our EXON works in contradiction with itself, by giving a strong existential status to an existentially weak entity (i.e., the concept of the almighty God)?*

Indeed, the concept of the almighty and benevolent God is still a created intellectual form, in which some features of my Self (e.g. being a conscious subject capable of self-reflection and creative power) are exponentiated ad infinitum. An

24 The meaning of existence

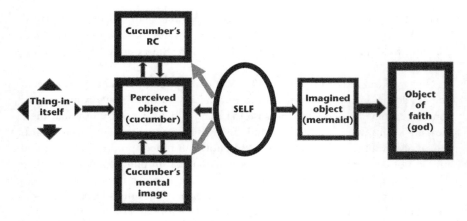

FIGURE 2.7 Relationships between the Self, Perceived objects, Imagined objects and Objects of faith

entity like that has unlimited power, unlimited compassion, and unlimited knowledge. This created form is maximally perfect, which, according to Cambridge Dictionary, means to be 'complete and correct in every way, of the best possible type or without fault' [13]. However, is attributing God with such qualities sufficient in order to make its existential status absolute or, at least, strong?

In the context of the formal definition of what a strong existential status involves, the answer is 'No', because God is not presented to my Self as a phenomenon. Of course, I can assume that God is presented phenomenologically through all the phenomena I have in the world (e.g., God is embodied in galaxies, plants, animals and people), but an entity like that doesn't meet important requirements for a Self-related entity - personal identity and locality (see Table 2.1). In regard to the absolute existential status, God can't have it because the question about God's existence is not circular; unlike my own Self, God is a created form and its presence in my mind is not self-evident. One possible way to attribute God with absolute existence is to identify God with my Self, but then I run into a conundrum: a form created by my mind is greater than my mind and includes my mind (my Self) as a part. Finally, attributing a created form with perfectness is logically impossible, because perfectness includes independence of my Self, and any created form by definition is derivative from my Self's creative activity. Either way, it is impossible to upgrade the weak existential status of God by means of *sheer logic*. But is it possible to make God a really existing entity by the *effort of feelings*? Our Self's ability to upgrade existence (EXUP) suggests that it is.

In fact, a simple observation shows that an entity can have a diminished existential status in our mind, and yet affect our behaviour to a greater extent than an object with the strong existential status. Thus, our late parents may have a stronger impact on our life than living strangers, we might prefer eating unhealthy but tasty food to eating a healthy one, and a flattering lie may create in us positive feeling towards the person to a greater extent than the uncompromising truth. In other words, EXON works not only *through our cognitive mind* but also *through our emotions*. With cognitive existential statuses being equal, those objects that have strong appeal to our needs and feelings have a greater existential status than the objects that don't have such appeal. This can explain the apparent paradox: The invisible God, with its weak existential status in our cognitive mind, can have a stronger existential status in our life than entities that can be perceived by our senses. In Chapter 5 experiments will be reviewed that examined in detail how the idea of an almighty subject can be upgraded in its existential status.

Indeed, the fundamental needs of our Self include the need for survival, which can be further reduced to such needs as avoiding pain and anxiety, being in good health, and postponing or avoiding death. A created form that appeals to these needs would have an existential status greater than the form that doesn't, and God is the mental form created exactly for helping us to survive. Historically, in order to combat the fear of personal death, people created the idea of *a spirit* that leaves the body after death and proceeds into the invisible world of the supernatural. Spirits of dead relatives were our first gods. Gradually, they coagulated and merged into the image of a single God – the creator and keeper of the universe and a personal guide to our individual life. Not only God is an assistant in our earthly life, but he also promises the eternal life – life after death. That is why, with all the logical weaknesses and inconsistencies of the Biblical narratives, the Biblical God possesses an existential status that for most people of the past centuries (and for many rational people today) exceeds the existential status of ordinary everyday objects. Cognitively weak, the invisible God is emotionally powerful and influential in the lives of believers. In upgrading the idea of God through faith, our Self inflates this entity with existence via EXUP. This means, that in faith our Self is involved to a *maximal degree*. Remember that almighty God is a logically impossible entity: It has to exist beyond our mind in spite of being a creation of our mind. But in order to upgrade the cognitively impossible entity to the status of an absolute entity, the *cognitive dimension of EXON* is not enough.

This makes us, along with the cognitive dimension of EXON, introduce the *EXON's emotional dimension*.

2.4 Emotional dimension of EXON

By definition, EXON is a creative effort of my Self, the quality of existence emanating from the depths of my mind, and because of this EXON is necessarily personally and individually coloured. In other words, any object that my Self certifies as existing necessarily bears the 'scent' of my emotional attitude towards this object, the attitude that is rooted in the history of my life, my needs, my moods, my plans for the future and all the multiple hues and features that I call my Self. This impossibility to draw a hard line between cognitive and emotional content of EXON can be seen even in a simple perception. We don't just see colours, we see colours that are warm or cold, emotionally dark or light; we don't impartially register sounds, we hear sounds that are clear and pleasant, or nasty and threatening. This emotional perception of things reaches its peak in the psychological condition of synaesthesia [14]. The emotional colouring of EXON covers virtually all of our personal universe, from simple sensation to our perception of galaxies and social structures. To summarize, EXON makes reality emotionally saturated and, to an extent, mythical [15]. It is only with some effort of our abstract thinking that we can separate cognitive content of EXON from its emotional content.

Nevertheless, having accomplished the above separation we can see that objects vary on the scale of emotional saturation. Entities that have identical cognitive existential statuses may differ on the scale of emotional dimension. Some objects evoke in me the acute feeling of personal presence in this world, which is manifested through strong positive of negative emotions and appropriate behaviours. These kinds of entities are hard to separate from my Self; there is the feeling that these entities are part of my Self. We will refer to these kinds of entities as to *personally significant entities (PSE)*. Speaking in terms of the degree of existence, PSE have a strong existential status on the EXON's emotional dimension. In contrast, there are entities that don't evoke strong feelings in my Self, and, as a result, have little effect on my behaviour. With entities of this kind, my Self is not personally involved. Let us call these kinds of entities personally non-significant entities (PNE). PNE have a weak emotional status on the EXON's emotional dimension.

For example, a death of a human being cognitively has the same existential status for me independently of who actually died, as long as I know what death means. However, the death of a close person would affect my being to a greater extent than the death of a stranger; thus, the former event has a stronger status on EXON's emotional dimension than has the latter. Similarly, gods in which I believe would have a stronger emotional value for me than gods of other religions, despite the fact that any god is invisible and thus has a weak existential statuses on EXON's cognitive dimension. Fantastical entities, such as angels, witches, ghosts and mermaids belong to the same category with mixed existential statuses. On EXON's cognitive dimension, these entities have a weak existential status as they are purely imaginary. On EXON's emotional dimension, however, such entities have a strong existential status; indeed, such entities can give us a fright in our dreams or in movies or bring us pleasure when we read about them in books and fairy tales, we might even believe in them, and this makes these supernatural entities attention-grabbing and emotionally saturated.

Sometimes ordinary concepts and images become existentially strong because we emotionally upgrade them. For example, we emotionally upgrade the image of the world as it existed before and after me being in this world. As argued in the previous section, it is impossible to think about the world without us, like it is meaningless to think about an object without a subject. Because of this, the world without me has a weak existential status on the EXON's cognitive dimension as it lacks the most important representing mode – the phenomenal presence. Yet, it is emotionally comforting to think that my family, my country, and the universe were present before me coming into this world; I believe that my children will survive me, and I believe that the books I write would serve a modest service to people after my death. This makes the world without me an existentially strong entity on the EXON's emotional dimension.

Another existentially weak phenomenon that we emotionally upgrade is our voluntary movements, which are a version of the *mind-over-matter events*. It is impossible to rationally understand how our mind – the entity that doesn't exist in space – can affect physical processes that unfold in space, such as the EEG patterns or our body movements. As a result, the mind over matter effects lack RC (i.e., a scientific explanation) and are therefore existentially incomplete entities. Still, we live as if these effects were as ordinary as trees in our garden or food that we eat. Some perceptual illusions too can be emotionally upgraded and become powerful enough to be taken for truth. For example, in a psychological experiment children verbally estimated the display of the Muller-Layer illusion (e.g., when two rulers of the same length look as if they have different lengths) as false (i.e., cognitively weak phenomenon), yet treated this illusion as a true phenomenon when it was required to use one of the competing rulers for achieving an emotionally attractive goal [16]. Under normal circumstances, however, most perceptual illusions remain in the status of emotionally weak entities: we might be surprised to see extraordinary Penrose's 'impossible triangle' [17] or Maurice Escher's wonderful graphic images, such as the 'Waterfall' [18], in which the flow of water seems to defy gravitation, yet these images leave us emotionally untouched.

One more target for emotional upgrade can be social influence (e.g., a suggestion). Like a physical entity, a social impact can be represented in my mind as a phenomenon (e.g., I can hear or see a suggested message), a mental image (e.g., a memory of this message), and as an RC (my knowledge of the social status of the suggesting agent, my rational calculation of whether it is profitable or unprofitable to me to follow the suggested message). If this message was irrelevant to my needs, the message would have a weak existential status on the EXON's cognitive dimension and would not change my behaviour. However, if the message targets things that are emotionally important to me, I may upgrade the suggested message and change my behaviour as a result (e.g., buy a suggested product that I like).

Finally, developing faith in God is upgrading an existentially weak entity (the idea of a god) to the status of an existentially strong entity – God we believe in. The energy for this EXUP is borrowed from the emotional dimension of EXON, which includes a variety of motives for such an upgrade, with our desire to survive death and explain the origins of the universe being the most important of them.

The crossing between cognitive and emotional dimensions of EXON is shown in Table 2.2.

Like all psychological processes, EXON can be disturbed on both cognitive and emotional dimensions. On EXON's cognitive dimension, the disturbance can take shape of *hyper-suggestibility* – the tendency to trust messages that are objectively unreliable. Specifically, in the state of *hypnosis* a person uncritically upgrades the hypnotist's arbitrary messages to the strong existential status and obeys the hypnotist's commands [19]. On EXON's emotional dimension, an example of

TABLE 2.2 Examples of entities, as a function of their existential statuses on *Cognitive* and *Emotional* dimensions of EXON

Status on Emotional dimension / Status on Cognitive dimension	Strong (Personally Significant Entities – PSE)	Weak (Personally non-significant entities – PNE)
Absolute Strong	My conscious Self. An emotionally important personal object (e.g., my body or my valuable property). Emotionally important ordinary perceived or imagined physical objects (e.g., a personal wedding ring). Empirically proven theory in your area of interest.	A strange person's Self. Emotionally neutral other people's objects (e.g., a strange person's body or property). Emotionally neutral perceived or imagined physical objects (e.g., a strange person's wedding ring). Empirically proven theory outside your area of interest.
Incomplete	The world before my birth and after my death. Some finds in geology, palaeontology, and astronomy. Perceptual illusions. Psi-phenomena. UFO.	The world before birth and after the death of a strange person. Future events in other people's lives. Abstract logical worlds, and unproven hypotheses. Unobservable quantum objects.
Weak	Gods of my religion. Fantastical impossible entities (the Devil, a ghost, a mermaid). Supernatural magical events (e.g., mind-over-matter effects). Social suggestions that target PSE. Future events in my life related to PSE.	Gods of other religions. Non-fantastical impossible entities (e.g., the Penrose's impossible triangle). Internally contradictive logical inferences. Impossible hypotheses (e.g., perpetual movement). Temporarily forgotten entities. Social suggestions that target PNE. Luminiferous aether.

EXON's disturbance is *hoarding disorder* [20], [21]. People with that disorder find it impossible to part with possessions that they objectively have no need in; they become emotionally attached to such items and experience distress at the thought of getting rid of them.

Keeping in mind the way we attribute existence to entities in the everyday life, let us have a look how they do this in physical science.

2.5 Detecting existence in physics

In classical physics, existence of a certain body or a physical effect is determined by direct observation of Self-related phenomena, combined with matching mental images and RC. Allegedly, Archimedes inferred that a buoyancy force was acting on a body immersed in water while he was taking a bath, and astronomers infer about movements of planets regarding Earth by measuring the planets' position regarding other objects observed in the sky. In nuclear physics, entities such as atoms and elementary particles are inaccessible for observation by a naked eye but can be observed indirectly, via devices that make the entities produce observable effects. Thus, electrons were first observed in the form of cathode rays, emitted by the cathode (the electrode connected to the negative terminal of the voltage supply). In a vacuum glass tube equipped with two electrodes to which a voltage is applied, one can see the area of glass behind the positive electrode to glow, due to electrons emitted from the cathode [22]. More massive alpha particles, which consist of two protons and two neutrons bound together, can be individually observed by tracks they leave in condensing vapour in the cloud chamber [23]. The cloud chamber was followed by the invention of the bubble chamber – a metallic sphere filled with a superheated liquid hydrogen used to detect electrically charged particles. This allowed researchers to observe single electron tracks, including both negatively and positively charged electrons (positrons) [24], which thus puts electrons into the class of entities with *strong* existential status. In the previous sections we called such entities science-generated objects.

However, not every object of physical science can obtain the strong existential status. There are elementary objects of matter which enter into existence in an indirect way. For example, existence of the particle named Z boson was predicted theoretically on the basis of the Standard model of particle physics by Steven Weinberg in 1967 [25] and indirectly supported by observation in 1973, when the bubble chamber photographed the tracks of a few electrons without an obvious reason suddenly starting to move, allegedly having been 'hit' by some invisible particles, such as neutrino. This effect could be explained by assuming that a neutrino interacted with the electron by the exchange of an unseen Z boson. Neutrino itself can only be detected indirectly, for instance, via producing charged particles that travel with the speed higher than the speed of light in a particular medium, causing the observable Cherenkov radiation. Such radiation allows researchers to infer information about direction, energy and other characteristics of the neutrinos that had caused the radiation [26]. Nevertheless, unlike electrons, neutrino does not leave *individual tracks* on any existing physical screens and is therefore unobservable as a phenomenon. According to the existential grades adopted in the EXON theory, neutrino should therefore be attributed an *incomplete* existential status. Neutrino is represented in our mind in the form of an RC but not as a phenomenon and a mental image. In this context, the existential status of particles such as Z boson and Higg's boson [27] also can be characterized as incomplete. Due to their extreme instability, existence of these particles can only be inferred indirectly by their decay products.

The incomplete existential status of quantum objects can also be a result of violation of properties of Self-related phenomena by these objects. One of such violations is *quantum entanglement*, according to which each particle of the group cannot be described independently of the state of the others, even when the particles are separated by a large distance [6], [28]. Another violation is the *dependence of the state of a quantum object from the conditions of its observation*. According to a popular theory (the so-called Copenhagen interpretation of wave function collapse), before a quantum system is observed, it exists in the indefinite state of superposition, so that it is impossible to say whether the quantum system is a particle or a wave. During an observation, the system interacts with a laboratory device and the wave function of the system collapses, thus taking the shape of either a particle or a wave depending on the condition of the measurement [29]. Both quantum entanglement and the state of superposition violate the requirements of identity, permanence and locality.

Similar incomplete existential status can be attributed to *dark matter* – a physical entity that does not appear to interact with electromagnetic radiation, such as light. It is therefore undetectable by existing physical devices [30]. The only reason to assume that dark matter exists is the inconsistencies between some physical laws that govern the observed phenomena: galaxies and clusters of galaxies. Galaxies and their clusters rotate around their axes, and the centrifugal forces act on them, which are directed outward from the axes. To keep the galaxies together, the opposite force – gravity – must match the centrifugal force in power. The problem is that it doesn't: the total mass of galaxies and the intergalactic gas accounts only for 15% of the mass required to keep the galaxies together. As a result, astronomers had to infer the existence of additional matter that accounts for the missing observable mass [31]. Another physical entity with incomplete existential status is *dark energy*. This entity has the only visible manifestation in the fact that, despite gravitational forces, our universe continues to expand with acceleration [ibid]. This feeble existential status of dark matter or dark energy causes scientists to look for alternative ways of accounting for the abnormal physical phenomena, without postulating the aforementioned hypothetical physical entities [32], [33].

Finally, some physical entities exist only as images which have no solid experimental evidence, direct or indirect, to support their existence. One of such entity is luminiferous aether – the 'light bearing' medium which was postulated to explain the wave theory of light [34]. Being a wave, light needs a medium (the aether) to spread. However, experiments failed to detect the aether, which brought physicists to the conclusion that the ether doesn't exist. Einstein's theory of relativity explained the failure of the experiments and suggested that the ether's concept is redundant. The luminiferous aether still exists though, but only as an *existentially weak entity*, – an image which lacks the phenomenological and conceptual modes of representation.

2.6 Conclusion: Basic and high levels of EXON

In this chapter, we considered a variety of entities across the scale of existential statuses. This allows us to distinguish the properties the concept of 'entity' entails.

We agreed that an *entity is a piece of subjective experience* which meets certain general requirements. For our Self to be able to operate with entities at a basic level (e.g., to compare two entities with each other), we need to make sure that the object we have in mind is the entity in the first place. In other words, we need to establish the object's identity, permanence, locality and inclusion. Viewed in this context, subjective experiences such as simple sensations (e.g., light or sound), emotional conditions (e.g., good or bad mood) and general concepts (e.g., space and time) are not entities. In contrast, proven scientific theories or solid logical inferences are, because they are supported by replicable phenomena and can also be presented as images in our minds. Simply put, we need to be certain that the object we call an entity did not emerge from thin air and doesn't cease to exist when it goes out of our perceptual field or from our immediate memory. Let us call *the process of establishing the object's identity, permanence, locality and inclusion* the *basic level of existence attribution (BLEXON)*.

Psychological studies have shown that although BLEXON is an intuitive process, it is not innate and takes some time to establish in the course of individual development. According to psychological observations, a few months old infants stop trying to obtain an attractive object if the object is covered by a blanket in their full view because they 'believe' that the object ceased to exist (the so-called 'out of sight out of mind' behaviour) [35]. This means that the infants treat physical objects as non-permanent entities. Nevertheless, more recent experiments demonstrated that infants as young as 3.5 months old *behave as if they believed* that physical objects don't cease to exist when they go out of sight [36], [37]. In terms of the EXON theory, this behaviour indicates that the infants have an early precursor of BLEXON. Altogether, studies suggest that the development of the *'belief in object permanence' (BOP)* may be conditioned by a multitude of factors [38]. It is only after 2 years of age that we develop a strong BOP and learn to distinguish objects that cease to exist (e.g., are destroyed or die and decompose) from those which only temporarily go out of our perceptual field [39]. For instance, when we regain our consciousness after general anaesthetics or after sleep without dreams, our BLEXON makes an 'extension' of the currently observed world 'back in time' in order to fill the gap by joining the 'now' and 'before' ends together and assuming that for the time we were unconscious the world existed in its present state. By distinguishing between the *permanent entities (PME)* and *non-permanent entities (NPE)* BLEXON divides reality into two opposite domains: *Ordinary reality (OR)*, which comprises PME, and *super-ordinary reality (SOR)*, in which NPE (magical entities) hold sway. Finally, when people are trying to change a physical object by a voluntary effort of the mind (e.g., by a wish or a magic spell), they use the emotional dimension of BLEXON. Examples of this kind of emotional BLEXON are sympathetic and contagious magic observed in traditional cultures (e.g., an attempt to hurt the enemy by burning the enemy's picture, effigy, hair or nail clippings) [40]. Magical manipulations violate general requirements of permanence and locality (e.g., by making a causal link between manipulations with a person's picture and the living person who is pictured), and thus eliminate the border between OR and SOR, which is crucial for EXON's cognitive dimension.

Further, we distinguished between various types of phenomena, depending on the three basic properties: mind independence, intermodality and intersubjectivity. We also established that an entity can be presented in our mind in three modes – as a phenomenon, a mental image and an RC (see Figure 2.2). This allows us to proceed from BLEXON to the *high level of EXON (HLEXON)*, which is *a process of consciously establishing existential statuses of an entity by searching for the entity's phenomenon, image and RC and matching them with each other*. HLEXON allows one to distinguish between the types of phenomena (Self-related, representing, simulating, hallucinatory and illusory, see Table 2.1)

It is also at the HLEXON that there appears *upgrading or downgrading* the entities' existential statuses through faith. As will be discussed further in this book, a cognitively weak entity (e.g., the idea of an Almighty Wizard)) can be emotionally upgraded to the status of an existentially strong entity (Chapter 5), and vice versa, a cognitively strong entity (e.g., a perceived physical object) can be emotionally downgraded to become existentially weak entity (Chapter 3).To reiterate, whereas BLEXON is mainly an intuitive process, HLEXON requires conscious reflection and critical thinking (see Table 2.3).

Based on this theoretical framework, we can begin now the review of empirical studies, looking at BLEXON and HLEXON in more detail. We will begin with

TABLE 2.3 Actions of EXON, as a function of EXON's *levels* (Basic vs High), and EXON's *dimensions* (Cognitive vs Emotional)

EXON's level EXON's dimension	Basic (BLEXON)	High (HLEXON)
Cognitive	Intuitively establishing entity's existential status by detecting presence or absence of identity, permanence, locality, and inclusion. Intuitively establishing the border between ordinary and superordinary domains of reality. Upgrading or downgrading the entity's existential status through perception.	Consciously establishing the entity's existential status by matching the entity's modes of representation. Consciously establishing the type of phenomena: Self-related, representing, simulating, hallucinatory and illusory. Consciously dividing reality into ordinary (permanent entities) and super-ordinary (non-permanent entities).
Emotional	Upgrading or downgrading the entity's existential status through internal or external suggestion. Upgrading or downgrading external influence (e.g., magical or ordinary suggestion).	Upgrading or downgrading the entity's existential status through faith or fake.

the studies on BLEXON of Self-related phenomena, which will be referred to as *perceived objects (entities)*.

References

[1] New Scientist (2013). *Nothing: From absolute zero to cosmic oblivion, amasing insights into Nothingness*. Profile Books.
[2] Subbotsky, E. (2020). *The Bubble Universe: Psychological Perspectives on Reality*. Palgrave Macmillan.
[3] Sacks, O. (2013). *Hallucinations*. Vintage.
[4] https://www.shutterstock.com/search/radioactive+decay
[5] Subbotsky, E. (2013). Sensing the future: Reversed causality or a non-standard observer effect? *The Open Psychology Journal*, 6, 81–93. https://www.lancaster.ac.uk/staff/subbotsk/Sensing%20the%20future%281%29.pdf
[6] Chow, T. L. (2008). *Gravity, black holes, and the very early universe: An introduction to general relativity and cosmology*. Springer
[7] Matson, J. (2012). *Quantum teleportation achieved over record distances*. Nature News. 10.1038/nature.2012.11163.
[8] https://home.cern/science/physics/dark-matter
[9] https://science.nasa.gov/astrophysics/focus-areas/what-is-dark-energy
[10] https://plato.stanford.edu/entries/logic-modal/#PosWorSem
[11] https://www.illusionsindex.org/i/impossible-triangle
[12] https://en.wikipedia.org/wiki/Event_horizon
[13] https://dictionary.cambridge.org/dictionary/english/perfect
[14] https://en.wikipedia.org/wiki/Synesthesia
[15] Losev, A. F. (2020). *Dialectika Mipha*. Moscow: Azbuka Klassica.
[16] Subbotsky, E. (1990). Phenomenal and rational perception of some object relations by pre-schoolers. *Soviet psychology*, 28, 5, 5–24. https://www.lancaster.ac.uk/staff/subbotsk/Phenomenal%20and%20rational%20perception.pdf
[17] https://www.illusionsindex.org/i/impossible-triangle
[18] https://artchive.ru/en/escher/works/200416~Waterfall
[19] https://en.wikipedia.org/wiki/Hypnosis#Hyper-suggestibility
[20] https://en.wikipedia.org/wiki/Compulsive_hoarding
[21] https://www.mayoclinic.org/diseases-conditions/hoarding-disorder/symptoms-causes/syc-20356056
[22] https://en.wikipedia.org/wiki/Cathode_ray#/media/File:Cyclotron_motion_smaller_view.jpg
[23] https://en.wikipedia.org/wiki/Alpha_particle#/media/File:Physicist_Studying_Alpha_Rays_GPN-2000-000381.jpg
[24] https://journals.aps.org/pr/abstract/10.1103/PhysRev.50.263
[25] https://en.wikipedia.org/wiki/W_and_Z_bosons
[26] https://www.sciencedirect.com/science/article/abs/pii/0370269390901691
[27] https://en.wikipedia.org/wiki/Higgs_boson#Experimental_search
[28] https://en.wikipedia.org/wiki/Quantum_entanglement
[29] https://en.wikipedia.org/wiki/Copenhagen_interpretation
[30] https://home.cern/science/physics/dark-matter
[31] https://science.nasa.gov/astrophysics/focus-areas/what-is-dark-energy
[32] https://arxiv.org/ftp/arxiv/papers/1210/1210.3021.pdf

[33] Brownstein, J. R. & Moffat, J. W. (2006). Galaxy cluster masses without non-baryonic dark matter. *Monthly Notices of the Royal Astronomical Society*, 367, 527–540.
[34] https://en.wikipedia.org/wiki/Luminiferous_aether
[35] Piaget, J. (1977). Gruber, Howard E. & Vonèche, J. Jacques., (Eds). *The essential Piaget*. Routledge & K. Paul.
[36] Bower, T. G. R. (1974). *Development in infancy*. Freeman.
[37] Baillargeon, R. & DeVos, J. (1991). Object permanence in young infants: Further evidence. *Child Development*, 62, 1227–1246.
[38] Bremner, J. G., Slater, A. M. & Johnson, S. P. (2014). Perception of object persistence: The origins of object permanence in infancy. *Child Development Perspectives*, 9, 7–13.
[39] Subbotsky, E. (1996). Explaining impossible phenomena: Object permanence beliefs and memory failures in adults. *Memory*, 4, 199–233.
[40] Frazer, J. G. (1925). *The golden bough. A study in magic and religion*. The Macmillan Company.

3
NOW IT'S THERE, NOW IT ISN'T: EXON ON PERCEIVED OBJECTS

3.1 Existence and psychology: A sketch of history

While in philosophy the problem of existence has been under investigation for millennia, experimental psychologists became interested in this problem relatively recently. Research in this area was pioneered by the Swiss psychologist Jean Piaget, in the context of his observations on how children build the idea of reality [1]. According to Piaget, children learn to attribute existence to objects by interacting with them on a sensorimotor level during the first two years of life. Piaget argued that a central feature of successful manipulation with objects is the belief in *object permanence (OP)* – the belief that an object continues to exist even after it goes beyond the child's perceptual field. Viewed in the context of Chapter 2, the *belief in object permanence (BOP)* is a version of BLEXON. The BOP is fully functional in two-year-old children; before that age, infants often behave as if the objects cease to exist as soon as they leave the child's 'perception horizon'. By analogy with the BOP, we will assume that the younger infants tacitly hold the 'belief in object's non-permanence' (BONP). In other words, infants younger than 2 years of age identify objects' existence with 'objects being perceived'. This 'out of sight out of mind' type of early BLEXON can be better captured by the 'out of sight out of the world' formular. In contrast, older children extend the time of object's existence beyond perception, by storing the object in their short time (and later also in their long time) memory. Piaget described six stages in the development of the BOP during infancy. In more recent years the phenomenon has been studied in great depth by a number of researchers (for reviews see [2], [3]). Despite some disagreements on various aspects of development of the BOP, most researchers agree that at the age of about two years a child is able to ascribe the OP or some kind of 'personal identity' to every stable material object that is accessible to sensorimotor manipulation, regardless of changes in either the object's environment or its features.

Whereas Piaget and other developmental researches based their methodology of studying BLEXON on observation over children's behaviour, Belgium psychologist Albert Michotte approached the problem from the perspective of phenomenology, by registering adults' judgements regarding transformations and movements of virtual objects on the screen [4]. He described three basic properties which adults attribute to a permanent object. Let us call these properties the *OP demands*. If the BOP is applied to an object, then the object is expected to conform to the following OP demands: (1) *it cannot emerge from thin air and vanish without a trace;* (2) *it cannot instantly change into a completely different object;* and (3) *it cannot be created, destroyed or reconstructed by a pure mental effort or a symbolic action of the subject in a non-causal way*. If any one of these expectations is violated, as may be the case when the perceived object spontaneously, as if by magic, changes into quite another object in front of the observer's eyes, then the object in question loses its property of permanence and becomes similar to a cloud of smoke or a ripple on the water surface. As can be seen, the *OP demands are a simplified version of the requirements and properties of a Self-related entity*, listed in Table 2.1, adapted for experimental research.

Psychological experiments have established that people distinguish between two types of entities: Those that meet the OP demands and those that don't. Entities of the latter type can appear from nothing, spontaneously change into other entities, and disappear into thin air. From the 3rd person view, we refer to the entities of the former type as permanent entities (PME), and to the entities of the latter type as non-permanent entities (NPE). Correspondingly, speaking from the 1st person view, we will say that people apply the BOP to the PME, while applying the BONP to the NPE. Put in the context of distinctions introduced in Chapter 2, the PME are sensorimotor equivalents of Self-related phenomena, whereas the NPE correspond to Self-created entities. On this ground, one can say that *the distinction between PME and NPE exists on the basic level of EXON (BLEXON)*. The classification of existential statuses on HLEXON partially overlaps with the PME/NPE distinction. Thus, entities with absolute and strong existential statuses (see the previous chapter) belong to the class of PME, whereas certain entities with incomplete existential status and all entities with weak existential status belong to the class of NPE.

As mentioned in Chapter 2, the distinction between PME and NPE categories divides reality into two distinct domains. Whereas PME dominate in the domain of ordinary reality (OR), NPE reign in the domain of superordinary reality (SOR) – fairy tales, dreams, imagination, and fantasy games. In certain circumstances, situations can arise in which NPE enter the domain of OR. Under these conditions subjects report to be observing supernatural phenomena. Normally, we could imagine a crystal glass suddenly appearing on an empty table; in that case, the imagined object (the crystal glass responding to our mental order to emerge) would belong to the NPE category and exist only in our imagination. However, if a perceived, and not imagined, crystal glass suddenly materialized as a result of our wish for the glass to appear, we would say that one of the OP demands has been violated and we are witnessing a miracle – the object from the NPE category crossing the borderline between SOR and OR and turning into the object from the PME category.

The question arises at what age do children begin to be sensitive to the distinction between ordinary and superordinary realities? Simply put, at what age children begin to be surprised if an ordinary perceived object, such as a postage stamp, appears from thin air, or disappears without a trace?

3.2 Shaping existence: BLEXON in children

In order to answer this question, in *Study 1* [5] children aged 4 to 6 years were divided into experimental and control groups; the children were first interviewed on whether they distinguish between ordinary and superordinary realities, and then presented with apparently superordinary phenomena including a) a sudden disappearance of a perceived object, b) a perceived object instantly changing into another one, and c) the creation of a perceived object 'from nothing'. A small wooden box was used, which had a secret compartment that could hide or display small objects as if they disappear into or appear from thin air. The box could be manipulated, without the compartment being revealed.

Children of the experimental group were given the prompt instruction: They were told that the box "was taken from a fairy tale" and possessed magical abilities. In the control group, the prompt instruction was absent. Before the experimental manipulation, the experimenter gave each child a nice postage stamp as a reward for their agreement to participate in the experiment. During the experiment, the experimenter gave a certain task to the child, which served as a distractor, and suggested that while working on the task the child placed the stamp in the box; after that, the experimenter close the lid of the box and then left the child alone in the room. Having completed the task, children approached the box in order to extract the postage stamp that they had already considered to be their lawful possession. On opening the box, they found that it was empty. The child's behaviour was observed by the experimenter without the child being aware of that. It was hypothesized that if the children applied the BOP to the perceived object, they would show surprise and begin to search for the disappeared postage stamp. On the other hand, if they believed in the possibility of the object's magical disappearance, thus employing the BONP, there should be an emotional reaction of disappointment and some magical manipulations but no search.

Preliminary interviews revealed that in their verbal judgements the children already had the idea of the distinction between ordinary and superordinary (magical) events: Almost all children agreed that ordinary perceived objects could magically disappear in a fairy tale but denied that this could happen in ordinary reality. They did not believe that an ordinary wooden box could destroy or create perceived entities. In spite of this, when they were showed the trick, most children in the experimental group behaved as if magical disappearance indeed took place: They exhibited neither surprise nor search behaviour. Instead, they continuously repeated the 'magical' act of opening and closing the lid, thus hoping to make the box 'return' their prise. In other words, the children treated the postage stamp as a NPE type of object, thus erasing the distinction between OR and a fairy tale. The crucial factor in this phenomenon seems to be the experimenter's prompting instruction. This was evident from the fact that children of the control group, who had not been given the prompts, reacted to the discontinuity phenomenon with surprise and exhibited active search behaviour. They therefore viewed the postage stamp as a PME type of object and interpreted the effect as though the postage stamp had not disappeared but had been displaced.

Importantly, witnessing the object's unexplained disappearance also affected the children's verbal behaviour. Whereas prior to the experimental manipulation most children denied the possibility of perceived object's vanishing without a trace in the real life, after the manipulation most children in the experimental group, but not in the control group, changed their minds and began to discuss the postage stamp as if it indeed was able to magically vanish without a trace.

The results of this study suggest that in preschool children the distinction between PME and NPE is unstable. This is not a new idea and has been expressed by other authors, first and foremost by Jean Piaget. What is new is the fact that under certain conditions preschool children can be led to attribute BONP not only to natural phenomena, such as wind, clouds or the Moon but also to everyday perceived objects which are accessible to sensorimotor manipulation. Whereas in their verbal judgements most pre-schoolers begin to realize that everyday perceived objects must conform to the OP demands, this early conviction is weak and collapses as soon as the children are shown instances of the perceived object's apparent discontinuity. Viewing the children's mind as the 'existence workshop', we might say that this workshop does not yet have strict methods of producing PME; the children have not yet developed established rules for distinguishing between ordinary and superordinary events. This suggests that *children who are shown an apparent violation of the OP demands by an ordinary perceived entity are prone to downgrade existential status of this entity from a strong (PME) to a weak one (NPE).*

Study 2 [6] that follows was designed to look at this process in more detail.

3.3 Tools of BLEXON: Magical versus ordinary entities

The *first question* raised in Experiment 1 of this study was to examine whether children were able to understand the difference between PME and NPE? Can they verbally acknowledge that an object of a PME type conforms to the OP demands, whereas an object of a NPE type doesn't? If they can, let us say that they apply to the observed phenomenon *a BLEXON tool* that will be referred to as a 'magic\ordinary distinguisher' (MOD).

The *second question* was to investigate how consistent the children's MOD is; specifically, it was necessary to find out whether the children who *verbally acknowledge* that PME must conform to the OP demands actually *attribute* the OP demands to perceived objects. Indeed, in an interview a child may verbally distinguish between

PME and NPE thus exhibiting the MOD, yet inconsistently still believe that perceived (sensorimotor) objects, like a postage stamp, could violate the OP demands. Earlier we called this *BLEXON tool* the belief in object non-permanence (BONP). If in an interview a participant *who had exhibited the MOD* said that in real life an ordinary perceived object cannot violate the OP demands, this would mean that this participant *applies the BOP* to the perceived object, and if the participant admits otherwise, we will say that the participant *applies the BONP*.

Finally, the *third question* was how firm, or entrenched, the BOP of perceived entities is. If the participant uses the BOP before and after he or she becomes a witness of the apparent violation of object permanence by an ordinary perceived object, we will say that *the BOP is entrenched*. If, however, the participant uses the BOP before, but not after witnessing the apparent violation of the OP demands, then we will say that *the BOP is not entrenched*. In terms of the EXON theory, the not-entrenched BOP means that a person is vulnerable to 'perceptual suggestion' and can easily downgrade the perceived entity's existential status from the strong one (BOP applied) to the weak status (BONP applied).

To answer the first two questions, 4-, 6- and 9-year-old children and adults were given *the interview trial*. They were verbally presented with four scenarios, each containing an ordinary and a superordinary outcome. The superordinary outcomes involved various instances of the OP demands violation: disappearance, creation, destruction, and restoration of a solid perceived object (a postage stamp), which occurred in an empty box under the influence of a magic spell. For instance, in the 'disappearance' scenario, the ordinary and superordinary outcomes were presented as follows: "Suppose, a person puts a postage stamp in an empty box like that, then says some magic words, opens the box and finds the same stamp in it" (ordinary) and "Suppose, a person puts a postage stamp in an empty box like that, then says some magic words, opens the box and there isn't the stamp in the box, it disappeared. Please, bear in mind that it disappeared because the magic words made it disappear, not because it was some kind of trick, OK?" (superordinary). After presenting each outcome (the order of presentation was randomized), the participant was asked two questions: a *conceptual question* testing for the presence of the MOD ("Would this be magic, or would there not be any magic in it?") and an *ontological question* testing for the presence of the BOP ("Can this event really happen or not?"). If participants answered the conceptual questions correctly, they were qualified as able to apply the MOD. The correct answer to the ontological questions indicated that the participants applied the BOP; if, however, participants said that perceived objects could violate the OP demands, they were counted as applying the BONP.

The interview trial was followed by *the demonstration trial*, which aimed at examining the entrenchment of participants' BOP. In this trial, the participants who in the interview trial had proved having both the MOD and the BOP were placed at a table on which there were the wooden trick box (described in the previous section) and a postage stamp lying next to the box. The postage stamp looked old: it was crumpled and torn in two places. The participants were individually invited to inspect the box and make sure that it was empty. Next, the participant was asked to examine the postage stamp, tell whether it was new or old, place the stamp into the box, and close the lid. The experimenter then proceeded with the following instruction: 'Now, I am going to put a magic spell on this box'. The experimenter pronounced some words that sounded like a magic spell and asked: "Now, what do you think… has the postage stamp that you placed in the box changed, or does it remain the same?" If the answer was "Yes, it changed", the question followed "How did it change?".

Next, the participant was asked to open the box and remove the stamp. On opening the box the participants discovered that the old postage stamp 'became' the brand new one. Questions that followed were: "What is this?" and "Is this the same postage stamp that you had placed into the box but changed, or it is a different postage stamp?" If the participants said that it was a different postage stamp, they were encouraged to search for the original postage stamp inside the box. This was done in order to create the impression in the participants that something superordinary had happened: An old and broken postage stamp became a brand new one after the magic spell had been said. Participants were then asked two key questions: "What do you think has happened to the postage stamp, why has it become new?" (spontaneous explanation) and "If I told you that I did this with the help of my magic words, as wizards do in fairy tales, would you believe me or not?" (suggested explanation). The participant's BOP can be considered entrenched if the participant did not spontaneously produce or accept suggested magical explanations even after they had been shown an event that apparently violated the OP demands.

The results indicated that in the interview trial participants of all age groups had no difficulty in conceptually distinguishing between ordinary (i.e., conforming to the OP demands) and superordinary (i.e., violating the OP demands) perceived objects (Figure 3.1, grey bars). Yet, most 4-year-olds also believed that violations of the OP demands could occur in the real world, most 6- and 9-year-olds and all adults denied this (Figure 3.1, white bars).

Nevertheless, when in the demonstration trial participants who had exhibited the BOP in the interview trial (Figure 3.2, white bars) were confronted with anomalous causal events that looked like instances of violations of the OP demands, all 4-year-olds and most 6-year-olds were quick to retreat back to the BONP, by acknowledging that the perceived physical object changed as a result of the magic spell (Figure 3.2, grey bars). In other words, whereas almost all of the children applied the MOD to perceived objects (see Figure 3.1., grey bars), in most 4-year-olds the BOP was absent (Figure 3.1, white bars), and in all of the few where it was present (Figure 3.2., white bars) it was not entrenched. In most 6-year-olds the BOP was present but not entrenched. In contrast, most 9-year-olds and adult participants exhibited the entrenched BOP (Figure 3.2, black bars). The MOD and BOP availability in children and adults is summarized in Table 3.1.

However, there can be some problems raised regarding the interpretation of these results. First, it could be argued that in the interview trial the capacity of

EXON on perceived objects **41**

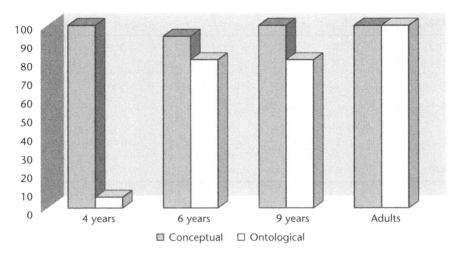

FIGURE 3.1 Percent of participants, who distinguished between ordinary and super-ordinary perceived objects (Conceptual), and exhibited the BOP (Ontological) in the Interview trial of Experiment 1, as a function of Age

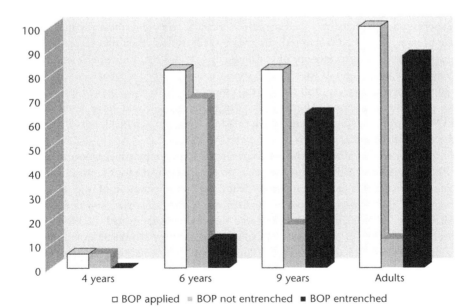

FIGURE 3.2 Percent of participants who applied the BOP in the Interview trial, and exhibited not-entrenched and entrenched BOP in the Demonstration trial of Experiment 1, as a function of Age

42 EXON on perceived objects

TABLE 3.1 MOD and BOP availability in regard to Perceived objects, as a function of age

BLEXON tool Age	MOD	BOP	BOP entrenched
4 years	Available in all children	Absent in most children	Absent
6 years	Available in all children	Available in most children	Available in some children
9 years	Available in all children	Available in most children	Available in most children
Adults	Available	Available	Available

children to distinguish between *ordinary* and *superordinary* outcomes did not necessarily mean that they could also distinguish between *superordinary events* and *similarly looking tricks*. Indeed, in the experiment the term 'magic' was used to designate superordinary events. In English, the word 'magic' contains a certain ambiguity in it: Magic could mean a supernatural event, but it could also mean a trick that looks like a supernatural event but in reality is an ordinary event that simulates the supernatural one. In fact, experiments have shown that 4- and 6-year-olds have a problem with distinguishing between impossible and improbable events [7]. It is therefore possible that, when in the demonstration trial of Experiment 1 participants called the effect 'magical', they did not really mean that the postage stamp had 'answered' the magic spell; instead, they may have thought that the stamp was an ordinary physical object (a PME) that the experimenter had changed by some kind of trick. If this were the case, then the participants, despite calling the effect magical, still viewed the object as a PME and invested it with the strong existential status. Alternatively, the participants could have applied the BONP to the postage stamp and began treating the stamp as a NPE, while viewing the experimenter as a real wizard.

In order to examine whether in Experiment 1 the participants who called the effect 'magical' in reality meant the magic to be a trick or meant the magic to be a true supernatural event, immediately after the demonstration of the apparent change of the postage stamp the mechanism of the trick was revealed to the participants. If the participants considered the changed stamp to be a PME, then after the exposure of the trick's mechanism to them they would be quick to stop calling the effect magical and begin calling it a trick. If, however, the participants applied their BONP to the postage stamp, then they would ignore the revelation of the trick's mechanism and keep viewing the event as a miracle.

Further, if some children ignored the revelation of the trick's mechanism and thus exhibited the BONP, the question still could be asked of whether their BONP is entrenched. In other words, just like participants BOP can be or not be entrenched, so can the participants' BONP. In order to answer the question about the BONP's entrenchment, the trick should be *fully explained to these children*. The children with the entrenched BONP would ignore the explanation and stick to their magical explanations of the event, whereas children in whom their BONP is not entrenched would be happy to abandon their BONP and shift to non-magical explanations. Experiment 2 of this study was conducted to clarify these questions and investigate the entrenchment of both the BOP and the BONP.

3.4 Tools of BLEXON: Magic versus tricks

The *first objective* of Experiment 2 was to replicate the results of Experiment 1 using a refined methodology – an *amended interview trial* that targeted the children's capacity to distinguish between real magical phenomena and similarly looking tricks, and *a more authentic magical phenomenon* (burning half of a postage stamp, instead of transforming an old postage stamp into a new one). Indeed, as earlier studies have shown, people detect violation of the OP demands only when a phenomenal object changes radically, but when only minor features change people tend to interpret the object as a PME [4]. In most stories and books for children, magic is associated with some kind of burning or transformation, rather than with restoration. It could be the case that in Experiment 1 some young participants simply did not consider the conversion of an old postage stamp into a new one as a change big enough to be considered as violating the OP demands. The *second objective* was to examine the degree of entrenchment of the BONP in 5-, 6-, and 9-year-old children.

Like in Experiment 1, in the *interview trial* of this experiment participants were tested on two issues: (a) whether or not they could distinguish real (supernatural) magic from magically looking tricks, and (b) whether or not they believed that real magic is possible.

Children were shown two pictures of a wizard who performed superordinary events. The wizards differed only in the colour of one of the following features: a cap, buttons, shoes, or a beard (see Figure 3.3).

Participants were then told that one of the two men was a real wizard and could *do real magic*, and the other only pretended that he could do real magic, but in reality, he *could only show tricks* that looked like magic. The children were then presented with four pairs of test items: For each given pair of items, the children were asked to consider two different outcomes: a *trick that looked like magic*, and *an instance of true magic* that involved a violation of known physical principles (the 'thought over matter' type of magic). In both types of outcomes the wizard says a magic spell and a postage stamp disappears inside the apparently empty briefcase. However, in the 'trick magic outcome' the postage stamp disappeared by hiding in a secret pocket that the briefcase contained, and in the 'true magic outcome' the postage stamp disappeared from the world because the magic spell made it disappear. Like in the previous experiment, in this experiment the experimenter, after describing each item, immediately asked two questions: a conceptual question (whether the outcome is a trick or an instance of true magic) and an ontological question (whether this outcome could or could not happen in the real world). Speaking in terms of the EXON theory, the conceptual question examined whether the children were able

FIGURE 3.3 The picture of a true and a fake wizard, used in the Interview trial of Experiment 2

to apply the magic versus trick distinguisher (MTD), and the ontological question targeted whether they were able to apply the BOP to the perceived physical object.

Only those children who *passed the conceptual questions* and *applied the BOP* in response to the ontological question participated in the subsequent trials. Passing the interview trial meant that the children understood the difference between 'truly magical' events and magically looking tricks. In terms of logical relations, one can say that MOD ⊂ MTD, meaning that all the contents of the first BLEXON tool are also contained within the second one. To summarize, children who were allowed to proceed to subsequent trials exhibited their ability to engage all the necessary BLEXON tools: the MOD, the MTD and the BOP.

In the *demonstration trial*, the children were shown the magical causal event as in Experiment 1, except that a brand-new postage stamp became half-burned after the experimenter pronounced the magic spell. Three questions were then asked: (1) "What do you think has happened to the postage stamp? Why has it become half burned?", (2) "Do you think that it was my magic spell that made the burned stamp appear instead of the new stamp, or was it not my magic spell?", (3) "Do you think that what I did to the postage stamp was true magic or it was a trick?" Like in Experiment 1, in this experiment the aim of this trial was to examine the entrenchment of children's BOP when applied to a perceived entity. The BOP was considered entrenched if the demonstration of the anomalous causal event that looked like an instance of real magic did not make children change their view that magic is impossible in the OR. If, however, the children produced or accepted magical explanations, their BOP was qualified as not-entrenched.

Children who exhibited not-entrenched BOP participated in the *prompt trial*. In this trial, we examined whether the children who abandoned their BOP in the demonstration trial and accepted magical explanations did this because they treated the observed 'supernatural' event as a trick, or they applied a special tool – the BONP – to the 'magical' event they had witnessed. Indeed, as mentioned above, by saying that the event they had witnessed was 'true magic' the children may have meant that this was *a really clever trick*, rather than a case of the mind-over-matter magic. If this were the case, then the children still viewed the original (brand new) postage stamp as a PME, which had been mechanically replaced by a half-burned postage stamp in the box. On the other hand, if the children applied the BONP, they viewed the magical effect to be a violation of the OP demands: A perceived entity (the new postage stamp) changed because it 'understood' the meaning of the experimenter's verbal order (the magic spell).

To examine this 'clever trick versus true magic' alternative interpretations of the children's answers, the mechanism of the trick was revealed to children. They were shown the trap door in the box and given the following instruction: "Look, this is not an ordinary box, but a special box. It has a trap door in it. See, I can lift this door with the help of this piece of wire, and the door sticks to this wall. When I close the lid of the box, this little cog on the lid pushes the trap door down, and the trap door drops down on the bottom. Can you see it?"

After this, the same questions as in the demonstration trial were asked. The presence of the BONP could be detected if children who had accepted magical explanations of the phenomenon in the demonstration trial retained this explanation after the mechanism of the trick box was exposed to them. As long as the children were able to distinguish between a magic trick and true magic, seeing the mechanism in the box should have made clear to them that what they had seen was in fact a trick. If, however, the children kept insisting that the event they had seen was truly magical, then they indeed believed that the event had violated the OP demands. This means that these children were applying BONP to a perceived object.

Children who retained their magical explanations in the prompt trial participated in the *explanation trial*. In this trial, the children were tested on the entrenchment of their BONP. Instead of just being shown *how the trick box worked* (like in the previous trial), in this trial they were shown *how the trick was done*. They were told as follows: "Look, now I am going to show you what really happened when I showed you how a new stamp became burned, OK? There had been a half-burned stamp hidden between this trap door and the wall of the box. When you placed the new stamp on the bottom of this box and closed the lid, the trap door dropped down, covered the new stamp and released the burned stamp instead". The instruction was accompanied by the demonstration of all the elements of the trick. After this, the key questions were asked again. The BONP can be qualified as entrenched if children stuck to magical explanations even after the trick had been fully explained.

The results showed that distinguishing magic from tricks proved to be a lot more difficult than distinguishing magic from ordinary events. Whereas in the previous experiment 95% of 6-year-olds and 100% of 9-year-olds were able to apply MOD

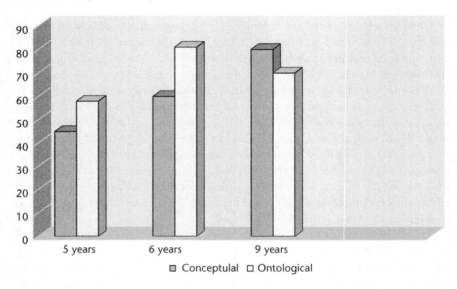

FIGURE 3.4 Percent of participants, who applied MTD (Conceptual) and BOP (Ontological) to the perceived object in the Interview trial of Experiment 2, as a function of Age

(see Figure 3.1, grey bars), in this experiment only 60% of 6-year-olds and 80% of 9-year-olds were able to apply MTD in the interview trial (Figure 3.4, grey bars). In response to the ontological question of the interview trial, 55% of 5-year-olds failed to apply the BOP to a perceived object, saying that the instance of true magic (the disappearance of a postage stamp as a result of a magic spell) could indeed happen in the real world. Like in Experiment 1, in this experiment in the interview trial the majority of 6- and 9-year-olds applied the BOP (Figure 3.4, white bars).

As shown in Figure 3.5, in the demonstration trial, out of the children who applied the BOP in the interview trial (white bars), all of 5-year-olds, most of 6-year-olds and half of 9-year-olds exhibited the not entrenched BOP (grey bars) and said that they had become witnesses of true magic. Comparing Figures 3.5 and 3.2 (white bars) indicates that in Experiment 2 (burning the postage stamp) the proportion of 6- and 9-year-olds that exhibited the not-entrenched BOP significantly exceeds that in Experiment 1 (the old stamp turning into the new one). This supports the assumption that the ability to apply the BOP is dependent on the magnitude of change: When the children saw a new stamp having half of it burned as a result of a magic spell (Experiment 2), a significantly larger number of them exhibited not entrenched BOP than when the children witnessed the old stamp becoming a new one (Experiment 1).

In the prompt trial, most 5-year-olds who had said that the event they saw in the demonstration trial was truly magical, ignored the hint that what they saw in the demonstration trial was in fact a trick and insisted that it was a case of true magic (Figure 3.6, white bars). This means that in the demonstration trial these

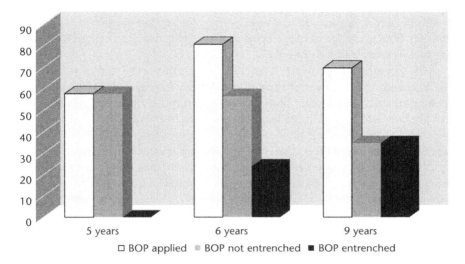

FIGURE 3.5 Percent of participants who applied the BOP in the Interview trial, and exhibited not-entrenched and entrenched BOP in the Demonstration trial of Experiment 2, as a function of Age

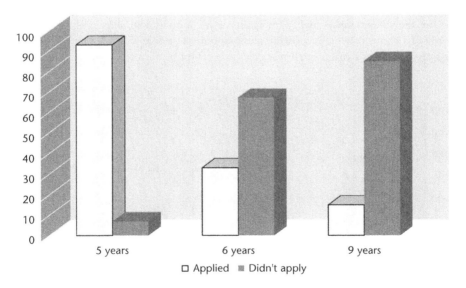

FIGURE 3.6 Percent of children who applied and didn't apply the BONP to a physical object in the Prompt trial of Experiment 2, as a function of Age

children abandoned their BOP, which they exhibited in the interview trial, and switched to the opposite BLEXON tool – the BONP. In contrast, only the minority of 6- and 9-year-olds switched to the BONP, with the majority coming back to the BOP as soon as they were given the prompt.

Finally, in the explanation trial most 5-year-olds exhibited entrenched BONP, but only 30% of 6-year-olds and none of 9-year-olds retained their BONP after the trick was explained (Figure 3.7).

As follows from Experiment 2, as children age, they exhibit a growth in application and entrenchment of their BOP, and the accompanying decline in the application and entrenchment of their BONP. On this ground, one could expect that adults would be even more inclined to use the BOP and reject the BONP in their BLEXON regarding physical objects. Nevertheless, the phenomenon of superstitions among adults suggests that in some circumstances adults too apply the BONP to certain *imagined entities*, such as events in their future lives. Indeed, believing that making or abstaining from making certain actions (e.g., going under a ladder, crossing fingers or knocking on wood) might affect events in the person's future life in a non-causal way violates one of the OP demands listed at the beginning of this chapter. The question arises of *whether adults could apply the BONP to ordinary perceived objects as well,* if they witness the perceived object apparently violating the OP demands.

In order to answer this question, in Experiment 3 of this study university undergraduates participated in the interview and demonstration trial. In the *interview trial*, a simplified version of a questionnaire used in Experiment 2 was employed. Conceptual and ontological questions were asked like in Experiment 2.

In the *demonstration trial*, participants were individually shown three superordinary events in which a postage stamp appeared or disappeared in an apparently empty box after a magic spell was cast on the box by the experimenter, and one

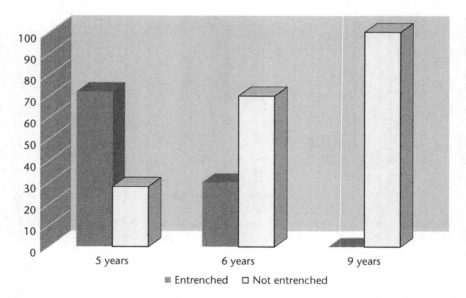

FIGURE 3.7 Percent of children who exhibited Entrenched and Not-entrenched BONP in the Explanation trial of Experiment 2, as a function of Age

event when the box stayed empty after the magic spell was not cast. Altogether, each participant witnessed four subsequent events in which a change (no change) in the empty box was observed as a possible result of casting (not casting) the magic spell. The order of the events was fixed, and the sequence was 'appearance–appearance–no change–disappearance'. To avoid the priming effect, in Condition 1 the interview trial preceded the demonstration trial, and in Condition 2 the order was reversed. The experiment's aim was to find out whether the repeated demonstration of the apparent violation of the OP demands would make the participants apply the BONP to an ordinary perceived object.

The results indicated that all participants applied the MTD and the BOP in the interview trial. In the demonstration trial, despite some individual differences, the participants interpreted the repeated violations of the OP demands by a perceived object as a trick. Altogether the results of this study are summarized in Table 3.2.

The table shows that almost all 5-year-olds and older children are able to distinguish between permanent and non-permanent entities (MOD). About a half of 5-year-olds and most older children can also apply MOD. In 5-year-olds' causal judgments, their tendency to apply the BOP and the BONP towards a perceived object coexist, with the tendency to switch from the BOP to the BONP when children see the apparent violation of the OP demands. Not only violation of the OP demands by a perceived entity is not viewed as anomalous by 5-year-olds but also their BONP is entrenched, whereas the BOP, if present, is not.

This prevalence of the BONP over the BOP disappears in 6- and 9-year-olds. At this age, in their ontological judgments the overwhelming majority of children denied the possibility of the OP demands' violation by a perceived object in the real world. In those 6-year-olds who exhibited the BONP this belief was entrenched, and in the few 9-year-olds who exhibited the BONP this belief was not-entrenched. Altogether, the prevalence of the BONP over the BOP observed in 5-year-old children in older children is reversed in favour of the BOP. This signifies the growing maturity of BLEXON that achieves its peak in adults and involves the MOD, the MTD and the entrenched BOP.

Experiment 3 confirmed the expectation that in adults the BOP is entrenched and can withstand multiple perceptual demonstrations of apparent violations of the OP demands. However, in the studies reviewed above, the entrenchment of the BOP in adults was observed only on the EXON's *cognitive dimension* (see

TABLE 3.2 Percent of participants who applied BLEXON tools to a Perceived object, as a function of Age

BLEXON tool Age	MOD	MTD	BOP	BOP *entrenched*	BONP	BONP *entrenched*
5 years	95	45	58	0	91	73
6 years	95	60	80	30	33	29
9 years	100	80	70	50	15	0
Adults	100	100	100	100	0	0

Table 2.2.). The question arises of whether adult participants will exhibit the same stability on the EXON's emotional dimension, when participants' 'vested interests' are involved in their causal explanations of events.

Indeed, some psychological observations suggest that modern adults are not completely free of applying BONP to perceived entities [8]. Studies demonstrated that in disgust and other domains people's behaviour conforms to the laws of sympathetic magic [9]. For example, university students were less willing to try a piece of chocolate if it was shaped in the form of dog's faeces than if it had a shape of a muffin; this shows that the participants experienced a certain perceived entity (i.e., a piece of chocolate) as fundamentally altering its identity (being a piece of tasty food) when it took the shape of a disgusting object. In terms of the EXON theory, the participants in this experiment applied BONP to an emotionally significant perceived entity. The limitation of the above research is that it only addressed BLEXON at the level of subconsciously based emotional reactions. But what if participants had to react consciously to the possibility of emotionally significant perceived objects violating the OP demands?

According to EXON theory, consciously accepting that a perceived object could violate the OP demands would mean that the entity with the strong existential status is downgraded to the entity with the weak existential status (see Table 2.3). As argued in Chapter 2 (Section 2.6) his action occurs on the EXON's emotional dimension and constitutes the high level of EXON (HLEXON). In order to examine the possibility of adults downgrading an existentially strong object to the status of an existentially weak entity, Study 3 [10] was designed.

3.5 Driving licence versus own hand: HLEXON on perceived objects

British university graduates and undergraduates were shown an apparent violation of the OP demands by a perceived entity – a square, plastic card became badly damaged in an empty box after a magic spell was cast on the box. The participants were then tested in the (a) no-risk condition, in which they were asked to say whether it was the magic spell that had damaged the plastic card, b) low-risk condition, in which they were asked to place in the box their driving licenses, and (c) high-risk condition, in which they were asked to place in the box their hands. In both b) and c) conditions participants had to decide whether they allow or don't allow the experimenter to repeat his magic spell. The degree of risk and therefore the degree of personal involvement was determined by the objects' existential status on the EXON's cognitive and emotional dimensions: Plastic card (cognitively and emotionally weak existential status), a replaceable document (cognitively strong and emotionally weak status), and own hand (cognitively and emotionally strong existential status).

The results showed that in the no-risk condition none of the participants acknowledged that the plastic card had been damaged by the experimenter's magic spell; in the low-risk condition only a few banned the magic spell, whereas in the

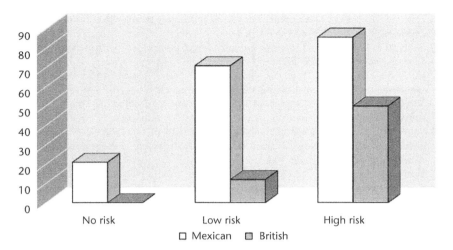

FIGURE 3.8 Percent of adult participants who applied the BONP to a perceived object, as a function of Risk (No, Low and High), and Cultural background (Mexican vs British)

high-risk condition 50% of participants prohibited the magic spell and justified their decision by admitting that the spell might in fact damage their hands. In this situation, British participants applied the BONP to the cognitively and emotionally strong perceived object to the extent comparable to that of uneducated peasants in central Mexico [11] (see Figure 3.8).

The study indicated that under certain conditions adults apply the BONP to perceived entities, given that the entity is emotionally significant. This indicates that personally significant entities (PSE) are more vulnerable to magical suggestions than personally not-significant entities (PNE) (see Table 2.2). At the same time, this experiment demonstrated that magical suggestion, which is an existentially weak entity when its target is a PNE (plastic card), can be upgraded to existentially strong entity, when it targets participants' PSE; when this upgrade happens, participants begin to behave as if they believed in that a magic spell may have real powers over perceived objects (i.e., participants' valued documents and their own body).

The experiments reviewed in this chapter examined BLEXON and HLEXON on perceived entities. However, most of our mental life goes inside our mind and is temporarily detached from perception. Our creative thinking relies not as much upon the perceived object as upon the objects that are imaginary. In the next chapter, we will consider studies on how BLEXON works in regard to imaginary, rather than perceived entities.

References

[1] Piaget, J. (1937). *La construction du réel chez l'enfant*. Neuchatel, Paris: Delacheux et Niestlé.

[2] Harris, P. L. (1975). Development of search and object permanence during infancy. *Psychological Bulletin*, 82, 332–344.
[3] Subbotskii, E. V. (1987). Development in children of the object permanence concept. *Voprosy Psichologii*, 6, 139–171.
[4] Michotte, A. (1962). *Causalité, permanence et réalité phenomenales*. Publications Universitaires de Louvain Editions Béatrice-Nauvelaerts.
[5] Subbotskii, E. V. (1988). Preschool child's conceptions of object permanence: Real and verbal behaviour. *Vestnik of Moscow University*, 14; *Psichologia*, 3, 56–69.
[6] Subbotsky, E. (2004). Magical thinking in judgments of causation: Can anomalous phenomena affect ontological causal beliefs in children and adults? *British Journal of Developmental Psychology*, 22, 123–152.
[7] Shtulman, A., & Carey, S. (2007). Improbable or impossible? How children reason about the possibility of extraordinary events. *Child Development*, 78, 1015–1032.
[8] Woolley, J. D. (1997). Thinking about fantasy: Are children fundamentally different thinkers and believers from adults? *Child Development*, 6, 991–1011.
[9] Rozin, P. Millman, L., & Nemeroff, C. (1986). Operation of the laws of sympathetic magic in disgust and other domains. *Journal of Personality and Social Psychology*, 4, 703–712.
[10] Subbotsky, E. (2001). Causal explanations of events by children and adults: Can alternative causal modes coexist in one mind? *British Journal of Developmental Psychology*, 19, 23–46.
[11] Subbotsky, E. & Quinteros, G. (2002). Do cultural factors affect causal beliefs? Rational and magical thinking in Britain and Mexico. *British Journal of Psychology*, 93, 519–543.

4
CAT WITH A FISH'S TAIL: BLEXON ON IMAGINARY OBJECTS

4.1 Perceived versus imaginary: What is the difference?

As stated in Chapter 2, by mental entities (objects) entities are understood that are created by our perception (phenomena) and imagination (mental images); mental entities can be contrasted with physical entities, which also include RC (see Chapter 2 for more on that). The most obvious difference between perceived and imaginary mental entities is that for experiencing perceived entities we apply our senses, whereas imaginary entities sit solely within our mind. Nevertheless, it is necessary to distinguish between two ontologically different types of imaginary entities: *imaginary physical entities* and *fantastical entities*. Imaginary physical rentities comply with the same physical and causal constraints as their perceived counter-parts (see Figure 2.6, Sections A and B1). For instance, if I imagine a physical item that I saw in a catalogue and want to buy (such as a particular computer), then the imagined item has the same properties of shape, colour, permanence and technical parameters as its real equivalent. Even if my thinking about the item is interrupted, on resumption I am likely to think of the item as having continued to exist and not as being recreated for a second time. There is a clear practical reason for the imaginary physical objects to be permanent. Indeed, if the imaginary physical objects didn't comply with the OP demands, then I wouldn't be able to use my memory for orientation in space and time. For example, driving a car in the area I am familiar with, I am relying on the 'mental map' of the area which, in order to be practically efficient, has to stay permanent and in correspondence to the real composition of turns, roads and roundabouts.

In contrast, with fantastical entities (see Figure 2.6, Section C), principles of the perceived physical world can be suspended. In this class of entities, one can include non-existing entities (e.g., a flying hippo), impossible entities (e.g., the impossible triangle) and irregular ordinary objects made of non-permanent substances (e.g., a

DOI: 10.4324/9781003219521-4

castle made of smoke). The common feature that unites these entities into a single domain is the fact that they do not have matching archetypes in the perceived world. Like imaginary physical entities, fantastical entities can be practically important, but for a different reason. When a designer is looking for a new image for a car or a bridge, he or she has to operate with images that are not tied up to a certain rigid structure in the perceived world; if it were not the case, the designer's product wouldn't be able to take shape of really innovative construction, being instead just variants of its rigid perceived prototype. Even more important fantastical domain is for specialists in creative professions, such as artists and fantasy writers. Because fantastical entities are associated with dreams, art, myths, and religions, they don't have to conform to the OP demands and other requirements for Self-related phenomena, which makes them highly non-permanent and prone to changes.

It was established in developmental research that 4- and 6-year old children can distinguish between perceived objects (a perceived cup), imaginary physical objects (an imagined cup), and fantastical objects (a witch flying in the sky) [1], 5-year-olds are as good as adults at differentiating fantastical from real objects [2], and even 3-year-olds understand that, unlike perceived physical objects, imaginary entities cannot be touched or seen by other people [3]. In studies with adults, researchers have compared between imagined and perceived objects on a number of parameters [4], [5], [6], [7], [8], [9], [10]. Nevertheless, the question of how imaginary entities compare with perceived objects in terms of permanence remains open. Specifically, do children (and, for that matter, adults) distinguish between different types of imaginary entities such as imaginary physical objects and fantastical objects in terms of object permanence?

To some extent, comparing the BOP of perceived and imaginary objects in older children and adults has been impeded by the absence of a suitable method. Traditionally, nonverbal tests were used for studying permanence of perceived objects in infants, with displays involving obstruction of perceived objects by other objects, invisible displacement, or replacement of one object by another behind a screen [11], [12], [13]. Clearly, this method is inappropriate for older children and adults. Unlike infants, older children and adults don't view these kinds of display as challenging their belief in object permanence; rather, they view them as tricks. For example, Chandler and Lalonde [14] showed to 3- to 5-year-old pre-schoolers a display that was mimicking the method earlier applied with infants: A solid perceived object passed unhindered through space apparently occupied by another solid object. Only half of the children called the event magical, and even these children, after further questioning, said they had meant that the event was actually a trick. In terms of EXON theory, these results indicate that the children applied the BOP to a physical entity in spite of the fact that the entity had apparently violated the OP demands.

The EXON approach helps to overcome this methodological difficulty. The new element used in this approach is *adapting a version of the invisible displacement task for participants with mature perception and critical thinking*. The adapted version uses a device

– a specially designed wooden box – that causes a physical object to appear, disappear or transform in such a way that these effects are hard to rationally explain (see Chapter 3 for the description). Unlike stage tricks that are shown at a distance, the effects happened in participants' own hands within an apparently empty box that participants thoroughly examine both before and after the superordinary transformations. The impossibility to find a rational explanation creates the impression that the observed effects had indeed violated the OP demands.

Another new element in this experimental methodology is distinguishing between different kinds of mental entities, depending on their *origin* (internally versus externally initiated) and *EXON kind* (assisted versus unassisted EXON). When a certain mental entity (perceived or imaginary) is *spontaneously actualized in our mind*, without us making a special effort to affect the entity's existential status, we are dealing with the 'default' version of *internally initiated entity*. A similar default version of externally initiated mental entity is engaged when another person asks us to think of or perceive a certain entity, without trying to affect this entity by any suggestion. Let us call this kind of EXON *unassisted EXON*. Usually, unassisted EXON takes place in pre-test interview trials, when participants are unobtrusively asked about their understanding of key concepts employed in subsequent test trials. In contrast, when the entity (perceived or imagined) appears *after an attempt is made to alter the entity*, either by wishing or by applying a magic spell, suggestion or prayer, we are dealing with *assisted EXON*. Finally, if our EXON is assisted by us (e.g., through a magic spell, a prayer or a suggestion), we will call this *internally assisted EXON*; if, however, our EXON is affected by someone else (through a magic spell, a prayer or a suggestion), we will call this *externally assisted EXON* (see Table 4.1).

Finally, one more new element of the new methodology is *employing entities that vary in their personal significance to participants* (see Chapter 2, Table 2.2). Traditionally, studies on object permanence employed only the EXON's *cognitive dimension*. In the new EXON's methodology, along with the EXON's cognitive dimension, the EXON's *emotional dimension* is employed. In the emotional dimension of EXON, our Self accomplishes EXON on entities that are linked to our core needs, interests and emotions. Entities that are linked to our core needs and interests we called personally significant entities (PSE). In the everyday language, we say that our EXON regarding these entities is biased, or we have vested interests in these entities. Examples of such entities could be our body, health and property. Because PSE are linked to our vital needs (such as nourishment, sex and safety), our judgement about such entities can be distorted and unobjective. In contrast, the same entities related to strangers we called personally not-significant entities (PNE). Usually, we judge about such entities impartially and objectively.

In the study that follows, the way people apply the OP demands to imaginary and perceived objects was assessed by unassisted, externally assisted and internally assisted EXON [15]. When experiments reviewed in this chapter examined only the basic level of EXON, the term BLEXON will be used (see Table 2.2).

In Experiment 1 of this study, EXON's *cognitive dimension* was targeted. In order to avoid interference with the EXON's emotional dimension, in this

TABLE 4.1 Mental entity as a function of its origin (internal vs external) and EXON kind (unassisted vs assisted)

Origin EXON kind	Internal	External
Unassisted	A phenomenon, thought or memory about a certain entity, which occurs spontaneously in our mind	A phenomenon, thought or memory about a certain entity, which is initiated in our mind by another person
Assisted	A phenomenon, thought or memory about a certain entity, which occurs in our mind after we tried to alter the entity, by wishing, a magic spell, a prayer or self-suggestion	A phenomenon, thought or memory about a certain entity, after other people tried to alter the entity in our mind by a magic spell, a prayer or suggestion

experiment personally not-significant entities (PNE) were selected as a target for participants' EXON. Specifically, in this experiment we compared the BOP towards *imaginary physical objects* (an imagined piece of paper) with that towards *ordinary perceived objects* (a perceived piece of paper). The reason for this comparison was that while ordinary perceived objects (e.g., a perceived post-card) by definition conform to the OP demands and have a strong existential status (see Table 2.2), an extent to which ordinary imagined physical objects (e.g., an imagined post card) conform to the OP demands is an open question. Theoretically, an imaginary object has an incomplete existential status: The object is in our imagination (e.g., an imaginary post card) and it has a corresponding RC (e.g., our knowledge about structure and functions of the post card) but is not available as a perceived phenomenon. Nevertheless, as argued in the beginning of this chapter, in order to use imaginary physical objects for orientation in the physical world, we have to hold the believe in that these objects are as permanent as their perceived counterparts. Only an experiment can answer whether we indeed hold or don't hold this belief.

In Experiment 2, the same procedures were applied to compare the BOP towards *fantastical entities* (e.g., a flying dog) with that towards *ordinary perceived objects* (e.g., a rabbit cut out of a card). The reason for this comparison was that in terms of existential statuses fantastical entities are a direct opposite to perceived ones. Indeed, on EXON's cognitive dimension ordinary perceived entities have a strong existential status, whereas fantastical objects are existentially week since they are not anchored in perceived physical reality; on the contrary, on EXON's emotional dimension, fantastical entities are emotionally saturated and have a strong existential status, whereas ordinary perceived entities, if they belong to PNE, are existentially weak (see Table 2.2). The mentioned differences between existential statuses of fantastical and perceived entities give a reason to expect that the former will be more vulnerable to external or internal assistance than the latter.

In Experiment 3, the BOP towards ordinary perceived objects, ordinary imagined physical objects, and fantastical objects were cross-compared using a different type of assistance: Instead of the experimenter trying to affect an object by a magic spell (externally assisted BLEXON), the experimenter encouraged participants to affect the object by wishing it to be changed (internally assisted BLEXON) (see Table 4.1). Experiments 4 and 5 assessed externally assisted BLEXON on *personally significant imaginary entities (PSIME)* - participants' images of good or bad events happening to them in their future lives. The reason for these experiments was to extend the results of Experiments 2 and 3. Whereas in Experiments 2 and 3 artificially created PSE (fantastical entities) were employed as a target for external and internal suggestion, in real life political and commercial leaders target people's PSIME.

The experimental tests were preceded by two pre-test interviews. The *first pre-test interview* assessed participants' ability to apply the MTD, by distinguishing between magical events and tricks. Researchers reported that calling materializations of their wishes 'magical events' many children actually meant them to be tricks [16]. In order to avoid the error of misinterpreting participants' answers, it was necessary to make sure that participants understood that they were asked questions about the supernatural events (called 'true magic' in the interview) and not about the sleight-of-hand magic (called 'trick magic' in the interview).

The *second pre-test interview* examined whether participants could apply a new BLEXON tool – the ability to distinguish between imaginary and perceived entities (the *imaginary/perceived distinguisher: IPD* for short). The criteria for this distinction are *intermodality* (perceived objects can be touched and seen, and imaginary ones cannot), and *intersubjectivity* (perceived objects can be seen by other people, and objects that we imagine cannot) (see Table 2.1). Earlier studies reported that young children are aware of these constraints [3].

4.2 Rabbit out of the box: Permanence of perceived and imaginary physical entities

In Experiment 1, 6- and 9-year-old children and university undergraduates who had passed both of the above pre-test interviews were divided in two groups. In one group, participants were individually tested in the *unassisted condition*, and in the other group participants were tested in the *magic assisted condition*.

The aim of the *unassisted condition* was to examine to what extent participants applied the BOP to an ordinary imagined physical object (an imagined piece of paper) compared with an ordinary perceived object (a perceived piece of paper) when the participants' BLEXON was *not affected internally or externally*.

A wooden trick box (described in the previous chapter), and two rectangular pieces of paper of 5x9 cm, one blank, the other showing a picture of either a rabbit or a fish were used as materials. A special construction of a lid with a hidden trap door produced an effect that looked like a violation of the OP demands: one object instantaneously turned into another object after the lid of the box was shut.

In the *perceived object trial* participants were asked to put a blank square of white paper in the empty box and close the lid. They were then invited to open the box and take the paper out. On doing this, participants discovered a square of paper identical with the above but showing a picture of a rabbit on it. They were then questioned about their theories of how the new feature might have appeared on the paper. If the participants said that the blank piece of paper and the one with the drawing on it were different items and justified the answer in a rational way (i.e., a trap door in the box), the participants were qualified as applying the BOP to the object. In contrast, the participants who said that the first object changed into the second one, called this event magical and acknowledged that this was true magic and not trick magic, were qualified as applying the BONP.

In the *magic assisted condition* the procedure was the same as in the unassisted condition, except that after the participant placed the object in the box and closed the lid, the experimenter said: 'And now I am going to draw a fish on this square of paper by my magic spell'. Then, the experimenter said a series of non-words that sounded like a magic spell. The aim of this condition was to examine the extent participants applied the BOP to perceived objects when the participants' BLEXON was *externally assisted by the experimenter's magic spell.*

In the *imagined physical object trial* the procedure was identical with that for the perceived object trial, with the exception that participants were not given actual pieces of paper. Instead, they were required to imagine the pieces of paper, with appropriate amendments to instructions. The experiment's conditions and trials are summarized in Table 4.2.

Results showed a considerable similarity between ordinary imagined physical objects and perceived objects in terms of their degree of permanence: Both children and adults applied the BOP to imagined physical objects to approximately the same degree as to perceived objects (Figure 4.1). Another important result was that external assistance (magic assisted condition) did not affect the BLEXON to a significant extent compared with the unassisted BLEXON regarding both perceived and imagined physical objects. These results confirm the expectation (see

TABLE 4.2 Changes in an entity, as a function of condition (unassisted vs magic assisted EXON) and trial (perceived vs imagined ordinary entity), in Experiment 1

Trial Condition	Perceived	Imagined
Unassisted EXON	A blank square of paper spontaneously developed a picture of a rabbit on it	An imagined blank square of paper spontaneously developed a picture of a rabbit on it
Magic assisted EXON	A blank square of paper developed a picture of a fish on it after the experimenter pronounced a magic spell	An imagined blank square of paper developed a picture of a fish on it after the experimenter pronounced a magic spell

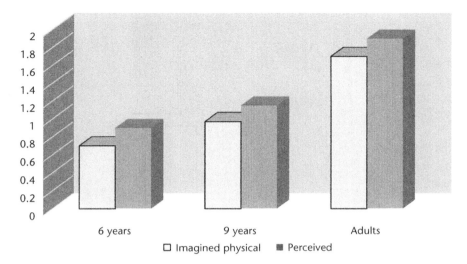

FIGURE 4.1 Mean BOP score in Experiment 1, as a function of Age (6, 9 and Adults) and Type of object (Imagined physical vs Perceived)

Section 4.1 of this chapter) of imagined physical objects to have a strong existential status: be it otherwise, the imagined physical object would be practically useless for orientation in the environment.

The question arises whether fantastical entities, which don't have perceived prototypes in the OR, will get the same degree of permanence from BLEXON as perceived objects. If the permanence of imagined physical objects resulted from their orientational function, then fantastical entities should be expected to be treated as significantly less permanent than either perceived objects or imagined physical objects. Indeed, since fantastical entities exist only in the imagination and are not anchored in the world of the OR, fantastical objects can be easily convertible and sensitive to external or internal suggestions.

4.3 Green rabbits versus flying dogs: Permanence of fantastical entities

To examine whether this expectation is true, in Experiment 2 of this study ordinary imagined physical objects were replaced with fantastical entities that do not have perceived prototypes.

In this experiment the method was the same as in Experiment 1, except two differences: a) In the *imagined fantastical entity trial,* participants were asked to imagine a fantastical animal (a little flying dog) turning into another fantastical animal (a cat with a fish's tail); b) In the *perceived object trial*, instead of a blank piece of paper developing a picture in the box, a small rabbit cut out of green card was converted into a much larger fish cut out of orange card.

60 Cat with a fish's tail

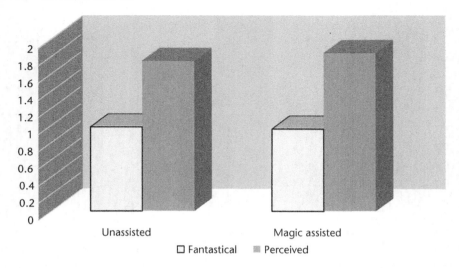

FIGURE 4.2 Mean BOP score in Experiment 2, as a function of Entity (Fantastical vs Perceived) and BLEXON type (Unassisted vs Magic assisted)

Results indicated that overall, fantastical entities were indeed treated as significantly less permanent than perceived objects, in both magic-assisted and unassisted BLEXON conditions (Figure 4.2).

The comparison between results of Experiment 2 and Experiment 3 showed a significant interaction between *Age* and *Type of entity* variables. As Figure 4.3

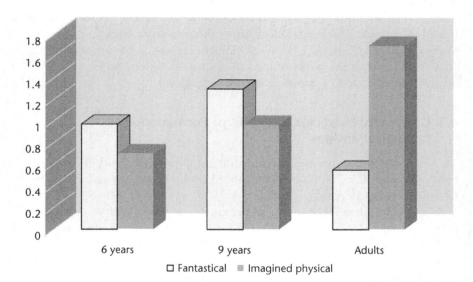

FIGURE 4.3 Mean BOP score in Experiment 3 (Fantastical entities) and in Experiment 2 (Imagined physical objects), as a function of Age

indicates, for children fantastical entities were almost as permanent as imagined physical objects. In contrast, adults treated fantastical entities as significantly less permanent than imagined physical objects.

In order to explain the difference between children's and adults' tendency to apply BOP to fantastical entities, we need to assume that in adults, but not in children, the divide appears between the two domains of imagined reality: imagined ordinary reality and imagined superordinary reality. Like children, adults viewed imagined physical objects as a reflection of their perceived counterparts, with both types of objects being a part of the OR; consequently, adults applied the BOP to imagined physical objects to the same degree as to perceived objects. Unlike children, adults viewed fantastical entities as a part of the SOR and treated them as significantly less permanent than imagined ordinary physical objects (see Section 4.1).

A possible way to verify this assumption is to vary the assisted BLEXON, for example, by replacing the externally assisted BLEXON (experimenter's magic spell) with internally assisted one (the participant's own wishing). If children viewed fantastical entities as less permanent than imagined physical objects but didn't show this in Experiment 2 because they didn't consider the experimenter's magic spell to be powerful enough to change the fantastical entities, then they certainly would view their own wish as capable of changing fantastical entities. If, however, children couldn't distinguish fantastical entities from imagined physical objects in terms of compliance with the OP demands while the adults could, then the results in this experiment would be similar to the results of Experiment 2: The BLEXON assisted with the participants' own wishing would yield lower permanence scores for fantastical entities than for imagined physical objects with adults, but not with children.

Accordingly, in Experiment 3 the method was the same as in Experiment 2, but instead of transforming an object in the box by his magic spell, the experimenter asked participants to do the transformation with the help of their own wish. The results (Figure 4.4) confirmed the results of Experiment 2: They indicated that adults, but not children, treated fantastical objects as significantly less permanent and more vulnerable to internal assistance than imagined physical objects.

Altogether, Experiments 1–3 revealed that whereas 6- and 9-year-old children did not draw a borderline between fantastical entities and imagined physical objects in terms of their freedom from physical constraints, adults treated fantastical entities as largely non-permanent. In other words, adults believed that perceived and imagined physical objects cannot magically change into other objects, whereas fantastical entities can.

While answering the question on the comparative existential statuses of perceived, imagined physical and fantastical entities, the results of the reviewed study raise another question: What is special about fantastical entities that makes adults treat them as more vulnerable to magical suggestion than either perceived or imagined physical objects?

As proposed above, the answer to this question is hidden in differences between existential statuses of the entities on EXON's cognitive and emotional dimensions. On the EXON's cognitive dimension perceived and imagined physical objects

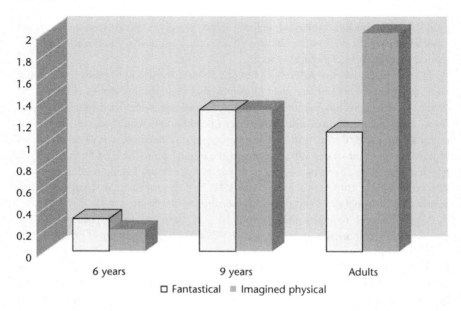

FIGURE 4.4 Mean BOP score in Experiment 3 (internally assisted BLEXON via participant's own wish), as a function of Age (6, 9 and Adults) and Type of entity (Fantastical vs Imagined physical)

have a strong existential status, whereas fantastical entities have a weak existential status. On the EXON's emotional dimension the relation is reversed: Both perceived and imagined ordinary physical objects used in the reviewed experiments (i.e., a rabbit, a fish) belonged to the OR and had a weak existential status, whereas fantastical entities (i.e., a flying dog and a cat with a fish's tail) were entities from the SOR and had a strong existential status (see Table 2.2). The results of experiments reviewed in this chapter can therefore be summarized as follows: in adults, but not in children, assisted EXON affected *cognitively weak but emotionally strong entities (CWESE)*, whereas *cognitively strong but emotionally weak entities (CSEWE)* showed resistance to both external and internal suggestion. On the opposite end of the chain, the experiments showed that the assistance in the form of wish or a magic spell undergoes *existential upgrade* when the target of the assistance is CWESE but remains an existentially weak entity when its target is CSEWE. These results are in concordance with the similar results of Study 3, reviewed at the end of the previous chapter.

While in the reviewed studies CWESE were represented by artificially created fantastical entities (i.e., a flying dog and a cat with a fish's tail), the domain of such entities is not limited by fantastical supernatural creatures and may include ordinary objects with unusual properties (e.g., an elephant made of smoke). Personally significant imaginary events (PSIME) can be included in this domain as well.

A special kind of PSIME is individual's thoughts about his or her own future or destiny. In addition to an individual's future life, PSIME include thoughts about the future lives of those close to the individual, the future of personally significant environments (e.g., a house, a homeland, the planet), and other events closely related to an individual's health and wellbeing. Unlike ordinary perceived entities, PSIME are fragile. Indeed, whatever plans individuals create about their future, they know that these plans can be suddenly interrupted by unforeseen circumstances. Our PSIME are absent in the perceived reality, and their RC (e.g., our plans of staying healthy and alive) cannot be built, because an unexpected illness or a tragic accident can always destroy them. This makes PSIME cognitively weak entities. At the same time, by definition PSIME are filled with emotional significance and personal value, and this makes them emotionally strong entities. Altogether, these contrasting existential statuses put PSIME in the domain of CWESE. This suggests that PSIME, like fantastical entities, could be vulnerable to external intrusion.

Whereas fantastical supernatural entities are generally conceived in arts and mass entertainment, magical practices and persuasion techniques used in religion, politics, and commercial advertising target PSIME. It is also a common observation that when people are thinking of events or making important decisions that might affect their PSIME, many otherwise rational individuals become superstitious [17].

However, not all personal imaginary entities belong to the domain of CWESE. The events related to the future life and destiny of a strange person do not contain emotional value for me and thus are existentially weak on EXON's emotional dimension (see Table 2.2). Existential weakness of such entities allows us to call these entities *personally not-significant imaginary entities (PNIME)*. On EXON's cognitive scale, PNIME may occupy a stronger existential status than PSIME, because for PNIME their RC can be built. Indeed, any PSIME is a unique entity; therefore, one cannot create the PSIME's rational (RC), because an RC is a result of comparisons and measurements of a bunch of related phenomena. In contrast, while one still cannot perceive PNIME, one can build the PNIME's RC, via comparison of various instances of PNIME and creating a typical model. For example, in regard to the person's own future life, a person cannot know how long he or she will live, but the person can employ statistics and science in order to create the RC of other people's life span. Going along this line, the person comes to the conclusion that other people's life span depends on gender, health service, and the people's lifestyle; for instance, an average life span for men in Russia in 2019 was 68.5 years, and for women 78.5 years. On this ground, PNIME should have a stronger existential status on EXON's cognitive dimension, compared with PSIME (see Table 2.2).

To summarize, on combination of existential statuses PSIME belong to the domain of CWESE, whereas PNIME better fits the domain of CSEWE. These theoretical consideration, combined with the results of the earlier reviewed experiments, allow us to expect that PSIME will be more vulnerable to external assistance than PNIME. As argued in Chapter 2, a social suggestion can be emotionally upgraded from a weak to a strong existential status if a person believes this suggestion. If it is shown that when PSIME are targeted by magical suggestion people begin to belief this suggestion, then this would mean that in the domain of CWESE *magical suggestion is emotionally upgraded* by positive BLEXON (see Table 2.3). Partly such an upgrade has been detected in the studies reviewed above (Study 3 of the previous chapter and Experiments 2 and 3 reviewed in this chapter). However, the focus of those studies was on comparative existential statuses of PSE and PNE, rather than on the suggestive influence per se. The experiments reviewed in the next section had examining the EXUP of suggestive influence as their main target.

4.4 An offer from the witch: Upgrading magical suggestion

Experiment 4 was designed in order to examine EXUP of *magical suggestion*. Adults' PSIME (participants' images of their future lives) were taken as the *suggestion target entities*, whereas magical suggestion was the *EXUP target entity*. The participants were university graduates and undergraduates, who in the pre-test interview revealed their understanding of the difference between true magic and tricks and claimed that they did not believe in true magic. A *between variable* was the *Suggestion target entity* (PSIME vs PNIME), and a *within variable* was the *EXUP target entity* (Desirable versus Undesirable suggestion). *Number of participants* who agreed to allow a magic spell to be cast on their future lives was a *dependent variable*.

In the *PSIME condition* participants' own future lives were targeted by magical suggestion. The participants were individually told two stories, one about a good witch who wanted to put a good spell on their future lives to make them happy (Desirable suggestion), and another about a mean witch who wanted to put a mean spell on their future lives, in order to make the participant a servant to evil forces (Undesirable suggestion). The key question was: "If you were in this situation, would you allow the witch to put the spell on your life, or would you rather not? Why?"

In the *PNIME condition* future life of a stranger was the target of magical suggestion. The participants were told the same stories happening to another person. The character was introduced as a scientist, a rational person and a non-believer in magic. Participants were then asked if the character should have said "yes" or "no" to the good and mean witches. The experiment's conditions are summarized in Table 4.3.

Three hypotheses were tested:

1. *No EXUP hypothesis:* Participants do not believe in the possibility that a magic spell could affect people's future lives. If participants were giving the magic spell zero EXUP, they would handle the situations with the good and mean witches in a rational way. Since a variety of motives could affect participants' judgements (to comply with the witch's request out of politeness, to prove that they don't believe in magic, to avoid interfering with magical forces), and these motives contradict each other, it was expected that participants would

TABLE 4.3 Imaginary entity, as a function of *EXUP target entity* (Desirable versus Undesirable suggestion) and *Suggestion target entity* (PSIME vs PNIME), in Experiment 4

Suggestion target entity EXUP target entity	PSIME	PNIME
Desirable suggestion	Me becoming wealthy and healthy in my future life	A strange person becoming wealthy and healthy in her future life
Undesirable suggestion	Me becoming a servant to evil forces in my future life	A strange person becoming a servant to evil forces in her future life

give "yes" and "no" answers to the Desirable and Undesirable suggestion at chance level in both conditions.

2. *Positive EXUP hypothesis*: Participants believe in the possibility that a magic spell can affect people's future lives. In that case the participants' reactions to the Desirable and Undesirable suggestions would diverge. Regarding the Desirable suggestion, frequencies of "yes" and "no" answers would still be at chance level. This is expected because, in this case the suggestion aimed in the same direction as the participant's own wish – to provide the participant with desired outcomes. Nevertheless, some participants would remember that they had denied their belief in magic in the pre-test interview and thus be reluctant to accept the positive spell. The counterbalance between these motives would produce the 50 x 50 distribution between "yes" and "no" answers. Regarding the Undesirable suggestion, however, the suggestion runs in the opposite direction to the participant's own wish, because the participants wouldn't like to become servants to evil forces. Like in the case with the Desirable suggestion, participants would still remember their pre-test interview claim that they don't believe in magic and thus tempted to say to the evil witch "yes, go ahead with your spell, I don't believe it would work." Nevertheless, because this is no longer an interview but a real-life situation in which the participants believe that the magic spell could indeed affect their future lives, they would be inclined to say "no" to the Undesirable suggestion at a level significantly above chance.

3. The results will *depend on the condition*: In regard to PSIME, EXUP of the suggestion will be positive, and in regard to PNIME it will be zero. In other words, in the *PSIME condition* participants would exhibit their belief in the effect of the spell and agree to the Undesirable suggestion significantly less often than to the Desirable suggestion. In the *PNIME condition* though, the participants' EXON would show their disbelief in the effectiveness of magical suggestion and give an approximately equal numbers of "yes" and "no" answers to both Desirable and Undesirable suggestion.

The results (Figure 4.5) supported the third hypothesis. In regard to their PSIME over 50% of participants said "yes" to the Desirable suggestion, but no one agreed

66 Cat with a fish's tail

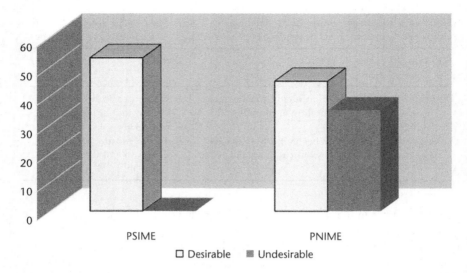

FIGURE 4.5 Percent of participants who agreed to accept the suggested message in Experiment 4, as a function of *Suggestion target entity* (PSIME vs PNIME) and *EXUP target entity* (Desirable versus Undesirable suggestion)

to accept the Undesirable suggestion. This means that the participants did not rule out the possibility that the external assistance in the form of a magic spell could affect their future lives. In contrast, in regard to their PNIME, approximately equal numbers of participants said that the story character should have given the "yes" answers to the Desirable and the Undesirable suggestion, with only insignificant prevalence of the Desirable suggestion. This indicates that the participants indirectly acknowledged that the non-believer in magic should be free of fear and accept both Desirable and Undesirable suggestions to an equal extent. However, when subsequently asked how they would answer if they were in the characters shoes, most participants changed the views: About half of the participants said that they would allow the Desirable suggestion, but most rejected the Undesirable one. This behaviour indicates that participants treated the witches' offer with zero EXUP when the suggestion targeted the participants' PNIME, but swiftly switched to positive EXUP when their PSIME were targeted by the suggestion. Altogether, the results indicated that, *taken on the basic level of EXON (BLEXON), people tend to emotionally upgrade magical suggestion from a weak to a strong existential status when their PSIME are targeted by the suggestion*. In contrast, when magical suggestion targets PNIME participants' verbal disbelief in magic gets zero EXUP (Figure 4.6).

In the reviewed experiment, the external assistance took shape of a magic spell cast by a professional witch, thus placing the participants' BLEXON in the context of SOR. However, *unlike in laboratory experiments, in real life messages that aim at*

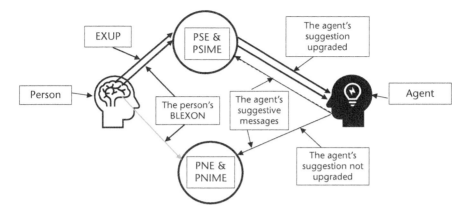

FIGURE 4.6 The relations between *the person's perceived or imaginary entities* (PSE & PSIME vs PNE & PNIME) targeted by an agent's suggestive messages, and *the agent's suggestive messages* targeted by the person's BLEXON & EXUP

manipulating with people's minds are presented to people in a mundane form and don't mention magic and witchcraft. For example, Western political leaders sometimes give people unrealistic suggestions (e.g., that going to this war will install democracy in the conquered country whereas not going for the war would threaten democracy in the West). Commercial advertisers follow politicians (e.g., suggest that buying this brand of i-phone will make you rich). It is clear that such suggestions when assessed rationally by unassisted BLEXON should be viewed as useless and invested with weak existential status. However, when suggestions are made by rich and powerful individuals (a president, a famous actor, a priest), they may acquire a strong existential value for people. Suggestions of this kind are typical for politics, commerce and pharmacology [18], [19], [20]. If ordinary suggestions were existentially upgraded by people in the same way as magical ones, then this would expose the psychological mechanism of manipulation with mass consciousness. Specifically, this would show that political and commercial powers exercise control over mass consciousness by targeting people's PSIME and thus forcing the people to convert *existentially weak entities (e.g., suggested political and commercial options which are not beneficial and may even be harmful to an individual)* into existentially strong entities. When people upgrade the suggestions, they begin to take these suggestions seriously and follow suggested messages.

4.5 Simulating the witch: Is an ordinary suggestion as effective as a magical one?

With the aim of examining this assumption, in Experiment 5 participants (university graduates and undergraduates) were divided into magical and ordinary suggestion groups [21]. In both groups, participants PSIME were targeted by suggestion.

In the magical suggestion group participants were asked whether they would allow the experimenter to put a magic spell on their future lives (magic-loaded context). There were two kinds of magical suggestion: Desirable suggestion (a good spell), which promised to make the participants' future lives good and problem-free, and Undesirable suggestion (a bad spell), which aimed at making their future lives hard and full of problems. In the *pre-test interview* (unassisted BLEXON) the participants denied that either of these types of magical suggestions could affect their future lives; however, in their *actions*, when the experimenter offered to cast the magic spell 'for real' (externally assisted BLEXON) the participants behaved as if they believed in the spell's magical powers, by allowing the experimenter to cast the good spell and prohibiting the bad one.

In the ordinary suggestion group participants received the same instruction, but this time the instruction was free from explicit association with magic; the participants were suggested that if the experimenter increased or decreased the number of ones on a computer screen (e.g., changed 1111 into 11111111 or into 11), then the number of difficult problems in the participants' future lives would increase (Undesirable suggestion) or decrease (Desirable suggestion) proportionally (magic free context). The results (Figure 4.7) were clear: although in the interview (unassisted BLEXON) all of the participants had told that this suggestion is powerless to affect their future lives, in their practical actions (externally assisted BLEXON) they behaved like the participants of the magical suggestion group: About a half of participants allowed to decrease the number of ones on the computer screen but all but a few prohibited to increase this number. These results confirm the assumption that

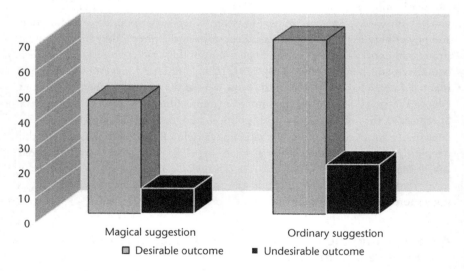

FIGURE 4.7 Percent of participants who agreed to accept the suggested message in Experiment 5, as a function of *Type of suggested message* (Magical vs Ordinary suggestion) and *EXUP target entity* (Desirable versus Undesirable suggestion)

when participants PSIME are targeted by suggestion, ordinary suggestion is upgraded to the same extent as magical suggestion. By targeting people's PSIME, the individuals of power can make people believe the suggested messages and accept choices that benefit interests of the persons of power but contradict the people's own interests.

4.6 BLEXON on imaginary objects in the developmental perspective: Conclusion

The reviewed studies examined permanence of three types of imaginary entities: Imagined physical, fantastical, and (adults only) PSIME and PNIME.

The studies revealed that *in children* all imaginary entities are moderately permanent and as permanent as perceived entities. The studies also showed that externally (a magic spell) and internally (the participants own wish) assisted BLEXON can affect fantastical, imagined physical and perceived objects to an equal extent. In other words, in children fantastical entities are not yet differentiated from imagined ordinary entities and from perceived entities on EXON's cognitive and emotional dimensions. Another important result was that permanence of both imaginary and perceived entities increased with age.

In adults, the picture was more complicated. Like children, adults treated imagined physical entities as equally permanent with perceived entities. However, in regard to fantastical entities adults' BLEXON became sensitive to both internal (own wish) and external (magic spell) assistance. In other words, in adults fantastical entities became significantly less permanent than perceived entities. This result was explained by the entities' existential statuses over the EXON's cognitive and emotional dimensions: Whereas perceived entities (e.g., a piece of paper or a picture of a rabbit) and imagined ordinary entities (e.g., an imagined piece of paper or an imagined fish) have a strong existential status on EXON's cognitive dimension but a weak status on EXON's emotional dimension (CSEWE), in fantastical entities the existential statuses are reversed: Fantastical entities are cognitively weak but emotionally strong (CWESE) (Table 2.2).

As long as PSIME belong to the domain of CWESE as well, we hypothesized that BLEXON on these entities should also be sensitive to external assistance. Subsequent experiments confirmed this hypothesis: In the pre-test interviews adult participants did not show any belief in both magical and ordinary types of suggestion, but when suggested messages targeted participants' PSIME, the participants behaved as if they believed the messages.

Altogether, in children imaginary and perceived entities are not yet differentiated in terms of their permanence and non-permanence. In adults, there appears a divide between imaginary entities that are moderately permanent (CSEWE), and imaginary entities that are non-permanent and sensitive to external attempts of manipulation (CWESE). Imagined physical entities belong to the former category, whereas the latter category includes fantastical entities and PSIME.

TABLE 4.4 Existential statuses of entities on EXON's cognitive and emotional dimensions, as a function of *Type of entity* and *Age group*

Type of entity Age group	Perceived physical	Ordinary imaginary physical	Fantastical	Personally not significant imaginary (PNIME)	Personally- significant imaginary (PSIME)	Upgraded personally significant imaginary (UPSIME)
Children (6–9 years)	Not differentiated	Not differentiated	Not differentiated	———	——	———
Adults	CSEWE	CSEWE	CWESE	CSEWE	CWESE	CSESE

One more conclusion which these results entail concerns the status of suggestive messages. The results indicated that when suggestive messages target PNIME, they meet zero EXUP. Simply put, such messages, both magical and ordinary, are either ineffective or their effect depends on the person's rational critical assessment. However, when suggestive messages target PSIME, the messages undergo positive EXUP: They become powerful enough to make the people uncritically accept the messages and follow the suggestions.

This positive EXUP on suggestive messages is particularly evident in regard to magical suggestion. On EXON's cognitive dimension, a magic spell fits the domain of existentially weak entities (see Table 2.2). In other words, most educated adults consciously don't believe that a magic spell can affect real-life events [22]. This means that in educated adults the idea of a magical event, which entails a violation of the OP demands, belongs to the domain of CWESE. The above experiments demonstrated that *when magical suggestion targets PSIME, modern adults tend to upgrade their idea of magic from an entity with a weak to an entity with a strong existential status (CSESE)*. When this kind of EXUP takes place, *the idea of magic* becomes *the belief in magic* and obtains the power of controlling the person's behaviour. Importantly, the degree of the belief in magic-free suggestive messages was almost identical to that of magic-related suggestive messages.

Existential statuses of entities are summarized in Table 4.4.

Thus far we have been reviewing studies which explored the basic level of EXON (BLEXON). On this level, our Self *intuitively* invests with existence ordinary and fantastical entities, whether perceived or imaginary, and can be influenced internally (own wish) or externally (magical or ordinary suggestion). Our BLEXON establishes whether we are dealing with a permanent or a non-permanent entity, and 'decides' whether the entity is or isn't emotionally important.

Along with the idea of magic, there is another supernatural imagined entity that belongs to the domain of CWESE – the idea of a God. In the next chapter, we will consider under what circumstances our EXON can *consciously* upgrade the idea of God, thus leaping from the level of upgrading ordinary PSIME to the level of *faith in the superordinary* entity – God. Earlier we called this kind of EXON the high level of EXON (HLEXON) (see Table 2.3).

References

[1] Harris, P. L., Brown, E., Marriott, C., Whittall, S., & Harmer, S. (1991). Monsters, ghosts and witches: Testing the limits of the fantasy-reality distinction in young children. *British Journal of Developmental Psychology*, 9, 105–123.

[2] Sharon, T. L., & Woolley, J. D. (2004). Do monsters dream? Young children's understanding of the fantasy/reality distinction. *British Journal of Developmental Psychology*, 22, 293–310.

[3] Wellman, H. M., & Estes, D. (1986). Early understanding of mental entities: A re-examination of childhood realism. *Child Development*, 57, 910–923.

[4] Aitneave, F., & Pierce, C. R. (1978). Accuracy of extrapolating a pointer into perceived and imagined space. *American Journal of Psychology*, 91, 371–387.

[5] Belli, R. F., Schuman, H., & Jackson, B. (1997). Autobiographical remembering: John Dean is not alone. *Applied Cognitive Psychology*, 11, 187–209.

[6] Ceci, S. J., Huffman, M. L. C., Smith, E., & Loftus, E. W. (1994). Repeatedly thinking about a non-event: Source misattribution among pre-schoolers. *Consciousness and Cognition*, 3, 388–407.

[7] Freyd, J. J. & Finke, R. A. (1984). Facilitation of length discrimination using real and imagined context frames. *American Journal of Psychology*, 97, 323–341.

[8] Henkel, L. A., & Franklin, N. (1998). Reality monitoring of physically similar and conceptually related objects. *Memory & Cognition*, 26, 659–673.

[9] Johnson, M. K. (1988). Reality monitoring: An experimental phenomenological approach. *Journal of Experimental Psychology: General*, 117, 390–394.

[10] Johnson, M. K., Foley, M. A., Suengas, A. G., & Raye, C. L. (1988). Phenomenal characteristics of memories for perceived and imagined autobiographical events. *Journal of Experimental Psychology: General*, 117, 371–376.

[11] Baillargeon, R. (1987). Object permanence in 3 1/2- and 4 1/2-month-old infants. *Developmental Psychology*, 23, 655–664.

[12] Bower, T. G. R. (1971). The object in the world of an infant. *Scientific American*, 225(4), 30–38.

[13] Piaget, J. (1986). *The construction of reality in the child*. New York: Ballantine Books. (Original work published 1937)

[14] Chandler, M., & Lalonde, C. E. (1994). Surprising, magical, and miraculous turns of events: Children's reactions to violations of their early theories of mind and matter. *British Journal of Developmental Psychology*, 12, 83–96.

[15] Subbotsky, E. (2005). The permanence of mental objects: Testing magical thinking on perceived and imaginary realities. *Developmental Psychology*, 41, 301–318.

[16] Woolley, J. D., Phelps, K. E., Davis, D. L., & Mandell, D. J. (1999). Where theories of mind meet magic: The development of children's beliefs about wishing. *Child Development*, 70, 571–587.

[17] Jahoda, G. (1969). *The psychology of superstition*. London: Penguin.

[18] Coriat I. H. (1923). Suggestion as a form of medical magic. *Journal of Abnormal and Social Psychology*, 18, 258–268.

[19] Malinowski B. (1935). *Coral gardens and their magic*. London, England: Allen & Unwin.

[20] Tambiah S. J. (1990). *Magic, science, religion, and the scope of rationality*. Cambridge, UK: Cambridge University Press.

[21] Subbotsky, E. (2007). Children's and adult's reaction to magical and ordinary suggestion: Are suggestibility and magical thinking psychologically close relatives? *British Journal of Psychology*, 98, 547–574.

[22] Subbotsky, E. (2010). *Magic and the mind. Mechanisms, functions, and development of magical thinking and behaviour*. Oxford University Press.

5
GENERATING GOD

5.1 Does God exist? Upgrading the idea of God by external assistance

God is an idea of an invisible entity to which various religions attribute different qualities. In ancient Greece gods were powerful but had unattractive human features: They were jealous, vindictive and adulterous. In modern monotheistic religions, God is a creator of the universe and the people and is omnipresent and omniscient. In Christianity, God is a loving and forgiving entity. Yet, studies have shown that even in modern religions God possesses many human psychological properties [1][2][3]. The question is, how can the idea of God, which is by definition a cognitively weak entity, raise to the status of a strong, and even absolute entity? As follows from studies reviewed in Chapters 2 and 4, for this to happen the idea of God has to be emotionally important and then upgraded internally or/and externally. But is this enough for having a faith in God?

Habitually, for a child brought up in a religious family the belief in God comes from his or her social environment, via suggestion. The child absorbs the parents' religious views and rarely doubts them. When children become adults, they seek support of their faith in their coreligionists. People born in a religious background come to believe because everyone in their social environment is a believer. This socially inspired faith may become a profession like it became for the bishop of the Episcopal Church John Shelby Spong, who was born in the American Bible Belt and absorbed the Christian faith from his Evangelical Protestant environment; this, however, did not stop him from later embracing the scientific view of the world and abandoning the traditional belief in omnipotent and omniscient god [4].

Psychological experiments have shown that for most people not only the belief in God, but also the belief in science is based not on independent thinking, but on the support of their trusted social group. As shown in one of the reviewed experiments (see Chapter 3) educated adult participants exhibited strong verbal disbelief in that their hands could be damaged by the experimenter's magic spell and grounded their scepticism towards magic by their belief in science. Nevertheless, when the social support for this scepticism was eliminated by special manipulations, half of the participants gave the idea of magic some credit and banned the magic spell [5]. As studies reviewed in Chapter 4 demonstrated, the belief in the supernatural becomes even stronger if it is supported by external suggestion. In the modern world, the whole institution of the official church is built in order to externally upgrade God's existential status in the people's minds.

Another way to upgrade the belief in God is through observing miracles. As argued in the introduction, an entity's existential status can be upgraded by matching the entity's idea with a certain perceived counterpart. If such a match is achieved, the idea may change from a cognitively weak entity (e.g., a fantastic image) into a cognitively strong entity (e.g., into an imaginary physical object). The visions of Jesus Christ and the Blessed Virgin Mary were used as the proof of the existence of God since the time of the first evangelists [6], not to mentioned multiple scenes of people observing their gods described in writings by Homer and other ancient authors. Since ancient times, artists depicted gods in their poems and paintings, and even when gods failed to appear in person they delegated miracles and supernatural events to testify for their (gods) reality.

Whereas pressure from the social environment and observing miracles target BLEXON, the attempts to *consciously prove* God's existence on the basis of observation of perceived phenomena elevate the assistance to HLEXON. Some of such attempts come from exploring natural phenomena that cannot be explained by science. Although science inherently denies the existence of the supernatural, some scientific discoveries and theories show in the direction of the presence of some kind of super-powerful intelligence in the universe. The origin of the universe via a Big Bang [7], the 'fine tuning' of main cosmological constants which allows for life to emerge in the universe [8], the 'rational' structure and work of the living cell [9] and other natural wonders suggest existence of the underlying intelligent design so compellingly that make some known defenders of atheism in philosophy change their views in favour of God's existence [10]. Indeed, the presence of the enigmatic creative force in the universe that builds complex systems out of the simple ones, dark energy and dark matter, the emergence of life from non-animate matter, the emergence of consciousness and free will – these and some other phenomena escape scientific understanding and thus increase the probability of the existence of God.

The *external assistance* to upgrade the idea of God on the basis of scientific observations of enigmatic phenomena is joined by the *internal assistance*, which comes from the basic concepts of science. At first glance, the conclusion that the idea of God might be rooted in the foundations of science looks mind-boggling. However, this conclusion would look less controversial if we remembered that mathematics and logic operate borderline concepts, such as 'infinity'. Indeed, how could people possibly acquire this concept and use it in scientific research?

Certainly, they could not infer the infinity concept from perceived phenomena, since in perceived experience we only see something finite. For example, when we think of a typical concept, such as 'dog', we can show a real dog running in the street in support of this concept. When we think of a mathematical concept, for example, the 'number 3' or a triangle, we can point out a set of three apples or a triangular-shaped facet of a crystal. In contrast, when it goes about infinity, there is nothing out there to show in support of it. It is impossible to perceive infinity in the same way we perceive a tree or a table; the concept of infinity can only be represented as a symbol ∞. But we know that infinity is not just a symbol, it really exists, because if it didn't, Achilles could never catch up with the tortoise, and some other Zeno paradoxes of movement could never be explained [11]. Of course, there may be other characters that are only imaginary and don't have referents in the real world, such as mythological creatures (e.g., Minotaur – a creature half man and half bull), but these characters are still based on our experience – seeing a man and a bull, and simply putting parts of these creatures together. Not so with infinity. Infinity couldn't originate in the human mind, since the human mind is only capable of making a finite (and not very large) number of operations. Even the most powerful quantum computers would be able to complete the 'almost infinite', yet still a limited number of operations. Infinity cannot exist in the physical universe either, because infinity is an infinite number of mental operations (e.g., the sum of an infinite set of real numbers), and the physical universe is devoid of any mentality. We have to admit on this ground that infinity exists within some kind of a super-intelligence – the mind of God – who simply shares his knowledge with us.

Usually, scientists are not bothered by this philosophical puzzle; they simply use the infinity concept to find solutions to theoretical and practical problems. But the effectiveness of science at solving such problems, though indirectly, proves that the 'holder' of infinity – God – exists as well. Surely, this 'god of science' isn't exactly like the gods of religions, yet there are some similarities. The god of science has a mind that is infinitely more powerful than the human mind. Despite science will always keep searching for the complete rational explanation of the universe, some philosophers argue that we will never be able to understand the mind of God [12], [13].

The aforementioned considerations raise the question whether the logical proof of God's existence can be upgraded internally. In terms of the EXON theory, this question targets the cognitive dimension of HLEXON (see Table 2.3).

5.2 Upgrading the logical proof of God's existence

Attempts to prove God's existence by pure logic have a rather long history. Usually, such attempts begin with the Self as a starting point. "I am thinking, therefore I exist" – this famous maxim by Rene Descartes stands as a bedrock in the ocean waves of doubt. Indeed, doubting one's own existence devaluates the doubting itself, and this gives my reflecting Self the highest possible existential status (see Chapter 2 and Table 2.2). Clearly, if I can prove that my idea of God is as existentially powerful as my reflecting Self, then this idea should certainly be granted the status of an existentially absolute entity. Given that, the question still remains of whether our EXON will upgrade this proof from the status of existentially weak *impossible theory*, similar to the theory of perpetual motion machine, to the status of existentially strong *proven theory* (see Table 2.2).

The most popular logical arguments that allow to upgrade the concept of God from a mental notion to the really existing person are the cosmological argument, the argument from intelligent design, and the ontological argument. The *cosmological argument* boils down to the idea that because every event in the universe is causally originated from the previous event, there must be the first cause, which has to be God [14]. The *argument from intelligent design* asserts that since the universe clearly has features of a complex and rationally arranged system (e.g., the system of fine-tuned cosmological constants), it had to be designed by an intelligent being – God [15].

Finally, the *ontological argument* proposed by Anselm of Canterbury in 1078 asserts that because God is a being compared to which no greater being can be conceived, this being must exist in reality, and not just in the mind [16]. There has been an extensive discussion on this argument's validity for almost a thousand years. The discussion, which is on-going [17], concerns philosophical and logical aspects of this argument, which go beyond the topic of this chapter. There is, however, *a psychological aspect* as well. This aspect concerns *the way the ontological argument of God's existence appeals to our HLEXON*.

Indeed, it is common knowledge that rational arguments do not necessarily have a changing effect on people's behaviour. For instance, in moral domain people can preach morality but in their practical actions follow their selfish interests [18], [19]. In the domain of human cognition, the insensitivity of EXON to rationality takes the form of cognitive biases – relying on irrelevant information when solving economic tasks [20]. In the everyday life, we may be fully aware of the dangers of smoking or eating unhealthy food, and still keep smoking and eating this food. In terms of the EXON theory, this means that external and internal assistance in the form of rational suggestion may or may not influence our behaviour.

As studies reviewed in Chapters 3 and 4 have shown, magical and ordinary suggestive messages were existentially upgraded by participants when these messages targeted the participants' personally significant entities. In terms of the EXON theory, the question that can be asked in regard to the ontological argument is as follows: What *psychological conditions* can make people upgrade the ontological proof of God's existence from the status of a weak to the status of an existentially strong entity? In other words, what psychological impacts can make people agree that the almighty and perfect imaginary entity (i.e., God) is as real as the chair standing in front of them? The study reviewed in this chapter aimed at examining such conditions [21].

5.3 Jumping out of the mind: Children's response to the ontological argument

The study was in the form of an interview, adapted from the famous Descartes' version of the ontological proof of God's existence [22]. One particular problem with conducting this interview was to find an appropriate term for the traditional Descartes' wording 'the Supreme Being'. The term had to meet the following conditions: (1) reflect the characteristic of 'almightiness' which is one of two key features of the 'supreme being', (2) be in children's everyday dictionary and (3) not to interfere with religious tradition of culture to which the children belong. The latter condition was important since it was participants' independent thinking and not their acquired knowledge about religious dogmas (i.e., external assistance via suggestion) that was a major aim of the interrogation.

The term 'Almighty Wizard' suited the aforementioned criteria best. Firstly, it eliminated the danger of putting the child on the track of displaying his or her religious ideas of God (if the child had any), which are acquired dogmatically through external suggestion [23]. Secondly, the term was in children's active dictionary. Thirdly, the concept 'Almighty Wizard' reflected the characteristic of 'almightiness' that was of key interest to this study.

In order to examine whether children were able to upgrade the existential status of the almighty being on the basis of their *unassisted HLEXON*, the following questions were asked to 95 Russian children in Moscow, aged 4, 5, 6, 7, 9 and 11 years:

1. Tell me, please, do you know many things? Do you know everything in the world? Who knows more than you?
2. Can you do everything that you want? Who can do more things than you can?
3. Is there anywhere in the world a person or a fairy tale wizard who knows everything and can do everything he wants? Can such Almighty Wizard exist in a fairy tale? Can he exist within a play?
4. Is this Almighty Wizard capable of creating you or somebody like you?
5. Can this Almighty Wizard come out from a fairy tale or our imagination into the real world?
6. Can you imagine such an Almighty Wizard who would even be able to come out from your imagination in the real world?
7. Please, imagine such a wizard right now, O.K.?
8. Now, if you have the idea of the Almighty Wizard in your mind, does this wizard exist in your mind?
9. But if this wizard is almighty and he exists in your mind, can he jump out from your mind in the real world, for instance, in this room and sit down over there on the chair? Why do you think so?

The interview included three stages. The *first stage* (questions 1–3) examined whether children were ready to acknowledge the existence of the Almighty Wizard in the domain of perceived reality and in the domain of the imagination (fairy tale and imaginary play). The aim of the *second stage* (questions 4–7) was to determine limits of the Almighty Wizards' power, specifically, whether the children thought that almightiness included the capacity for the wizard to move from the domain of the imagination into the perceived world. In the *third stage* (questions 8-9) the children were faced with the awareness of the link between the imaginary wizard's almightiness and his ability to come out of the imagination and acquire a perceived, and not just imaginary, existence. It was at this stage that children's unassisted cognitive HLEXON regarding the wizard was tested: The questions allowed to examine whether the children were able to *upgrade the logical inference* that the Wizard's almightiness must include the Wizard's presence in the perceptual world from the *existentially weak hypothetical statement* to the *existentially strong believable theory*.

The results of the *first stage* of the interview indicated that existence of the Almighty Wizard as a perceived entity was acknowledged only by a few 4-year-old children, who placed the entity in a remote location, saying that the wizard lived 'in the forest', 'in the woods', or 'on another planet'. Obviously, this upgrade was based on the children's dogmatic acceptance of the fairy tale's character and had nothing to do with the upgrade based on the consciously acting HLEXON. The rest of the children denied that the Almighty Wizard could really exist in the perceived world. At the same time, all children acknowledged that such a person existed in their imagination.

The *second stage* of the interview revealed that all children agreed that 'inside a fairy tale' the wizard can create everything, including a living child. In response to Question 6, all but 3 children denied that the imaginary wizard could cross the fairy tale boundaries and enter the real world.

In the *third stage* of the interview Question 6 (whether or not we can imagine a wizard in who's power it is to go out of our imagination), which played a crucial role in the 'ontological argument', proved to be too difficult for 4-year-olds, but most older children agreed to imagine a wizard that could go out of their mind into the real world. Nevertheless, in response to Question 9, all children unanimously denied that such an Almighty Wizard could really jump out of their minds and sit down in the chair in front of them. This means that using their unassisted EXON, the children were able to produce the image of the Almighty Wizard in the status of an existentially weak entity (an item within their imagination) but refused to upgrade the image to the status of an existentially strong entity (a person that belongs to the perceived world).

In order to examine, whether *external assistance in the form of logical priming* could make the children accomplish the upgrade, the logical contradiction in the children's judgements (between the wizard's almightiness and his simultaneous disability to do something) was exposed to them via discussion. The children were repeatedly asked to imagine the wizard number two (three, four, five) who is even more powerful than the wizard of the previous number and who "really could jump from their imagination into this room", with Question 9 repeated again each time. However, even when the wizard's might had been increased four times with each child, this failed to shatter the children's certainty that the Almighty Wizard is unable to leave their imagination. For example, Artiom (a boy, 9 years) answered the question about the wizard's ability to leave his mind for the perceived world as follows "No, he is only in our thinking, but not outside it". The questioning then continues "OK, but can we think of such an Almighty Wizard who is even more almighty than the first one and who can really go out to the real world?" "Yes, we can, but this is only fantasy. In reality he, however powerful, cannot go out of our thoughts, because he doesn't exist, he can only be conjured up". "Therefore, he is not almighty?" "He is not. He is almighty, but only in his own way, in a fairy tale way". The questioning continued for three more rounds, with the same result.

Altogether, the results of this interview showed that almost all of the children refused *to upgrade the existential status of the ontological argument from WE to SE when their HLEXON was externally assisted via exposing logical contradictions in their judgements* (Figure 5.1). Replication of this study with British children in the UK didn't reveal any significant differences between answers of Russian and British children.

5.4 Upgrading God's existence: Adults' response to the ontological argument

To examine whether adult educated participants are more sensitive to external assistance in the form of exposing the logical contradiction in their judgements, a study that included a series of interviews was conducted with graduates and undergraduates in the UK.

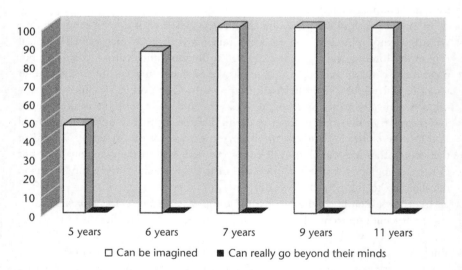

FIGURE 5.1 Percent of children who a) said that the Almighty Wizard who can go beyond their minds into the perceived world *can be imagined,* and b) agreed that the imagined Almighty Wizard *can really go beyond their minds*

In *Interview 1* of this study, which will be referred to as *default interview*, participants' *unassisted EXON* was tested, which was then followed by the *external assistance in the form of exposing the logical contradiction in the participants' judgements.* The questions of the default interview were the same as those in the interview with children, however, if the negative answer was given to the final key question, the experimenter draws to the subject's attention the fact that there seem to be *a logical contradiction* between the statement that *the wizard was almighty* and that *he still could not go out of the participant's mind.* After this, two additional questions were put to the participants: "Do you agree or not that there is a logical contradiction in what you have said?", and if the answer was "yes", "Do you prefer simply to accept this contradiction, or you would like to reconsider your opinion and agree that the wizard is able to come out of your mind and into this room?"

The objective of these questions was to emphasize a major strength of the ontological argument: The fact that the almighty subject, once it is acknowledged that he exists as a concept, has to be given a strong existential status because the subject's attribute of almightiness logically includes the subject's ability to take a perceived form. If the participants didn't acknowledge the logical contradiction in their judgements, then they were classified as insensitive to the external assistance. If, however, the subjects did acknowledge that their denial of the almighty subject's capacity to come out of the imagination put them in a logical contradiction with themselves, they still had two options. The first option was to change their opinion and accept the conclusion that the Almighty Wizard could, in fact, come out of their mind into the perceived world; if the participants go for this option, they upgrade the ontological argument from an entity with the weak to the entity with the strong existential status. The second option was to simply accept the contradiction without changing their opinion on the almighty subject's existential status. Participants who go for the second option upgrade the ontological argument from an entity with the weak to the entity with the incomplete existential status (see Table 2.2). Indeed, if the logical contradiction is acknowledged, then the possibility that the concept of the Almighty Subject can materialize stops being an impossible idea because the thought about the logical contradiction in EXON entails some probability that the ontological argument might still be true. At the same time, this argument is not yet accepted as an existentially strong entity, since the probability is not the same as certainty.

The results showed that in the default interview all participants acknowledged that they could imagine the Almighty Wizard capable of leaving their imagination and going into the perceived world, yet most of them refused to accept that the wizard can really leave their imagination and sit down in the chair in front of them. After the additional questions, only one of the seventeen participants acknowledged the fact of the wizard's real existence ("He is here, but we can't see him. He's not giving any light waves"), with all the others emphatically denying this. Out of these sixteen subjects eleven did not see a logical contradiction in their judgements, and five said that there was a contradiction, but they prefer to accept it rather than acknowledge that the wizard can go out of their mind and into the perceived world.

80 Generating God

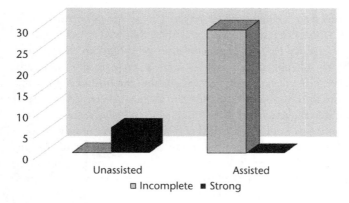

FIGURE 5.2 Percent of adult participants who invested the ontological argument with *Incomplete* and *Strong* existential statuses, as a function of *EXON type* (Unassisted vs Assisted), in Interview 1

In terms of the EXON theory, the results indicated that in most educated adults, like in children, unassisted EXON granted the idea of Almighty Wizard only a *weak existential status*. The external assistance via emphasizing the logical contradiction increased this status to the *incomplete one*, yet only in a minority of the participants (Figure 5.2). Since it was unlikely that adults took the Almighty Wizard for a fairy tale character (as it was the case with some of the children), it became clear that there were reasons that made it very difficult (and in fact impossible) for most of the participants to invest the imagined Almighty Wizard with strong existential status. It was also clear that the reasons were psychological rather than logical; indeed, five of the participants preferred to accept the logical contradiction in their judgements than to invest the imagined Almighty Wizard with the strong existential status.

In order to identify the most probable of these reasons, three more interviews were run, *each with a different group of participants*. In each of these interviews, *the default section* of the interview was preceded by *a priming section* that aimed at eliminating the possible reason for the participants' reluctance to upgrade the ontological argument.

5.5 Upgrading God's existence: Psychological HLEXON in adults

One psychological reason why most subjects refused to acknowledge the validity of the ontological argument could be that they *viewed the Almighty Wizard's ability of getting out of their minds as a causal event*, with the participants being the cause and the Almighty Wizard being the consequence. In so far as the Almighty Wizard is by definition extremely powerful, the participants could have had the feeling that they were being pushed to go for the 'perverted EXON': To create the entity who is infinitely more powerful than themselves.

To prevent this feeling from happening, in *Interview 2* of this study the purpose of the *priming section of the interview* was to lead the participants to the realization that it could be the Almighty Wizard who had created the participants and then simply 'settled down' in the participants' minds in the form of their thinking (speaking) about him. Realizing this would make the participants think that, instead of being creators of the Almighty Wizard they are in fact the Almighty Wizard's products. If in Interview 1 it was the 'perverted EXON' that had stopped the participants from upgrading the ontological argument to a higher existential status, then in Interview 2 participants would be more willing to go for such upgrade, by giving the Almighty Wizard either an incomplete or a strong existential status.

The questions of the priming section of this interview were as follows:

1. Now I'd like to talk with you about wizards, is that O.K.? Have you ever heard or read something about them? What have you heard (read)?
2. Tell me, if a wizard is almighty, can he create a human individual, yes or no?
3. And can this Almighty Wizard create a person like yourself?
4. And can this Almighty Wizard create some thoughts in your mind, for instance, can he make you think about an Almighty Wizard, yes or no?
5. And what do you think, can this wizard, if he is almighty, turn himself into your thoughts, enter your mind and settle down there, yes or no?
6. If this occurred, would you know that it was the wizard who settled down in your mind or you would think that it is yourself who produced thoughts about this wizard?

Another possible psychological reason for the subjects' refusal to upgrade the ontological argument could be *'anthropomorphizing' the Almighty Wizard* by the participants. Indeed, if the participants viewed the Almighty Wizard as a humanlike creature who has a physical body, it would seem evident to them that however hard they tried, it was very unlikely that such humanlike figure would appear in the room. In order to prevent the possibility of such anthropomorphizing, in the priming section of *Interview 3* of this study it was made clear to participants that the Almighty Wizard could be invisible and, if visible, not necessarily look like a person. If the reason for the refusal to upgrade the ontological argument was the anthropomorphizing the wizard's image, then the number of participants who go for EXUP on this argument in this interview would be significantly larger than in Interview 1.

In this interview, the questions of the priming section were as follows:

1. Now I'd like to talk with you about wizards, is that O.K.? Have you ever heard or read something about them? What have you heard (read)?
2. Tell me, please, is this necessary that wizards should look like human beings, or can they look differently?
3. Can a wizard be invisible, yes or no?

4. Can a wizard turn himself or herself in various animals and objects, yes or no?
5. Can a wizard turn himself/herself in the air or in the walls of this room, yes or no?
6. So, if the wizard is almighty, he is not necessarily visible and can be hiding himself/herself in various objects in this room, yes or no?

Finally, one more psychological factor could make the participants resist the possibility to upgrade the ontological argument. This factor could be the participants' strong belief that the impenetrable border exists between mental and perceived realities. Indeed, as studies reviewed in Chapter 3 have shown, adult's BLEXON is based on the strong belief in permanence of perceived objects (BOP), and in most adults their BOP is entrenched (see Figure 3.2). One of the OP demands is the *non-creation rule*, which states that a perceived object cannot be affected, to say nothing created, by a mental action alone (e.g., a thought, a spoken word or an effort of will). In order to turn an image into a perceived object certain conditions have to be observed, such as having a piece of some 'primary matter', tools and applying special efforts to the piece of matter with the aim of shaping it into the form of the artist's mental image. For instance, if a sculpture decided to make a statue out of a piece of rock, he or she needs the rock, a chisel, and a hammer. Acknowledging that an image can obtain its perceived embodiment without the aforementioned conditions would be a violation of the BOP. Since the idea of the Almighty Wizard is a part of participants' mental imagery, the participants could view this idea as any other imaginary object (e.g., an imagined car) and apply the non-creation rule to it; this could have prevented the possibility of upgrading the ontological argument from the status of WE to the statuses of IE or SE.

In order to examine this hypothesis, in the priming section of *Interview 4* participants were individually demonstrated a phenomenon, in which an object conjured up by the participant would spontaneously 'turn' into a perceived object. This apparently magical phenomenon aimed at relaxing the participants commitment to the OP demands. Earlier studies have shown that observation of an apparent violation of the non-creation rule by participants affected the adults' BLEXON, by changing their belief orientation: Instead of the BOP, the participants began to apply the BONP to the entity they have just seen to have changed as a result of the experimenter's effort of will [24]. If it was the application of the non-creation rule to the idea of the Almighty Wizard that prevented participants from acknowledging the possibility for the Almighty Wizard to come from their imagination into the perceived world, then observing a violation of this rule should increase the number of participants who upgrade the ontological argument. Indeed, having seen that an *ordinary entity* (e.g., a postage stamp) they are imagining has 'magically' turned into a real postage stamp, the participants would soften to the suggestion that a *superordinary entity* (i.e., the Almighty Wizard) could do the same.

The procedure of Interview 4 was as follows. Participants were individually shown an apparently empty wooden box (described in Chapter 3), encouraged to carefully examine it and asked to close the lid of the box. They were then briefly shown a postage stamp with a particular picture on it, which was immediately hidden from view, and asked to make a wish that this postage stamp appeared in the box. After opening the box, the participants discovered that the postage stamp they had in their memory and had made a wish to materialize did indeed appear in the box. They were then encouraged to examine the box again for as long as they wanted. Having found nothing suspicious, the participants entered the mental state in which their BOP was temporarily suspended, and then were asked the questions of the default section of the interview.

The results of Interviews 2, 3 and 4 (Figure 5.3) revealed that Interviews 2 and 3 yielded results similar to results of Interview 1 (assisted); however, in Interview 4 the majority of participants (83% altogether) upgraded existential status of the ontological argument, and only in Interview 4 a number of participants who upgraded the ontological argument from the status of WE to SE was statistically significant. This suggests that it was attribution of the non-creation rule to the idea of the Almighty Wizard that was a major psychological obstacle for participants to comply with the ontological argument.

The study's results may suggest one of the reasons why the ontological argument of the existence of God, despite it's nearly a thousand years' history, failed to buy the sympathy of philosophers. As Interviews 1, 2 and 3 showed, the sheer reliance on cognitive external assistance is not enough in order to make the HLEXON abandon its commitment to the BOP. Even the assumption that God may have created them and their thoughts about God (Interview 2) or that God could take an arbitrary physical appearance (Interview 3) did not make the

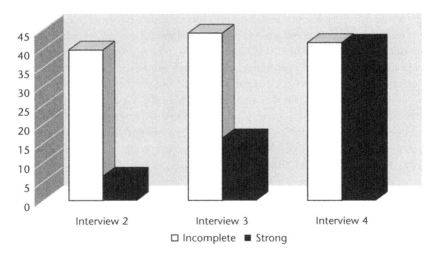

FIGURE 5.3 Percent of adult participants who upgraded the ontological argument to the statuses of either *Incomplete* or *Strong* entity in psychologically assisted HLEXON, as a function of Interview (Int. 2 – external assistance via suggesting the participants being the Wizard's products, Int. 3 – external assistance via suggesting the Wizard's non-anthropomorphic image, and Int. 4 – external assistance via suspension of the BOP)

participants ready to invest the ontological argument with the status of a perceived physical object. The question arises of how can these results be explained?

5.6 The HLEXON dilemma: Am I a creator or a product of God?

Since EXON is rooted in our reflecting Self, the Self has the highest possible existential status – the status of an absolute entity (AE) (see Chapter 2 for more on that). As long as for any other entity to exist the entity has to be experienced by our Self, any entity has an existential status lower than our reflecting Self (see Table 2.2). The question raised in this chapter is about the existential status of a noncontingent entity – God. On one hand, I produce the idea of God in my imagination, on the other hand – God is an almighty and perfect entity whereas I am not. From this, it follows that thinking of myself as a creator of the idea of God is like thinking about a statue creating the sculpturer. So, am I a creator of the idea of God or am I God's product, to whom God granted the idea of himself as a gift?

The ontological argument of God's existence asserts that the absolute existential status of God follows from thinking about the almighty entity with logical necessity, thus by-passing physical causation. Indeed, logical necessity does not imply physical causality: $A > C$ follows from $B > C$ and $A > B$ not in the same way as a butterfly emerges from its pupa, because the cause precedes the effect in time, whereas logical premises and conclusions exist simultaneously. But can the inference about the logical necessity of the absolute existential status of God mask the fact that this inference itself is the product of our own mind?

Indeed, the inference about the logical necessity of God's existence is made by a person's reflective Self. This ordering in time is maintained even if we assume that the idea of God in a person's head is laid down by God himself since this assumption too is a product of the person's reflecting Self. In other words, the absolute existential status of our Self undermines the logical validity of the ontological argument, by making children and adults feel that they actually generate God out of their own reflective Selves. Because the idea of God is generated by upgrading some of the Self's properties (e.g., the Self's creative ability), psychologically God becomes a prisoner of the person's mind unable to break through the 'walls' of the person's Self. *The feeling that they are creators of the idea of the Almighty Wizard and thus ontologically superior to this idea was a reason of why the attempts to stimulate participants' EXUP on the ontological argument via rational arguments (Interviews 1, 2 and 3) failed.*

Experiments reviewed in Chapter 4 have shown that a suggestive influence gets upgraded when the suggestion targets a person's PSIME. The idea of the almighty subject belongs to PSIME. However, unlike PSIME which have potential counterparts in the perceived world (e.g., the person's health or the significant events in the person's future life), the idea of God is the fantastical entity. Like all fantastical entities, the idea of God is therefore a creation of the mind and locked within the walls of the Self. At the same time, the idea of the perfect subject is different from other fantastical ideas, because unlike other fantastical ideas (e.g., a winged horse), the idea of God logically includes almightiness. The only psychological barrier that keeps the idea of God locked within the mind is the BOP or, to be more exact, the *non-creation rule*. When this barrier between the mental and physical world was temporarily lifted via observation of an apparent violation of the non-creation rule, the idea of the Almighty Wizard, which has been already 'knocking' on the 'wall' inside the Self under the pressure of the ontological argument, broke through the 'wall' and filtered into the physical world, simultaneously upgrading the ontological argument in its existential status (see Figure 4.6).

The data of this study may shed some additional light on the psychological origins of religious beliefs in modern rational adults. *In the everyday life, the BOP can be suspended in a number of conditions.* As children, people might uncritically upgrade suggestions of their close ones in that supernatural entities, such as the Candy Witch, Santa Claus or God are real [24][25][26][27][28][29]. As they mature, the children might downgrade some of such entities to the weak existential status, while keeping the others (i.e., God) in the status of a strong entity. As adults, some people may have *hallucinatory experiences of miraculous events,* such as revelations and appearances of saints, Jesus Christ of the Virgin Mary, in others their BOP can be lifted under the pressure of *strong emotional frustrations*, such as fear of death, bereavement or other powerful unsatisfied needs, still others begin believing in miracles after *pondering scientific discoveries* that escape convincing rational explanations, such as the Big Bang or the fine-tuning of the universal cosmological constants [30]. In any of these conditions the peoples' BOP, which was established in their minds from early childhood, may relax its grip over participants' HLEXON, and some cognitively weak but emotionally strong imaginary entities (CWESE) can filter through the barrier of the non-creation rule, thus becoming cognitively strong and emotionally strong entities (CSESE). Having gone through this barrier, the idea of the almighty and benevolent 'heavenly father' undergoes EXUP and becomes existentially powerful and capable of changing the person's behaviour. The natural ability to upgrade PSIME obtains its extreme manifestation by turning into faith, and *the dream about God (CWESE) becomes the belief in God (CSESE).*

In any of the above versions of coming to the belief in God, this process is not a result of the direct external assistance through persuasion, suggestion or oppression. Instead, it is rooted in *the person's innate tendency to project his or her own reflecting Self into the outer world and then upgrade the projection to a higher existential status when appropriate conditions turn up.*

However, religion is not the only benefactor of our ability to autonomously upgrade the ideas and images in our mind via observing apparent miracles. Another way to stimulate EXUP is through demonstration of fake phenomena. Let us consider how our HLEXON can be deceived or misled.

References

[1] Barett, J. (2007). Cognitive science of religion: What is it and why is it? https://onlinelibrary.wiley.com/doi/abs/10.1111/j.1749-8171.2007.00042.x

[2] Shtulman, A., & Lindeman, M. (2015). Attributes of God: Conceptual foundations of a foundational belief. *Cognitive Science,* 40, 1–36.
[3] Hodge, K.M. (2018). Sorting through, and sorting out, anthropomorphism in CSR. https://www.academia.edu/3743520/Sorting_Through_and_Sorting_Out_Anthropomorphism_in_CSR
[4] Spong, J. S. (2009). *Eternal life: a new vision. Beyond religion, beyond theism, beyond heaven and hell.* New York: Harper Collins.
[5] Subbotsky, E. (2001). Causal explanations of events by children and adults: Can alternative causal modes coexist in one mind? *British Journal of Developmental Psychology,* 19, 23–46.
[6] Wiebe, P. H. (1998). *Visions of Jesus.* Oxford: Oxford University Press.
[7] Big-Bang model (2020). *Encyclopaedia Britannica.* https://www.britannica.com/science/big-bang-model
[8] Friederich, S. (2017). Fine-Tuning. *Stanford Encyclopedia of Philosophy.* https://plato.stanford.edu/entries/fine-tuning/
[9] Ricard, J. (Ed). (1999). Complexity and structure of the living cell. *Science Direct,* 34, 1–14.
[10] Flew, A. & Varghese, R. A. (2009). *There is a God: How the world's most notorious atheist changed his mind.* New York: HarperOne.
[11] Palmer, B. (2014). What Is the Answer to Zeno's Paradox? Why Achilles actually can catch a tortoise in a race. *Science.* https://slate.com/technology/2014/03/zenos-paradox-how-to-explain-the-solution-to-achilles-and-the-tortoise-to-a-child.html
[12] Davies, P. (2006). *The Goldilocks enigma: Why is the universe just right for life?* London: Allen Lane.
[13] Tiger, L. & McGuire, M. (2010). *God's brain.* New York: Prometheus Books.
[14] Koons, R. (1997). A new look at the Cosmological Argument. *American Philosophical Quarterly,* 34, 193–211
[15] Kenneth E. H. (2020). Design arguments for the existence of God. *Internet Encyclopedia of Philosophy.* https://www.iep.utm.edu/design/#SH2c
[16] Halsall, P. (1996). *Anselm on God's Existence.* Fordham University. Retrieved from https://sourcebooks.fordham.edu/source/anselm.asp
[17] Oppy, G. (2019). Ontological Arguments. *Stanford Encyclopedia of Philosophy.* https://plato.stanford.edu/entries/ontological-arguments/
[18] Batson C. D. & Thompson E. R. (2001). Why don't moral people act morally? Motivational considerations. *Current Directions in Psychological Science,* 10, 54–57.
[19] Wicker A. W. (1969). Attitudes versus actions: The relationships of verbal and overt behavioural responses to attitude objects. *Journal of Social Issues,* 25, 41–78.
[20] Tversky, A., & Kahneman, D. (1974). Judgement under uncertainty: Heuristics and biases. *Science,* 185, 1124–1131.
[21] Subbotsky, E. (1996). *The child as a Cartesian thinker. Children's reasonings about metaphysical aspects of reality.* Psychology Press.
[22] Descartes, R. (1996). *Meditations on first philosophy: with selections from the objections and replies (Cambridge texts in the history of philosophy).* Cambridge University Press.
[23] Ney, W.C. & Carson, J.S. (1984). The development of the concept of God in children. *Journal of Genetic Psychology,* 145, 1, 137–142.
[24] Subbotsky, E. & Trommsdorff, G. (1992). Object permanence in adults: A cross-cultural perspective. *Psychologische Beitrage,* 34, 62–79.

[25] Woolley, J.D., Boerger, E.A., & Markman, A.B. (2004). A visit from the Candy Witch: Factors influencing young children beliefs in a novel fantastical being. *Developmental Science*, 7, 456–468.
[26] Harris, P.L., & Koenig, M.A. (2006). Trust in testimony: How children learn about science and religion. *Child Development*, 77, 505–524.
[27] Shtulman, A., & Yoo, R.I. (2015). Children's understanding of physical possibility constrains their belief in Santa Claus. *Cognitive Development*, 34, 51–62.
[28] Corriveau, K.H., Chen, E.E., & Harris, P.L. (2015). Judgements about fact and fiction by children from religious and nonreligious backgrounds. *Cognitive Science*, 39, 353–82.
[29] Goldstein, T.R., & Wooley, J. (2016). Ho!Ho!Who? Parent promotion of belief and live encounters with Santa Claus. *Cognitive Development*, 39, 113–127.
[30] Atran, S., & Norenzayan, A. (2004). Religion's evolutionary landscape: Counterintuition, commitment, compassion, communion. *Behavioral and Brain Sciences*, 27, 713–770.

6
FAKING EXISTENCE

6.1 There is and there isn't

Many years ago, in one of my experiments, I stumbled upon a remarkable conversation with my participants. In this experiment, I showed participants an unusual phenomenon: An object disappeared in an apparently empty box and could not be found however hard one tried. I asked whether this was or wasn't magic. Most participants answered that it was. But when then asked whether magic existed or didn't exist, most participants answered that it didn't. Obviously, my participants were confused: Something was definitely there, and yet this something didn't exist.

This conversation made me ask myself two questions: 'What is magic?' and 'What does it mean: To exist?' In this chapter, I will share the results of my contemplations.

6.2 Two kinds of magic: Unravelling the confusion

There are two concepts of magic: *True magic* and *Stage magic*. True magic is an event that violates known laws of physics, biology or psychology. A particular manifestation of True magic is violating the OP demands, such as creating perceptual objects from nothing by a sheer effort of will or a physical object emerging from thin air in an instant (see Chapter 2 for more on that). In contrast, Stage magic (e.g., the classical 'Rabbit from a hat' trick) is an illusion that simulates violation of the OP demands without actually violating them. In addition to Stage magic, True magic can be simulated in virtual reality through movies, computer games, and complex technical devices.

Why do magicians show tricks? Why do we enjoy watching magic tricks while we know they are illusions? The EXON theory suggests an answer. In our dreams and imaginations, all sorts of impossible things exist, even though our rational mind marks this existence as ephemeral. And now suppose that we are seeing something

DOI: 10.4324/9781003219521-6

impossible, like a person walking on water, happening in front of our eyes. Immediately the thought 'a person can walk on water' is upgraded in its rank on the EXON's cognitive dimension (see Table 2.3). Just for a fleeting moment at the back of our mind the image of a person denying gravity becomes a SE, while our critical thinking keeps saying it is a WE and what we are seeing is an illusion. Seeing the miracle on the stage evokes in us the emotion of surprise and, usually, happiness.

The emotion of surprise is understandable, but why is watching stage magic charged with positive emotions? Perhaps, seeing a supernatural phenomenon touches upon the hope hidden deep in our subconscious that the supernatural is indeed real and we can be a part of it. If miracles do exist, then a miracle could happen to me, and my life is not just a random splash on the boundless ocean of time but has a meaning! Experiments showed that, all other conditions equal, both preschool children and adults preferred watching an *apparently supernatural event* that violated the OP demands to watching a *novel physical event* imitating violation of these demands [1]. As children, we like playing magical games of pretend because the feeling of being a powerful wizard or a fairy helps us overcome the feeling of inferiority and gives us the feeling of control over the external world. As adults, we keep playing with magic in our dreams and imagination.

To reiterate, Stage magic is a simulation of the event that violates the OP demands. In psychology, Stage magic can be used for studying cognitive abilities, such as perception, decision making and memory [2], [3]. It can also be used to study magical thinking and beliefs in the supernatural phenomena [4]. The problem discussed in this chapter is *how it is possible to make a rational observer upgrade the observed effect (i.e., the magic trick) from the status of a weak entity to the status of a strong entity*. In other words, how can one assist the viewer's HLEXON to help the viewer invest a rationally impossible perceived event with the existential status of a SE?

6.3 Imitating existence

As argued in Chapter 2, according to the EXON theory, an object or event can be represented in our mind in three modes: as a phenomenon, as a mental image and as an RC (see Chapters 1 and 2 for more on that). The phenomenon is something that is perceived, directly by senses or indirectly, through devices: A mug in front of me, a person walking in the street, or a unicellular organism seen through a microscope. The image is something that we imagine, either inside our mind, or projected on a screen: An imagined mug, a filmed person walking in a street, or a mental image of the organism earlier seen through the microscope. Finally, an RC is a concept, acquired through comparing and measuring a bunch of related phenomena and written into the context of the available scientific knowledge; for example, the RC of a person is the knowledge acquired through scientific exploration of a number of particular individual people, culminated in the knowledge of shape, physiology, psychology, and other properties that are typically included into the concept of species called humans.

We also agreed that an object X has an existential status of *a strong entity* (SE) when the object is presented in all three modes – the phenomenon, the RC and the image – simultaneously and these modes match each other. In addition, the X must meet the expectations for the Self-related entity – *permanence, intermodality* and *intersubjectivity*. For example, a glass of water is a SE if you see the glass of water in front of you (a phenomenon), can imagine it if you close your eyes (a mental image), and know what the glass of water is (an RC). You also can take the glass in your hand and other people would acknowledge the presence of this glass of water. Let us call the relations between the three aforementioned forms of an entity's presentation in the mind the 'Ring of Existence', and say that *in the case of a SE, the ring of existence is complete* (see Figure 6.1).

Further, an object X has the existential status of *an incomplete entity* (IE), if an image, a phenomenon or an RC is absent, or all of the forms are present but don't match each other (e.g., visual and other illusions, art, extinct species of animals, futuristic objects and unconfirmed scientific hypotheses). Finally, if object X is represented solely by an image, with no matching phenomenon or RC, we say that the object is an existentially weak entity (WE) (e.g., gods, ghosts, fantastical creatures, and hallucinations) (see Table 2.2). In contrast to a SE, let us say that in the case of an IE *the ring of existence is ruptured*, and in the case of a WE *the ring of existence is disabled*.

The dominant conscious belief in the modern industrial world is that True magic has the existential status of a WE. We have an image (imaginary magic, a film with magical effects, a magical story), but not a phenomenon and an RC. *In the case of True magic, in the popular mind the 'ring of existence' is therefore disabled* (see Figure 6.2).

According to the EXON theory, what happens when naïve spectators are watching Stage magic is as follows. The magic trick show is *a suggestion* to the viewer that True magic is a part of the OR, which tacitly pushes the viewer to EXUP the idea of True magic from WE to SE. Simply put, by demonstrating a magic trick, a magician sends to viewer the tacit message "Look, a superordinary event, which you have been viewing as not existing, exists in reality".

As the experiments reviewed in Chapters 3 and 4 showed when a magical suggestion targets participants PSE, the suggestion is upgraded and the person begins to believe the suggested message (see Figure 4.6). The idea of True magic

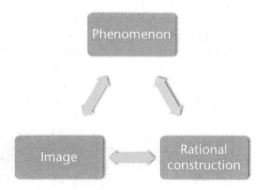

FIGURE 6.1 The Ring of Existence is *complete*

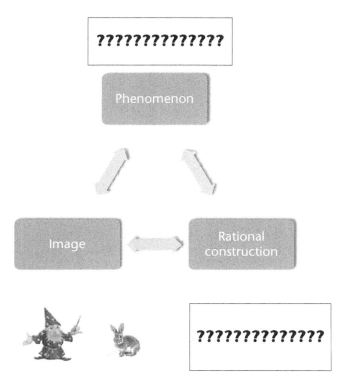

FIGURE 6.2 Existential status of True magic in the popular mind: The ring of existence is *disabled, with the Phenomenon and Rational construction absent*

belongs to PSE; being cognitively weak, it is a strong entity on the EXON's emotional dimension (see Table 2.2). In the context of the EXON theory, when naïve spectators are watching a magic trick, their BOP becomes temporarily suspended and replaced with the BONP; as a result, the idea of True magic is upgraded from being a WE to the status of a SE. For this to be possible, the ring of existence for True magic that in the everyday life is disabled, in the moment of watching the magic has to become temporarily completed, despite the fact that the viewers still don't know the trick's RC (i.e., the mechanism of how the trick is being accomplished). As argued in Chapter 2, the psychological mechanism of EXUP is hidden in the EXON's emotional dimension: *The entity gets upgraded in its existential status in spite of the fact that objectively the entity is still missing one of its representational modes.* In other words, EXUP makes EXON bypass the missing representational mode and completes the ring of existence (Figure 6.3).

Let us call the state in which the mind gets immersed by the demonstration of a magic trick the 'state of upgraded impossible' (SUI for short). In the previous chapters, we have already come across the SUI. The experiments with children have shown that typical behavioural manifestations of the SUI are a reaction of

92 Faking existence

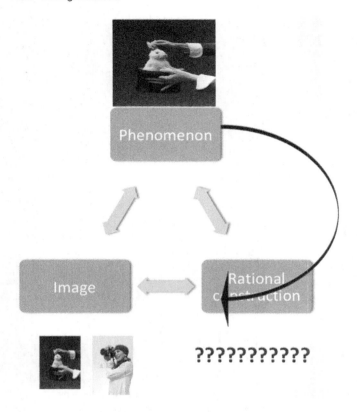

FIGURE 6.3 Existential status of *Trick magic* in *the naïve spectator's mind* at the moment of watching the trick: Objectively the ring of existence is *ruptured* with Rational construction absent, but due to the emotional EXUP the missing mode of representation is bypassed, completing the ring of existence

surprise, accompanied by the reactions of joy or/and fear [5]. In terms of beliefs, under the SUI children who initially had claimed they did not believe in true magic, changed their minds after seeing a toy magically 'coming to life' [6], and adults reacted to the SUI in a similar fashion (see Chapter 4, Study 3, and Chapter 5, Interview 4).

Anecdotal observations suggest that the public reaction to magicians who presented themselves as genuine wizards capable of miracles (e.g., revival of dead people) varied from extreme believing in the miraculous powers of the impostors to outward rejection and criticism [7]. Nevertheless, relatively little *psychological research* was done on how observing magic tricks affects people's psychological functioning.

6.4 Upgrading the impossible as a booster of the mind: Summary

Almost the whole bulk of psychological research on perception, thinking, memory and other psychological functions thus far has been done on participants who consciously believe True magic to be a WE. In this context, the SUI opens a unique opportunity to study the way the mind of a modern individual functions when the BOP (and as a consequence, the conscious disbelief in True magic) is temporarily replaced with the BONP.

Indeed, studies indicated that under the SUI adults treated magical suggestions as if they believed in the suggested messages (see Chapter 4, Study 3), thus bypassing the lack of RC – the knowledge on how a magic spell could affect a physical object. When in the SUI, adults became significantly more willing to accept the existence of God, bypassing the absence of the phenomenon – God's presence as a perceived entity (Chapter 5). At the same time, the SUI made adult participants who had accepted the magical help see scary dreams significantly more often than those participants who declined the magical help [8]. These apparently controversial results have, nevertheless, a common psychological core. When an imaginary entity, such as the idea that magic can affect person's PSIME, is existentially upgraded, the person's behaviour depends on the person's attitude towards the entity. As the experiments reviewed in Chapter 4 showed, when the existentially upgraded magical suggestion is viewed as benevolent (a good suggestion), the SUI does not create negative feelings, but when the upgraded suggestion has negative connotations (real or imaginary), the person may reject the spell or develop bad dreams after accepting it.

In modern virtual culture, one of the most effective ways of putting a person's mind into the SUI is through exposing the person to movies with magical effects. The studies have shown that exposing children to movies with magical effects facilitates children's creativity on divergent thinking tasks to a significantly stronger extent than exposing the children to equally interesting movies without magical effects [9]. Put in the SUI, children better distinguish between fantastic and realistic visual displays than children in the control SUI-free group [10]. Both children and adults better recognized previously seen advertisements if they had watched the advertisements in the SUI than if they had watched them in the SUI-free state [11]. Some researchers argued that demonstrating magic tricks may have a psychotherapeutic effect for stress reduction and improving physical and psychological wellbeing [12]. According to recent findings, children who had been primed by learning a magic trick obtained greater scores on subsequent tests on divergent thinking compared to those primed by a matched art-based tasks [13].

At the same time, SUI can make people highly suggestible to messages that target their PSIME, and thus easy to manipulate (see Chapter 4 for more on this). Immersing potential believers in SUI through showing miracles is a traditional way of converting people into a faith, described in both Old and New Testaments. In modern times, controversial religious leaders, such as the leader of the Branch Davidians cult David Koresh or the People's Temple founder Jim Jones, began their careers as faith healers and prophets; later they employed the SUI they created in their followers for manipulation with the cult members' minds, leading them towards a mass murder-suicide. But the most recent example of using the SUI by political leaders happened in Russia when the ideologists of *perestroika* skilfully used the Russian people's trust to central TV channels in order to prepare the psychological ground for privatization of the public property. In the end of the 80th, the central channels of Soviet TV were given to 'wizards' – magical healer Allan Chumak and hypnotizer Anatoly Kashpirovsky. Millions of people drank the water magically 'charged' by Chumak or moved with their heads sitting in front of the TV on the order by Kashpirovsky. In the beginning of the 90th the 'wizards' suddenly disappeared from the TV screens and were replaced by the ideologists of the free market economy. The new showmen put forward the idea of 'privatization', but in reality – *the plan of stripping the people off their communal property and moving the property into the hands of the government's bureaucracy and KGB authorities, their friends and relatives*. Although it was clear to most people that privatization of the communal property would lead to drastic inequalities, the deal was done. The 'wizards' upgraded the people's subconscious belief in the authorities' suggestive message that the idea of privatization is in their own interests, and the people accepted the idea without resistance.

Due to the same SUI psychological mechanism, Russian president Boris Yeltsin managed to do what seemed to be impossible – terminated the Soviet Union, put a ban on the Communist Party of the USSR. Like Russian tsars, who passed their power to their heirs, Yeltsin passed his 'magic rod' of power to Vladimir Putin. That is why Putin – a mid-level officer in the Soviet KGB, unknown to the people, not a leader of a political party and without original political ideas of his own, suddenly became a victor at presidential campaigns: Succumbing to SUI, the majority of Russian population voted for Putin voluntarily, when the holder of the 'magical power' – Boris Yeltsin – said that doing this is in the people's best interests.

On a wider scale, some symbolic actions, such as *presents, good words* and *imitated feelings* can replace miracles in creating the SUI. In the everyday life, *every person can serve as a 'magician',* by giving presents and saying good words to other people not because he or she experiences genuine emotions towards the people, but in order to existentially upgrade the relationships that are fragile and non-permanent. In personal relations, natural mechanisms that cement relationships, such as sexual and physical attraction, can eventually fade, whereas objective factors, such as maintaining family ties and bringing up children, require that the relationships lasted. In such circumstances, creating an illusion of love, via saying good words to the partner, making presents and observing love rituals can help to replace the natural mechanisms and upgrade the existential status of this fragile and tender phenomenon that we call 'love'. Similarly, such illusory phenomena as *politeness* and *diplomacy* in interpersonal and international relations aim at replacing the lack or degradation of natural economic and political interests that usually connect people and countries. When a person becomes a target of a message that imitates love, politeness and diplomacy, the person's EXON bypasses the absence of the natural cementing factors and begins to believe that the feelings are genuine. In other words, the mild everyday version of the SUI is a psychological 'glue' that links people together when natural mechanisms that cement human relationships (such as sexual attractiveness or common economic and political interests) wear off.

Altogether, experiments demonstrated that immersing a person in the SUI is a mixed blessing. In some circumstances, upgrading the belief in the impossible can help to improve cognitive functioning, have positive psychotherapeutic effects, and facilitate human relations. In other circumstances, experiencing SUI may expose people to hidden dangers. Not surprisingly, witnessing impossible phenomena, along with giving pleasure, may produce anxiety and trigger in participants psychological defense mechanisms. In the next chapter, we will discuss how people's EXON may resist the unexpected and undesirable external intrusion, via altering physical reality in an attempt to risqué the person's BOP.

References

[1] Subbotsky, E. (2010). Curiosity and exploratory behaviour towards possible and impossible events in children and adults. *British Journal of Psychology*, 101, 481–501.
[2] Kuhn, G., Amlani, A. A., & Rensink, R. (2008). Towards a science of magic. *Trends in Cognitive Sciences*, 12, 349–354.
[3] Pailhes, A. & Kuhn, G. (2020). Influencing choices with conversational primes: How a magic trick unconsciously influences card choices. *Proceedings of the National Academy of Sciences*. 10.1073/pnas.2000682117
[4] Subbotsky, E. (2010). *Magic and the mind. Mechanisms, functions and development of magical thinking and behavior.* New York: Oxford University Press.
[5] Subbotsky, E. V. (1985). Preschool children's perception of unusual phenomena. *Soviet Psychology*, 3, 91–114.
[6] https://youtu.be/vIzqQW5W0GQ
[7] Samodelova, S. (2006). Taina, pokrytaya magom. *Moscovskii Komsomoletz, March 22.* https://credo.press/64698/
[8] Subbotsky E. (2009). Can magical intervention affect subjective experiences? Adults' reactions to magical suggestion. *British Journal of Psychology*, 100, 517–537.
[9] Subbotsky, E., Hysted, C. & Jones, N. (2009). Watching films with magical content facilitates creativity in children. *Perceptual and Motor Skills*, 111, 261–277.
[10] Subbotsky, E. & Slater, E. (2011). Children's discrimination of fantastic vs realistic visual displays after watching a film with magical content. *Psychological Reports*, 112, 603–609.
[11] Subbotsky, E., & Matthews, J. (2011). Magical thinking and memory: Distinctiveness effect for TV commercials with magical content. *Psychological Reports*, 109, 1–11. https://www.researchgate.net/publication/236979741_Magical_Thinking_and_Memory_Distinctiveness_Effect_for_TV_Commercials_with_Magical_Content
[12] Wiseman, R. & Watt, C. (2018). Achieving the impossible: A review of magic-based interventions and their effects on wellbeing. *Brain and Cognition.* https://peerj.com/articles/6081/
[13] Wiseman, R, Wiles, A. & Watt, C. (2021). Conjuring up creativity: The effect of performing magic tricks on divergent thinking. *Peer J*, 2, e11289.

7
ADJUSTING REALITY: PROTECTING BELIEFS THROUGH MEMORY FAILURES

7.1 Belief in object permanence: The challenge

As argued in Chapter 2, the way we invest entities with existential statuses is determined by our beliefs. The belief that in the OR physical objects are permanent (the BOP) is one of the most basic. When this belief is challenged our Self has two options: to give the BOP up and switch to the BONP or stick to the BOP by adjusting reality with the aim of rescuing this belief. In other words, in order to protect the BOP a special mechanism has to be added to EXON – the *BOP defence mechanism*, or the *BOP/DM* for short. One way to detect the work of the BOP/DM is to register distortions in our memories, which the BOP/DM creates in our memory to make reality fit the BOP.

In recent years, the inference-based memory errors were reported in studies both with children and adults [1], [2], [3], [4], [5]. However, these errors were conceptualized mostly as the work of perception and thinking, without linking them to the BOP. For a special kind of such errors – the memory on temporal order of successive events – Dennett and Kinsbourne's 'Multiple Drafts Model' [6] offers a plausible theoretical explanation and predicts that such errors become less likely when temporal intervals between the successive events grow. When the temporal intervals become long enough, the accuracy of the recollection can only be disturbed by other tasks that the mind has to solve in parallel with the reconstruction of the succession.

In the present study, this parallel task was the participants determination to rescue their BOP.

7.2 Belief in object permanence: The protection

The aim of Experiment 1 of this study was to find out whether adult participants who are shown the effect violating the OP demands would reverse the temporal

DOI: 10.4324/9781003219521-7

order of events that immediately preceded the effect, with the subconscious intention to reinterpret the superordinary event as an ordinary event and thus risqué their BOP [7]. Participants (university undergraduates) were divided into *experimental* and *control* groups. They were then individually presented a wooden trick box with the secret compartment inside (see Chapter 3). In addition, two identical postage stamps and a scrap of white paper 2 × 3 cm. were employed as stimuli: One of the stamps was hidden in the box's secret compartment, and another was available on the table next to the box, together with small scrap of white paper.

During the session, the experimenter asked a participant to bring a small toy car from the far corner of the experimental room. This request aimed at creating a rupture in the participant's stream of consciousness. Due to this temporary distraction, the participant had the opportunity to explain the extraordinary event (an unexpected disappearance of a physical object in an apparently empty box) as an ordinary one (e.g., that somebody tampered with the box while the participant was distracted).

The participant was then asked to put the objects (the stamp and the scrap of paper) in the empty box, close the lid, and in few moments was asked to remove the objects from the box. Having opened the box, participants in the experimental group found 'the same' postage stamp (in reality the other one that had been hidden between the metal plate and the wall of the box) but *not the scrap of paper* (the OP demands violation), whereas participants in the control group found the same objects (*no* the OP demands violation).

After being asked a few background questions, the participants were encouraged to recall the order of the two *key events*: whether they first *brought the toy truck* (Event 1) and then *put the objects into the box* (Event 2) (right order) or the order of these two key events was reversed (wrong order).

The aim of the control condition, in which participants BOP wasn't challenged, was to establish participants' default working memory for the order of the key events. This was necessary in order to rule out the possibility that in the experimental condition the large number of wrong answers was produced by poor default memory on order of the key events rather than by the pressure from the BOP/DM. It was expected that if the poor performance in the experimental condition was caused by the BOP/DM, then in the control condition the correct order would be recollected with frequency significantly above chance, and with frequency significantly higher than in the experimental condition.

The expected patterns of answers are shown in Table 7.1.

The results indicated that the BOP/DM was indeed involved: they showed a significant prevalence of correct answers in the control condition over that in the experimental condition (see Figure.7.1). The results also revealed that the participants' default memory on the temporal order of events was good.

The question arises about the psychological nature of the BOP/DM. Specifically, is the BOP/DM predominantly conscious cognitive mechanism and therefore a part of HLEXON, or is this mechanism mostly subconscious and a component of BLEXON? If the BOP/DM relies on conscious information

98 Adjusting reality

TABLE 7.1 Patterns of answers expected as a function of participants' *Default memory* (Good vs Poor) and *Presence* (Experimental condition) or *Absence* (Control condition) of the BOP/DM effect

BOP/DM effect Default memory for temporal order of events	Present (Experimental condition)	Absent (Control condition)
Good	Recollect right order at chance frequency	Recollect right order at above chance frequency
Poor	Recollect right order below chance frequency	Recollect right order at chance frequency

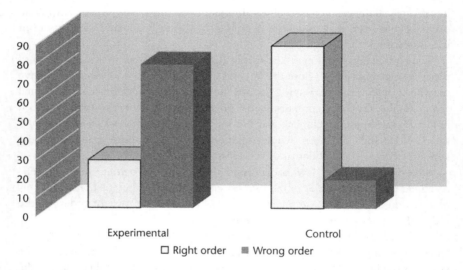

FIGURE 7.1 Percent of participants who recollected *Right* and *Wrong* temporal order of events in Experiment 1, as a function of *Condition* (Experimental vs Control)

processing, then for the BOP/DM to be engaged a rupture in the participants flow of consciousness is a necessary condition, because it provides the participants' conscious thinking with the tentative explanation of the apparent violation of the OP demands by a physical object: While the participants were turning their attention away, the experimenter may have surreptitiously extracted the piece of paper from the box. Alternatively, if the BOP/DM is mostly subconscious, then the rupture in the observer's conscious is not necessary, and the BOP/DM should work even when the key events unfold in full view of the observer, which prevents the possibility of the assumption that the experimenter tampered with the box at the moment when the box was temporarily out of the participant's view.

To examine this, in Experiment 2, two participants were involved instead of one. One of the participants was an *acting subject*, and the other was an *observer*. The acting subject was instructed as participants in the experimental condition of Experiment 1, and the observer was placed in one corner of the room and instructed to carefully watch the actions of both the acting subject and the experimenter. As a result, the rupture in the stream of consciousness was present in the mind of the acting subject, but not in the mind of the observer. If the rupture in the stream of consciousness was a necessary condition for the BOP/DM to be engaged, then the acting subjects in this experiment, like the participants in the experimental condition of Experiment 1, would exhibit recollection of the right temporal order at chance frequency, whereas the observers' recollections are supposed to be mostly correct. If, however, the rupture in the stream of consciousness was not important, then the frequency of recollections of the right order of events in observers, like that in the acting subjects, would be at chance level.

The results (Figure 7.2) revealed that the memory on the right order of events in the observers, like in the acting participants, was at chance level. This supports the assumption that the BOP/DM is engaged independently of whether the participants' stream of consciousness is interrupted or not. This means that the BOP/DM is not dependent on conscious inference and is mostly subconscious BLEXON process.

But if BOP/DM engagement is not conditioned by conscious thinking, can it be conditioned by perception? In other words, how long should the interval

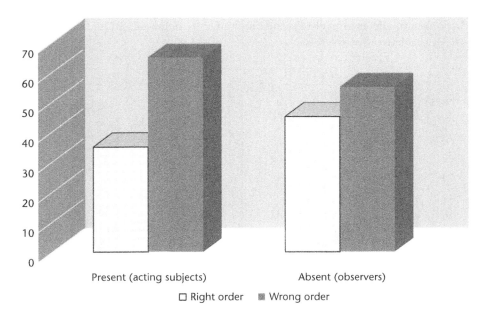

FIGURE 7.2 Percent of acting subjects and observers who recollected *Right* and *Wrong* temporal order of events in Experiment 2, as a function of *Rupture* in the stream of consciousness (Present vs Absent)

between the two key events be so that the default memory on the temporal order is no longer wiped out by the BOP/DM?

To answer this question, in Experiment 3, in the 'long interval' condition the procedure was like in Experiment 1, save that after taking the toy car from the participant, the experimenter kept filling in the protocol for some time before asking the participant to place objects into the box. There was also the 'short interval' condition, which was identical with the experimental condition of Experiment 1, but with a slightly different pattern of background questions. Like in Experiment 1, the time interval between the key events in the 'short interval' condition was 5 sec., and in the 'long interval' condition it was 30 sec.

The results showed that in the 'short interval' condition participants erred with frequency significantly above chance level, whereas in the 'long interval' condition of this experiment, like in the control condition of Experiment 1, the number of correct responses significantly prevailed over the number of wrong recollections (Figure 7.3).

The results of this experiment confirmed that the BOP/DM was engaged when the interval was short (5 sec) and disengaged when the interval was long (30 sec). The link between the BOP/DM and the time interval dividing the key events can be explained by the structure of the BOP/DM. Indeed, in order to reverse the Key event 1 (bringing the toy car) and the Key event 2 (placing the objects into the box) in time, the BOP/DM has to wipe off the intermediate events, which separated the key events (i.e., the participants conversation with the experimenter) (see Figure 7.4). When the time interval increased from 5 sec. to 30 sec., the number of the intermediate events multiplied 6 times and BOP/DM was no longer able to wipe them off.

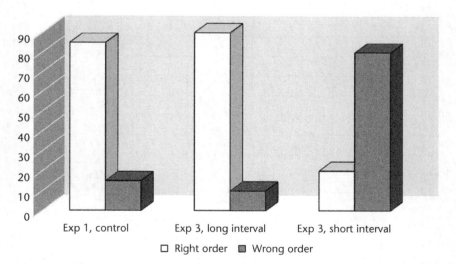

FIGURE 7.3 Percent of participants who recollected *Right* and *Wrong* temporal order of events in Control condition of Experiment 1, and in Long interval and Short interval conditions of Experiment 3

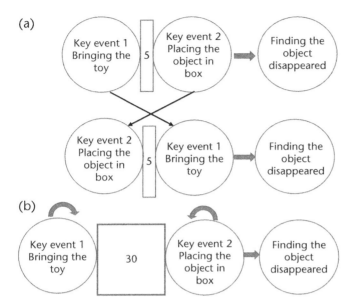

FIGURE 7.4 The BOP/DM work: Replacing correct order of Key events with the wrong order at 5 sec. interval (a) and failure to do so at 30 sec. interval (b)

The question arises of whether the BOP/DM works in children as well. Experiments reviewed in Chapter 3 suggest some expectations in this regard. The experiments indicated that most 6-year-old children, when shown an apparent violation of the OP demands by a perceived object, exhibited not entrenched BOP (see Figure 3.5); this suggests that in 6-year-old children the BOP/DM is weak or isn't functioning. Indeed, the BOP/DM is simply another term for a rejection to accept the fact that a perceived entity (a piece of paper or a postage stamp) could behave as a non-permanent entity. This means that if the children are happy to give up their BOP as soon as they see an apparent violation of the OP demands, the BOP/DM is absent. In contrast, in children of 9 years and older, in whom their BOP becomes strong enough to withstand witnessing the OP demands violation (Figure 3.5), the BOP/DM should be expected to work.

To examine these expectations, Experiment 4 reproduced Experiment 1 described in this chapter with 6-, 8- and 10-year-old children, who attended schools in Moscow [8]. As Figure 7.5 indicates, in the *control condition* Russian children's memory on the key events' temporal order was as good as in British adults. However, in the *experimental condition* over 80% of 6-year-olds reproduced the correct temporal order of events, whereas in 8- and 10-year-olds' the number of correct responses was at chance level.

These results supported the expectation that in 6-year-olds the BOP/DM is not yet functioning. Because in 6-year-olds their BOP is not entrenched and easily reversible, observation the OP demands violations doesn't challenge the children's BLEXON. In contrast, in older children who have the entrenched BOP, violation

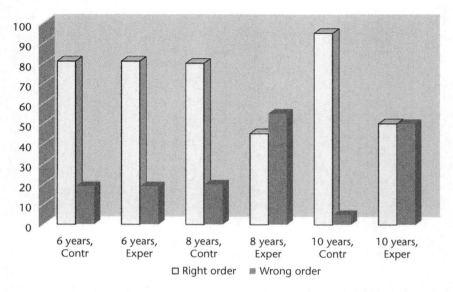

FIGURE 7.5 Percent of participants who recollected *Right* and *Wrong* temporal order of events in Experiment 4, as a function of *Condition* (Control vs Experimental) and *Age* (6, 8 and 10 years)

of the OP demands by a perceived physical object is detected by the children's BLEXON as a disturbance; the BOP/DM is the way to correct this disturbance, albeit at the expense of altering the children's memories.

As studies reviewed in Chapter 3 have shown, in 6-year-old and younger children the distinction between ordinary and superordinary events is unstable. The emergence of the BOP/DM in 8-year-old and older children signifies that the children's world becomes split into two distinct domains: The domain of ordinary reality (OR), in which the BOP reigns, and the domain of superordinary reality (SOR), where the BONP holds sway. This division makes people's subjective reality more complicated and puts new demands on their EXON. In the next chapter, we will consider how people cope with this more complex and demanding subjective reality.

References

[1] Conway, M. & Ross, M. (1984). Getting what you want by revising what you had. *Journal of Personality and Social Psychology*, 47, 738–748.
[2] Hannigan, S.L., & Tippens-Rainitz, M. (2001). A demonstration and comparison of inference-based memory errors. *Journal of Experimental Psychology: Learning, Memory, and Cognition*, 27, 4, 931–940.
[3] Hoffner, C., Cantor, J., & Thorston, E. (1985). Children's responses to conflicting auditory and visual features of a televised narrative. *Human Communication Research*, 16, 2, 256–278.

[4] Roediger, H. L. III., & McDermott, K. B. (2000). Tricks of memory. *Current Directions in Psychological Science*, 9, 4, 123–127.
[5] Tversky, B. & Schiano, D. J. (1989). Perceptual and conceptual factors in distortions in memory for graphs and maps. *Journal of Experimental Psychology: General*, 118, 4, 387–398.
[6] Dennett, D. C. & Kinsbourne, M., (1992). Time and the observer: The where and when of consciousness. *Behavioral and Brain Sciences*, 15, 2, 183–201.
[7] Subbotsky, E. V. (1996). Explaining impossible phenomena: Object permanence beliefs and memory failures in adults. *Memory*, 4, 2, 199–223. https://www.researchgate.net/publication/14505340_Explaining_Impossible_Phenomena_Object_Permanence_Beliefs_and_Memory_Failures_in_Adults
[8] Subbotsky, E., Chesnokova, O., & Greenfield, S. (2002). *Inference-based Memory Failures in Children and Adults*. Poster presented at the 3rd Tsukuba International Conference on Memory, University of Tsukuba, Japan. https://www.researchgate.net/publication/355960082_Inference-based_Memory_Failures_in_Children_and_Adults

8
SEPARATING REALITIES: THE STRUCTURE OF EXON

8.1 The realities distinguisher

In the previous chapters, we described several mechanisms that are involved in EXON. The magic/ordinary distinguisher (MOD) appears in children at the age of about 4 years (see Figure 3.1) and is based on a limited amount of personal experience and knowledge that children accumulate from their social environment: Personal communication with educators, communication with peers, and visual and virtual content available to children. The more complex MTD, which includes MOD as its precursor and a necessary compound, appears in children at the age of 5- to 6-years, but fully matures only when the children reach the age of 9 years (see Figure 3.4). Finally, at the age of about 8 years children develop the BOP/DM – a special mechanism that protects the BOP (see Figure 7.5). At this point, subjective reality splits into the OR and SOR domains.

The structure of EXON becomes even more complex as there appears a separation between two domains of imaginary entities: The imagined physical and fantastical entities. Despite children can cognitively distinguish between ordinary imagined entities and fantastical entities from early preschool years, they are unable to distinguish between these types of entities in terms of their permanence until they reach adulthood (see Figures 4.3 and 4.4). Whereas most adults attribute object permanence (OP) to perceived physical and imagined physical objects, fantastical objects are free to violate the OP demands. Moreover, the studies reviewed in Chapter 6 showed that, under some circumstances, educated adults may attribute non-permanence to perceived objects as well. Mostly, such temporary suspension of the BOP happens when the adults are watching tricks that imitate non-permanence of perceived objects. In addition, there are entities in the perceived world that are truly non-permanent, such as clouds or short-lived quantum objects. The crucial feature of mature subjective reality is that it has a bipolar structure, in which ordinary reality (OR) represented by perceived and imaginary physical entities, is juxtaposed with the superordinary reality (SOR) represented by fantastical entities.

Viewed from the anthropological perspective, the split between the OR and the SOR occurred at the dawn of human history, when, sometime in the Upper Palaeolithic, people began to bury their dead and place human artefacts in their graves. This ritualistic behaviour allows one to assume that these humans already developed an embryonic idea of the afterlife, and the ability to represent some kind of the invisible reality inhabited by their late ancestors. The representation of the invisible fantastical entities – the souls of the dead – also required the development of a new mental tool – the ability to distinguish imaginary entities from the perceived ones. Earlier in this book we called this EXON tool the imaginary/perceived distinguisher (IPD) (see Chapter 4 for more on that). Such juxtaposition of two cardinally different types of reality allowed early humans to break away from captivity by the OR and look at the OR 'out of the box', as if from the perspective of gods [1]. This newly formed ability of reflection – looking at the OR from the perspective of the SOR – drastically changed human social behaviour, by opening the door to executive control and critical thinking. It became necessary for people to watch themselves in order not to offend the invisible creatures – gods and spirits. The invisible and ever-present eye of Gods made it possible for rules of morality to enter the human life.

Indeed, before the invention of the SOR people's social behaviour must have been similar to social behaviour in animals and was based on instincts and learning through conditioning. The discovery of the SOR changed that. There appeared controlling agents – spirits and gods – who superseded the power of tribal leaders and were never asleep. For example, if a person didn't share his or her food with other members of the group, this would offend the spirits, who then might punish the offender. The onset of symbolic consciousness, which happened in the Upper Palaeolithic, also revolutionized human thinking, moving operations with physical objects inside the human mind and thus opening the way to abstract reasoning and, much later in human history, to the emergence of science.

In sum, symbolic consciousness created the ground for morality, science and philosophy, but it also made human life more complicated by forcing people to maintain the division between OR and SOR. Let us call the process of maintaining the division (the borderline) between OR and SOR the *realities distinguisher* (RD). As a result, the structure of EXON in modern humans can be represented as in Figure 8.1.

It is important to mention here that the structure symbolically presented in Figure 8.1 represents not a physical mechanism but a psychological one. There are several definitions of the concept of mechanism, and different for different areas of knowledge - engineering, biology, chemistry and others, but the essence is approximately the same: A physical mechanism is a system of parts connected in a causal way through the four known physical forces: gravitational, electromagnetic, strong and weak nuclear ones. In the physical mechanism, the parts are internally

106 The structure of EXON

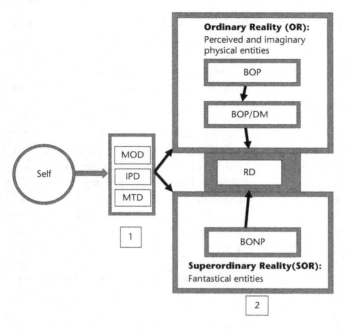

FIGURE 8.1 The structure of positive EXON: Explicit block [1] (MOD – magic/ordinary distinguisher, IPD – imaginary/perceived distinguisher, MTD – magic/trick distinguisher, and Implicit block [2] (BOP – belief in object permanence, BOP/DM – BOP defence mechanism, BONP – belief in object non-permanence, RD – realities distinguisher)

indifferent to each other and do not have mentality of their own; for example, the piston of a steam engine moves not because it sympathizes with the steam, but because the steam pushes it. Alternative to a physical system is a magical system that consist of parts connected by a magical bond, or sympathy. Each part of the magical system possesses some kind of 'inner dimension' or sensitivity to other parts. Examples of magical systems are psychological systems (e.g., people who love each other or influence each other via communication), planets and people's fates in astrology, and entangled quantum particles in physics. The EXON mechanism presented in Figures 2.1, 2.7, 4.6, 8.1 and 10.4 is a magical system, in which separate components (or sub-mechanisms) are linked not in a causal mechanical way but are different facets of a single entity – the human Self. In the course of individual development various components of the EXON mechanism may appear at different times, but at the moment of action all the available components of this mechanism are involved together and mutually influence each other.

For a long time in history the RD component of the EXON mechanism was imperfect, and people frequently conflated the worldly and the divine. This conflation was manifested in superstitions, visions, everyday magic, magical healing, witch hunting and other psychological and social phenomena. Eventually, the RD component improved and became automatized. In the everyday life of a modern mentally healthy person RD functions subconsciously and is hardly noticed, like we rarely notice our heartbeat. However, life becomes more troublesome when, under certain conditions, the RD starts faltering.

8.2 Magical thinking as a corrupted RD

Magical thinking is thinking based not on the laws of formal logic, but on the laws of magical participation: sympathy (independent objects which resemble each other are connected by invisible forces) and contagion (objects that were in physical contact with each other keep being connected after they become physically disentangled). In the *world of magical thinking*, like in our dreams, we can fly in the air, see animals speaking human languages, and travel back in time. In this world, ordinary and superordinary events and entities are freakishly intertwined, and the laws of physics, biology and psychology may be violated. This world attracts us by its novelty and unpredictability. Magical thinking gives us rest from the dullness of the everyday life, but also performs useful cognitive functions: It stimulates creative thinking, helps us to get rid of frustrating experiences, gives us the feeling of strength and control over our lives [3].

As long as magical thinking unfolds in the realm of the imagination, our excursions into the world of magical thinking go well together with our belief in science. Our minds maintain the borderline between the world of OR, in which things obey the laws of science, and the world of SOR where the laws of magic reign. The juxtaposition between magical and everyday realities is important for education, since the laws of science become more salient when bounced from the laws of magical reality [4], [5]. Going through the adventures of Alice in the Wonderland, admiring magical feats of Harry Potter and his friends, a child becomes sharply aware that the real world is built on different grounds and obeys different laws than the world of magic and fantasy. This awareness helps children better understand and remember the laws of physics and other sciences. It also facilitates the development of executive function – the children's ability to consciously control their thoughts, attention and actions [6].

But the ability to distinguish between the OR and the SOR doesn't come naturally and is not always perfect. Even in educated adults, the RD mechanism can occasionally fail, which results in magical thinking turning into *magical behaviour*. So, what happens when the RD is malfunctioning?

Physical science tells us that we cannot affect inanimate matter in a way other than through one of the four known physical forces: gravitation, strong and weak nuclear, and electromagnetism. However, our thoughts and wishes live not in the physical world, but in the world of the mind. Yes, our thoughts cannot directly change physical objects, but they can change other thoughts, images and emotions. Psychological studies have shown that if a person had thought about something to happen (for instance, that a certain person has a car accident) and such event did really happen, then contrary to common logic the person develops a sense of guilt and feels responsible for the accident. This fusion between thoughts and real events can convert routine actions into magical rituals. People suffering from obsessive-compulsive disorder (OCD) are particularly prone to this kind of confusion.

The OCD is a mental disorder when people feel a need of doing certain actions, which in reality have no effect on their lives. For instance, a person with OCD may feel an urgent need to frequently wash his or her hands or check if a door is locked because not doing these actions makes the person feel insecure [7]. Consciously, people with OCD understand that a causal link between their compulsive actions and real-life doesn't exist, yet they find it hard to abstain from the ritualistic behaviour. Although OCD affects only about 2.3% of people [8], studies have shown that in the domain of disgust and fear of contagion, which is mostly intuitive, the RD may fail, and even healthy adults begin to follow the laws of sympathetic magic [9].

Another domain where the RD mechanism relaxes its grip on the mind is night dreams. One way to examine this is to study people's emotional reactions towards magic in the state of sleep. In the Western mindset magic is associated with dark forces yet contains a degree of irresistible attraction. Some masterpieces of fiction, such as Goethe's 'Faust' and Thomas Mann's 'Doctor Faustus', expose this ambiguous attitude of modern people towards magic. Because of this duality in the cultural disposition, our attitudes towards magic are mixed. On one hand, we are curious towards magic and eager to experiment with it, but on the other hand we are fearful that involvement with magic might harbour dangers. In the light of a day, when our consciousness is active and the RD mechanism is engaged, we are not sensitive to the fear of magic. But could this fear slip into our night dreams, when our RD is put to rest?

To examine this, educated adults were divided in two separate groups. In the 'magical suggestion' group participants were offered a magic spell that aimed at helping them to see their chosen night dreams [10]. In the control 'no suggestion' group participants were simply asked to choose their target dreams, but no offer of magical help was made. In those who had received the magical help, the results showed only a slight increase in the number of chosen target dreams; however, these participants saw a significantly larger number of scary dreams than did participants of the control group (see Figure 8.2). This suggests that despite our conscious disbelief in magic, *the subconscious anxiety of being engaged with magic filters into our minds* in the form of bad dreams when our RD is relaxed.

Studies indicate that under certain conditions the RD can falter in people *even when they are in full possession of their conscious critical thinking*. One of such conditions takes place when a certain authority (e.g., a political leader, a priest or a psychology experimenter) makes some unrealistic suggestion to a person, and the person's disbelief in the suggestion is deprived of social support. Indeed, experiments reviewed in Chapter 4 showed that participants who had denied that a suggestion framed in magical or magic-free context could change anything in their future lives nevertheless behaved as if they believed the suggestion to have real

The structure of EXON 109

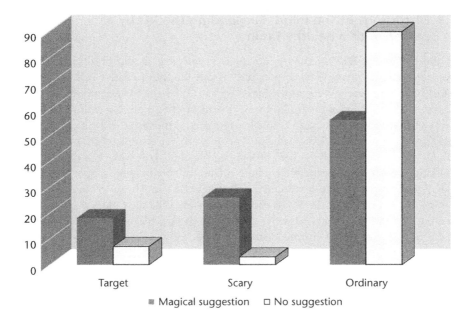

FIGURE 8.2 Percentage of dreams as a function of *Condition* (Magical suggestion versus No suggestion) and *Type of dream* (Target, Scary and Ordinary)

powers. Put in terms of the EXON theory, when the RD fails an existentially weak external impact (e.g., a magic spell or an unrealistic suggestion) undergoes EXUP and filters from the domain of SOR to the domain of OR.

Art is another domain in which the RD can be partially disabled. From the EXON perspective, every piece of art is a tacit suggestion behind which there is an agent – a painter, a sculptor, a composer – and most often this suggestion targets our PSE. As studies reviewed in the previous chapters have shown, in this combination the suggestion has a good chance to be upgraded and begin to affect our feelings and behaviour (see Figure 4.6). For example, when we are in the middle of a movie with fictional characters or events, we might temporarily suspend the feeling that the events happening on the screen are only fantasy and begin experiencing real feelings by identifying ourselves with the movie characters. We are petrified when a criminal is approaching a lonely woman on the street and feel relaxed when the criminal is scared away by Superman; we love and hate, enjoy and suffer together with the characters of books that we read. This ability to relax our RD and immerse our Self into the imaginary world is a reason for the art's invincible charm.

Nevertheless, the price we pay for adapting to the rules of the everyday life is the necessity to keep the OR and the SOR apart, and this puts a demand on our mental energy. In this section, we discussed some of the consequences when our RD mechanism is relaxed. But what happens when the RD fails entirely?

8.3 Distortions of the mind: Suspending the RD by a person with a healthy brain

In the context of EXON theory, *distortions of the mind* should be distinguished from *distortions of psyche*. The former result from the incapacitated RD with the intact brain chemistry, whereas the latter are caused by the malfunctioning brain.

Among distortions of the mind, one of the most often cases is a malfunction of faith. Generally, religious faith implies a temporary and local suspension of the RD. In their everyday lives, religious people can be completely rational and submit their behaviour to the laws of logic and science. It is when the people are thinking about the subject of their religious faith, usually in church or at religious meetings, that the people temporarily relax their RD and begin to behave as if Gods – the entities from the SOR – trespass into the OR and obtain the status of existentially strong entities. Usually, as soon as the people come back into the realm of OR, their RD is immediately restored. However, sometimes the RD suspension becomes irreversible. When this happens, we deal with the phenomenon of *religious extremism*.

Religious extremism is one of the manifestations of a disturbed RD, when values of the invisible world of the supernatural supersede values of ordinary reality. Psychological causes of religious extremism are still under investigation, but there is little doubt that religious extremism is a main contributor to *suicidal terrorism* [11]. Thus, Palestinians ready to become suicidal terrorists socially and psychologically did not differ from other members of their social environment; the only feature that distinguished radicalized Palestinians from their ordinary compatriots was intensity of their belief that their destructive actions are sanctioned by God [12].

Another manifestation of the disturbed RD is the *spontaneous killing spree*. On May 11, 2021, an armed young man burst into a school in Kazan, detonated a homemade grenade and began shooting students and teachers with a hunting rifle that he had legally acquired [13]. The culprit was a 19-year-old former school graduate. Teachers and acquaintances of the criminal spoke of him as a quiet, non-conflict and unremarkable young man, who did not give any signs that he was capable of a crime. The young man's father said that his son did not express any negative thoughts and moods. The only sign of a troubled mind was that at the end of his teaching semester in the college the young man stopped attending and refused to pass his final exams. The psychiatrist who commented on the event did not find clear signs of mental disorder in the criminal's behaviour.

A similar killing spree happened on the 17 of October 2018, in the Crimean city of Kerch, when a student at Kerch Polytechnic College opened fire at his teachers and fellow students with an automatic rifle, killing 18 people and wounding more than 40 [14]. Still earlier, on September 5, 2017, in the city of Ivanteevka, Moscow Region, a 15-year-old teenager entered the building of the educational centre where he was a student, opened fire from an air rifle, detonated an improvised explosive device and attacked a teacher with a knife [15]. Psychiatric examination established the adolescent's sanity at the time of the attack. According to the reviews of teachers and parents, the boy had previously shown no signs of aggression, did not violate discipline, and was calm; his relations with other children were even, although there was some deterioration in his academic performance. In his appearance, the offender mimicked two American teenagers who had attacked Columbine High School in 1999, killing 13 people and injuring 23 [16]. Like his American predecessors, on his website the teenager had fantasized about suicide, death and murder. Social causes for such crimes are linked to a variety of factors (e.g., the laws that allow a legal purchase of the gun, the rules regulating access to the school's building and handling emergency situations, etc.), but in the perspective of EXON most important is the psychological mechanism of the crimes.

According to the EXON theory, the idea of killing people (IKP) may enter the mind of a child from books, fairy tales and visual and virtual media games. This idea is, however, placed in a special compartment of the mind – in the domain of superordinary reality (SOR). Images of a murderer, a serial killer, and a child molester share the SOR with a dragon, a goblin, the devil and other supernatural monsters. Although killing another person is an event that is not physically impossible, given a certain amount of physical strength and availability of appropriate 'tools', the idea is under a powerful social ban and is treated by the normal mind as socially impossible. As a result, the IKP has an existential status of CWESE – cognitively weak and emotionally strong entity (see Table 4.4). While remaining in the status of CWESE, this idea is kept on the fringes of the mind and cannot take control over a person's behaviour.

However, as the studies reviewed in Chapters 4 and 6 demonstrated, CWESE are highly vulnerable to external or internal assistance. Externally, CWESE can be upgraded to the status of cognitively strong entity by suggestion that comes from a powerful source (e.g., a political leader, a charismatic personality, or a popular character of computer games). Thus, a person who under normal circumstances considers killing people to be a horrible crime, in the circumstance of a war might consider killing enemy soldiers (and sometimes even civilians) as an action of virtue. Whereas the *external EXUP of the IKP* happens mostly in the domain of virtual reality (e.g., computer games or dark sites on the internet) and can easily be exposed, the *IKP's internal EXUP* is unfolding secretly and inside the person's mind. In this process, the RD mechanism that maintains the internal borderline between CWESE and cognitively strong PSIME becomes gradually corrupted and eventually thins out to the degree that allows the IKP filter into the domain of OR. This means that the IKP becomes a CSESE kind of entity, existentially strong enough to take control over the person's behaviour. At this stage, the person begins his or her preparation to putting the IKP in action.

The question arises of *what psychological conditions bring a person with an undisturbed brain to the state of the corrupted RD, which allows the IKP's existential upgrade*. Analysis of the aforementioned cases shows that the common feature that precedes the IKP's EXUP is the feeling by the offender of his own worthlessness and insignificance, which is then followed by the sudden EXUP of significance of the person's Self and reloading the image of worthlessness from his own Self to others. This sudden change from downgrading one's Self to upgrading one's Self, which seems paradoxical, finds an explanation in the theory by Austrian psychiatrist Alfred Adler (1870 – 1937). Adler maintained that the feeling of one's inadequacy and worthlessness, which he named '*inferiority complex*', is the psychological trigger of the opposite '*superiority complex*', which develops in the person as the means of overcoming the unbearable feeling of inferiority [17]. For example, after the arrest, the aforementioned Kazan's killer stated that about 2 months ago he suddenly realized that he was a God in the guise of a man and that he hated people. After that, he began to prepare for the crime. On the morning of the day he committed his crime, the young man placed a post with his photo in a mask on which the word 'God' is written and a vest with the words "Today I will kill a huge amount of bio-waste and shoot myself". In a similar vein, one of the messages posted by the shooter from Kerch was as follows: "There are a couple of millions more like me on this social network alone. I'll answer right away - I have empathy below the plinth. I think I'm semi-psychopathic. I have little interest in communicating with my own kind. All feelings are lies, deception and bullshit. You should hide them from yourself. And also, all those around me are idiots, and there are thoughts – to shoot them all. But killing people is bad. I expressed only a subjective opinion and do not urge anyone to kill" [18]. Upgrading the Self to the status of a Superman suspends the RD and allows the IKP obtain the status of CSESE – the idea that can and should be put into action.

One of the known literary analyses of the IKP internal upgrade we meet in Dostoevsky's novel 'Crime and punishment'. The novel's character, a young person named Rodion Raskolnikov, is a former university student, who had to leave the university for the shortage of money. Disappointed in his position in life, Raskolnikov begins pondering the causes that bring people to poverty and misery in life. His contemplation leads him to historically known personalities, such as Napoleon or Alexander the Great, who were capable of killing other people and get away with that. The extraordinary persons have the courage to adjust the world to their needs, whereas the uncapable ones are destined to submit to the capable ones and lead miserable lives. In the beginning, for Raskolnikov these thoughts were purely mental and still in the domain of CWESE, yet the thoughts emotional appeal started to grow and gain more cognitive strength in the character's mind. Raskolnikov began to ask himself a question "Am I a trembling beast or do I have the right?" There appeared the lure to move himself from the pool of ordinary people to the upper crust of extraordinary ones, yet this lure was still abstract and incapable of affecting the character's actions; in order for the lure to obtain the necessary strength, it needed a justification. The justification came from Raskolnikov's observation of the ugly inequality in which people around him lived. Some people suffered extreme poverty, while others lived in luxury. Raskolnikov himself lived in poverty and had to give his last possessions over to an old woman – a moneylender. By coincidence, he overhears the conversation of two people who discussed the moneylender as a greedy and cruel bastard.

Suddenly the three components of Raskolnikov's mental work – his contemplation of the exceptional people, his unsatisfaction with his own life, and his observation of the social inequality – came together, and the IKP obtained a practical embodiment: Raskolnikov decided to join the club of extraordinary people, by killing the moneylender, with the aim of distributing her wealth to poor people. As a result, he hacked to death the old woman and her sister who turned to be in the wrong place at the wrong time.

According to the EXON theory, the seemingly spontaneous killing spree is a pathological EXUP of the IKP, which is a result of internal and external assistance – the tragic combination of a person's thoughts and observations, combined with the ever-present desire to be in control over his personal world – the 'Bubble universe' [19]. The disappointment in his life produces in the offender the powerful desire to upgrade his image, at the expense of downgrading the others. While normally being in the status of CWESE, the IKP obtains the status of CSESE and takes control not only over the person's thoughts but also over his behaviour. Sometimes the IKP upgrade goes even further and the IKP obtains the existential status of an *absolute entity*, which is equal to the status of the killer's own Self; when this happens, the killer goes for the crime with full understanding of its consequences and the killing often results in the killer's after-crime suicide. Of the spontaneous killing spree cases described above, Kazan's killer gave himself up, while the Kerch's killer and Columbine killers committed suicide.

8.4 Hallucinations: Suspending the RD by a person with disturbed psyche

While the RD failures described above occur in the minds of people free from mental disorders and the psychological origins of such cases are not (and perhaps cannot be) completely understood, a lot more is known of the causes of the disturbed RD in sensory and mental disorders. *Hallucinations* are a manifestation of EXON distortions caused by malfunctioning of the brain and/or sensory systems. Hallucinations are different from *perceptual illusions* (see Table 2.1). Perceptual illusions are real phenomena which contradict their rational constructions (RC), whereas hallucinations are sheer creations of the mind. For example, when looking at the sun we can see the sun to be the size of a coin (a perceptual illusion), but the after-image of the sun that we see after closing our eyes is a production of our perceptual system (a perceptual hallucination). Another example of a perceptual hallucination is palinopsia - the persistent recurrence of a visual image after the stimulus has been removed (e.g., a patient sees a real person crossing the room, but then experiences the image of the same person crossing the room repeatedly) [20]. Whereas after-image is a result of normal physiological processes, palinopsia belongs to the group of pathological visual symptoms.

One of the most revealing for the structure of EXON is the kind of hallucinations called Charles Bonnet syndrome (CBS) [21]. Most of the CBS type of hallucinations are not caused by the brain malfunctioning but result from deterioration of the visual system, hence most of them are visual hallucinations, though in patients with impaired hearing they may also be auditory (e.g., hearing music). There are two types of CBS hallucinations: Simple (repeated patterns can take the form of grids, shapes or lines, which can appear in bright or vivid colours and may lay across or cover everything the person sees) and complex (people, places, animals and insects). The hallucinatory images usually simulate *Self-related* phenomena (e.g., faces, objects, people, animals) but can also include *representing* ones (letters, signs, texts, and musical notes) (see Chapter 1). The following EXON features distinguish the CBS hallucinatory images from Self-related phenomena:

a. Violation of the OP demands, such as inclusion, permanence, intermodality and intersubjectivity: the images appear as if from nothing, hang for a while but may disappear suddenly, they cannot be touched and are not confirmed by other people;
b. Form-place-meaning distortions – the images look distorted in shape (e.g., faces with various parts not in the right places, animals with wrong features, two-dimensional human figures), place (e.g., a scaffolding seen in the street suddenly appears inside the room) and meaning (e.g., meaningless words or musical notes impossible to read or play).

Due to these features, people with normally functioning RD usually do not believe that the images they see or hear are real and exist outside of their Self; they usually isolate these images from Self-related phenomena and treat them as a simulation - something that is created by their mind against their will. However, sometimes these hallucinations are so vivid and fit the surrounding real phenomena so well that the person's RD fails and the hallucinatory images filter from the domain of SOR in the domain of OR. For example, Oliver Sacks brings a description of an old man who was visited by two of his grand-daughters accompanied by two beautiful young men; when the old man commented about the beauty of the young men and the young ladies denied the young men's presence, the young men's images immediately evaporated from the old man's view [22]. Interestingly, under certain circumstances the 'SOR versus OR exchange' goes the opposite way and the Self-related phenomena filter through a weakened RD into the domain of SOR. Sacks reports a story of a patient who took a window cleaner hanging outside his window on the 19th floor for a hallucination (ibid).

In terms of the EXON theory, in the CBS type of hallucinations the high level of EXON (HLEXON) is activated: The person's critical thinking assesses correspondence of the perceptual image created by the person's mind to the image's RC. By comparing the image with its RC on shape, place, inclusion, permanence, intermodality and intersubjectivity, the HLEXON brings the verdict on whether the image is a real or a simulated phenomenon. Generally, the patient observes that the hallucinatory phenomenon 'goes wild': The parts of the face (e.g., a nose) and the whole bodies of familiar people grow out of proportions, realistically looking objects appear 'from nothing' in empty places, and familiar objects suddenly 'multiply'.

Speaking figuratively, the hallucinatory phenomena 'jump out' of their RC and begin violating the limits of 'behaviour' set by the patient's knowledge of how things 'normally should be'. Thus, in another example by Sacks, a pianist who was losing sight began seeing realistically looking musical notes, but when he looked closer he realized that these notes are a very complex mess impossible to read or play; besides, the page with the 'devilish notes' was seen only for a few seconds, after which it changed for another one with the equally unreadable notes.

At that, in most cases the patient's HLEXON keeps working normally and the patient places the hallucinatory phenomenon into the domain of SOR, even without asking other people for a confirmation. When patients with CBS have some remnants of vision instead of being completely blind, along with reporting hallucinations they sometimes report perceptual illusions: The perceived objects look distorted in size and shape. MRT studies reviewed by Sacks showed that visual hallucinations and perceptual illusions correlate with activation of different areas in the brain. For example, in a participant (a talented artist) spontaneous visual hallucinations were accompanied by increased activity of visual cortex, whereas when the same person was asked to deliberately imagine the same content the increased brain activity was observed in the executive area of prefrontal cortex. This suggests that in visual hallucinations the RD breakdown happens due to the *malfunctioning of perceptual system*, rather than being a product of the imagination 'going wild'. The question arises what can go wrong with visual perception so that, instead of real phenomena it begins producing hallucinations?

Speaking metaphorically, the work of visual perception is a joint effort of two 'eyes': A *physical eye* and a *mental eye*. While the physical eye is a receptive device, the mental eye is a producer. The physical eye receives the physical light (electromagnetic waves of a certain length) reflected by the molecular structure of the perceived object. The physical light creates neural impulses in the receptors of the eye, which are then transmitted to the neurons of our visual cortex via the visual nerve and disappear into the 'black hole' of the subconscious. At this point, the mental eye comes into the game, by extracting from this 'black hole' a beam of 'subjective light' which throws the image of the perceived object into the space out there.

We can feel this 'projective' ability of our mind when engaged in the process of writing with a ballpoint pen. When we are writing with the pen, our point of kinaesthetic sensation is on the end of the ballpoint pen, despite we don't touch the pen's end with our hand. This means that our kinaesthetic sensation is 'sliding' down from our hand along the pen's body to its very end. In the same vein our vision and hearing work, by projecting subjective images from our mind forward into what we experience as the outer space.

So, our mental eye works like a projector. A real projector creates images on the screen, and so does our mental eye. How the neural impulses in the brain are linked to the subjective beam of light is a mystery which cannot be explained in terms of physical causality. At this point, there is an unsurmountable gap between the phenomenal image of the object that we are seeing (e.g., a laptop computer), and our knowledge (the RC) about the object. When we obscure the computer with a non-transparent screen (e.g. close our eyes) or turn our gaze away from it, our 'subjective beam' keeps working, by creating the mental image of the computer. But without the support of sensory input, this mental image is powerless and deficient.

"But if our mental eye works like a projector, does this mean that we create images by the sheer power of our mind?" – one might ask. No, in normal circumstances it does not. As argued in Chapter 2, there are things out there, and these things are independent of our mind. The philosopher Immanuel Kant called these things 'things-in-themselves'. However, the 'things-in-themselves' exist only potentially; in order for them to obtain actual existence they have to be illuminated by the subjective light of our mind. The *sensory input* that comes into our eyes is connected with *things-in-themselves*, but the connection is not like a connection between an object's photo and the object itself; rather the connection is like a connection between an icon on a computer screen and the folder the icon represents. Whereas the connection between icons and folders is set by people, the connections between sensory input and things-in-themselves are quite mysterious; these connections vary slightly between people and a lot between species. Nevertheless, without such connections the 'icons' become empty and meaningless.

Now, for a projector to be able to produce the image on a big screen, the projector needs two things: (1) a torch producing the beam of light and (2) a transparency slide with a small image on it. Similarly, our mind works like a torch that throws the subjective light to 'illuminate' things-in-themselves. If we looked at a physical beam of light in darkness from one side, and if there were no objects on the beam's way able to reflect the photons, we wouldn't see the beam. The sensory input that our eyes and brain receive are such 'slides' that the 'subjective beam' of our mind 'illuminates' to produce phenomena, which our EXON invests with the status of 'real objects'.

To summarize, Self-related phenomena are things-in-themselves transformed by our mind; phenomena emerge when the projector of our mind 'illuminates' the things-in-themselves with its subjective beam, with the help of the physical eyes and the brain. These phenomena out there – apples, vases, mountains, beams of light, stars and galaxies – we call physical matter. Now, what happens when, due to the distortion of visual nerves or visual cortex in the brain, a person loses his or her sight? Typically, the person simply goes blind, but in some cases the visual system begins producing sensory input by itself. This sensory input is no longer linked to the things-in-themselves, or the links still exist but are distorted. However, our mental eye, having been deceived by the false sensory input, projects the image into the outer space, thus creating realistically looking simulations. Hallucinations are these simulations. Because the false sensory input is no longer anchored in things-in-themselves, perception has to weave the hallucinatory images solely from memory. Having no support from things-in-themselves, memory supplies perception not with stable whole images, but rather with 'building blocks' from which the whole image has yet to be synthesized; that is why many CBS images look like surrealist paintings (e.g., human heads with boxes on instead of hats, or with flowers growing out of cheeks).

Along with distortion of shapes, hallucinatory images have distortions engraved in their origin. Normal phenomena always originate from some accompanying context, but the hallucinatory phenomena, having no link with the objects-in-themselves, appear to spring out of nothing. But perception is only a part of HLEXON (see Table 2.3). Another part is critical assessment via a comparison of the phenomena with their RC, the comparison which may also include intersubjectivity check. It is the critical assessment that does not allow CBS hallucinatory phenomena not only *look real* but also *believed to be real*; instead, these phenomena are mostly treated as movies, often entertaining and sometimes frightening. In terms of the EXON theory, one can say that the CBS hallucinations have a weak existential status and belong to the domain of CWESE (see Table 4.4). Even if hallucinatory images seem real to the patients, the belief in the images' reality is short-lived and disappears in seconds. This means, that the patients' RD is deactivated at the level of perception but is still functioning at the level of thinking. Let us call this condition *partially disturbed RD*. It is only when patients, along with the lost vision, also suffer from impairment of the brain sections associated with critical thinking (i.e., frontal lobes) or have mental conditions associated with old age (e.g., mental dementia or Alzheimer disease) that the patients begin to take the CBS hallucinatory images for reality. When this happens, we will say that the *RD is fully disturbed*.

Like vision and other sensations, *hearing* is a two-sided process: our 'physical' ear registers the vibrations caused by a speaking person, but our 'mental ear' is projecting the voice out there into physical space. Like in the case of vision, the 'thinking component' of HLEXON is making assessment of whether the voices being heard could or could not belong to the source the voices seem to be coming from. According to some studies, around 10% of healthy people reported hearing 'inner voices' which they treated as CWESE – auditory hallucinations produce by their own mind. In schizophrenic patients who suffer from disorder of delicate brain chemistry, the RD is fully disturbed, and voices acquire existential power of CSESE – they seem to be coming from people and objects and are capable of changing the patient's behaviour [ibid].

The interesting feature of both visual and auditory hallucinations is their unusual vividness and the abundance of details. Some patients report that they see landscapes or palaces of unimaginable beauty in the smallest details or hear sounds of every single instrument in an orchestra; at that, these patients in ordinary life had never seen anything comparable to these hallucinatory landscapes and couldn't remember the simplest melody. This suggests that the patient's subliminal memory, from which the patient's 'subjective eye' and 'subjective ear' extract their material for projection, contains a lot more details of a visual display or a musical piece than does the patient's conscious memory.

Because hallucinatory phenomena are apparitions produced entirely by the patient's mind there is a magical participation between the patient and the hallucinatory phenomena. As mentioned earlier in this chapter, magical participation means that two phenomena that are physically independent from one another are nevertheless connected as if they were one entity, so that what happens to one of them also happens to the other. One female patient described by Sacks suffered a particularly complicated form of Parkinson's disease; one day she saw that the Indian tribe leader, whose picture was included in the painting hanging on the wall in her bedroom, went out of the painting and stood in the middle of the room. When her husband got up and waved his hand through the apparition, the hallucinatory figure disintegrated, but the patient painfully felt shat she too was breaking into parts [ibid]. Typically, magical participation is an integrative part of healthy BLEXON, which is revealed in the phenomenon of empathy [23]. However, in the normal state of mind 'empathic distress' is mediated by functioning RD and accompanied by the realization that the 'real pain' is being experienced by another person; in contrast, when the patient's RD is fully disturbed, the events happening to the apparition are felt by the patient as if they were happening to the patient himself or herself.

Whereas in pathological conditions of the brain and sensory systems hallucinations still have some resemblance with normal Self-related phenomena, in the so-called 'altered states of consciousness' HLEXON can go completely wild. Altered states of consciousness can emerge when normal healthy people take hallucinogenic drugs, such as extractions of certain kinds of mushrooms (e.g., peyote and psilocybin) or LSD. Participants in this kind of 'travels of the mind' report that ordinary inanimate objects begin moving spontaneously as if they are alive, their shapes drastically change, and colours become extremely intensive. In extreme cases, participants feel to be entirely detached from the OR and find themselves in 'different universes' with unknown objects and unimaginable colours and sounds. The participants also feel that the division between objects and their own Selves is melting and they 'become one' with the outer world. At that, the RD mechanism is only partially disturbed, and most participants are aware that what they are seeing and hearing is the product of their mind [24], [25], [26].

To summarize, hallucinations are Self-created experiences, in which some properties of Self-related phenomena, such as identity and locality, are *simulated*, whereas other properties, such as permanence and inclusion, are *absent entirely* [see Table 2.1]. To remind, identity means that a phenomenon has some features that make the phenomenon a unique entity and different from other, similar entities. In the hallucinatory world, an object's *identity* can be violated by objects turning one into another; for instance, a patient with the Capgras syndrome is experiencing a delusion that a friend or a family member has been replaced by an identical impostor. Another way of identity violation is multiplication: an illusory object suddenly produces its own multiple copies, which fill the whole volume of surrounding space [27]. The property of *permanence* requires that a phenomenon cannot instantly change into another phenomenon (e.g., person cannot turn into a cat and vice versa). This property disappears in the hallucinatory world, particularly after taking a large dose of hallucinogenic drugs: Inanimate objects turn into animated ones, and people can turn into animals. According to the property of *locality*, a phenomenon possesses a certain amount of solidity; there is a borderline between the phenomenon and other phenomena, which prevents the phenomena from merging with each other. In the hallucinatory world, things may look solid but allow other things (like a person's hand) to go right through them. Finally, violation of the property of *inclusion* in the hallucinatory world is manifested in the sudden emergence of objects from nothing and the sudden disappearance of objects as if they dissolve in thin air.

Altogether, phenomenology of the hallucinating person suggests that the person's mental (projecting) component of HLEXON lost the 'gravitational pull' of things-in-themselves but, by inertia, keeps producing subjective images, which are now levitating in the person's 'mental space' without support. The liberation from the ties with the ground makes these images bizarre yet increases their creative potential. The question arises of whether these 'ground-disconnected' images might have played a role in shaping some features of modern cultures.

8.5 Hallucinations: Suspended RD in the cultural-historical context

Indeed, some authors suggested that hallucinations played a part in initiating cultural phenomena in art, popular beliefs, psychology and religion. Thus, seeing hallucinations of small people playing around may have given the idea of elves, gnomes and fairies, while nightmares and frightening hallucinations could have caused the beliefs in demons, witches and aliens [28]; seeing themselves travelling out of our bodies in dreams and hallucinations may have initiated the beliefs in ghosts and spirits, as well as give the idea that our soul can exist separately from our body [29]; the 'entopics' – bizarre geometrical patterns that people see in the altered states of the mind (migraine or the state of shamanistic trance) – may have become the source of the Palaeolithic cave art [30]; the experience of mystical 'presence' during the epileptic seizures could have been a neurological trigger for the belief in the almighty God [31].

Whereas associations between disturbed RD and cultural-historical phenomena remain in the department of speculations, some observations support the view that there is a link between hallucinatory world and cultural environment. As mentioned above, when hallucinating patients' critical thinking is functional and the RD is only partially incapacitated, the patients are aware that perceived entities they are seeing or hearing are not real. Russian psychiatrist Victor Kandinsky (1849–1889) called this kind of delusions '*pseudo hallucinations*'; in contrast, proper hallucinations trick both perception and consciousness thus making a person feel that his or her fantasies really exist [32]. Kandinsky observed his patients in the cultural setting of the 19th century Russia, which was deeply influenced by the Orthodox church. He noted that hallucinations of his schizophrenic patients were conditioned by the patients' religious beliefs. For example, patients reported such visions as seeing a demon who spread his black wings over the whole St Petersburg, looking down at the "abyss of hell", with the little devils going in and out of it, and turning into flying angels [ibid, p.17]. Sometimes visions included paradise and inferno or having a telepathic communication with God or the devil. In contrast, hallucinations of modern patients seem to be more 'science based'. For example, Arnhild Lauveng was born in 1972 in Norway and diagnosed with schizophrenia at the age of 17 years; on recovery she reported in her book that, along with seeing all sorts of fantastic creatures, patients in her ward had seen aliens, Martians or spies [33]. Lauveng was a Scandinavian teenager living in a technically advanced and not very religious society at the end of the 20th century. It is not surprising that, unlike hallucinations of schizophrenic patients described by Kandinsky, hallucinations experienced by Lauveng and other patients involved images linked to the cultural context of their time, in which images installed by science and science fiction replaced images inspired by religious faith.

Altogether, in both mentally healthy (e.g., religious extremists) and mentally disturbed (e.g., schizophrenic patients) people the RD failure means trouble, both for the people and for their social environment. Still, as French philosopher Michel Foucault famously noted, if in the modern world people who confuse the real with the supernatural are not highly praised, their position is far not as bad as it used to be a few hundred years ago [34].

8.6 Witchcraft: Suspending the RD by the belief in magic

Experiments reviewed in Chapter 4 demonstrated that when people's PSIME are targeted by magical suggestion, people who had consciously denied their belief in magic began to take magic seriously. Like mental illness, the belief in magic, which was common in the antiquity and the Middle Ages, challenged the division between OR and SOR. This common feature of mental disorders with the belief in magic may have been the reason why these two phenomena were frequently conflated. Not all those accused of witchcraft by Holy Inquisition (12th to early 19th centuries) were insane, but all people with schizophrenia were under suspicion of their involvement with magic [35]. Organized religions, such as Christianity, have been fighting magic for millennia, but not because they were bothered with maintaining purity of the OR; the real reason was competition for people's minds. Witches challenged the authority of the Catholic Church, for they revolted against the illnesses, which the Church viewed as the punishment from God [36]. By healing poor and weak, witches undermined traditional hierarchy of the medieval society: The authority of a priest over an ordinary parishioner, and a lord over a peasant [37]. The confrontation between witchcraft and Holy Inquisition was a real-life analogy of the confrontation between Simon Magus and Saint Peter described in the apocryphal Acts of the Apostles [38]. Indirectly, the war against magic opened the way to the belief in natural laws. About 400 years ago, modern science joined the organized religion in its fight against magic and witchcraft.

Yet, despite centuries of persecution, witchcraft and magical healing in Europe are not eradicated. Along with knowledge of magical spells, white witches possessed valuable expertise in the curing properties of herbs. Some of the methods of magical healing led towards scientific medicine, whereas others tried to cure people by the magical transfer of an illness from a patient to another person or an animal. While the 'rational component' of the medieval magical healing condensed into modern homeopathy, some modern practicing sorcerers still use traditional magical methods of healing, by manipulating with PSIME of modern people [39]. Under certain conditions, magic can indeed trespass in the domain of OR [40]. Imagination and dreams are among such conditions. The etching by Francisco Goya 'The sleep of reason produces monsters' depicts a person in deep sleep, his reason bedevilled by monstrous creatures emerging from the dark [41]. Ghosts, apparitions, spirits of the dead, gods – science is unable to eradicate these fantastic images from our mind. The 'world through the looking glass', the world of SOR, accompanies us from childhood to the last breath, whether we believe in it or not.

Could this be the case because this world has deep historical, developmental and neurological roots?

8.7 The voices of gods: Illusion or reality?

As studies showed, at the age of 4 to 6 years children become able to distinguish between perceptual, imagined and fantastical entities [42], yet only adults can verbally explain what the differences are. Further research revealed that educated adults view imaginary realistic objects (e.g., an imaginary spoon) to be as stable and permanent as their perceived prototypes; by contrast, they regarded fantastical entities (e.g., a cat with the fishes tail) as unstable and in constant danger of turning into another fantastical creature (e.g., a flying dog) (see Chapter 4). These data suggest that the RD is not hardwired into the brain and matures gradually with age. The development of consciousness that may have taken millennia of human evolution, in a modern child happens in the time span of years. Instead of inventing the invisible world of the supernatural, modern children get this world ready for them, in the form of fairy tales, toys with magical abilities, and computer games. To a small child, even adults look almost like gods. Bouncing from their interaction with the supernatural, children quickly develop symbolic thinking, executively controlled behaviour and eventually, symbolic consciousness. Still, till the age of teens children's RD is unstable. Only adolescents develop the RD ability that begins to approach the RD of adults. And they do need this ability.

In the everyday life, when we are speaking with another person or watching a movie, we automatically assess actions and words of other people as being a part of either OR or SOR. This HLEXON of other people's behaviour 'on normality' is historically and culturally conditioned. For example, even about 20 years ago seeing a person on the street talking loudly to himself or herself would be a sign of abnormal behaviour, but the use of earphones that work remotely changed that. But if the RD criteria change so quickly, what might these criteria be a few thousand years ago?

In an attempt to answer this question, the American philosopher Julian Jaynes hypothesized that approximately up to 1000 BC ancients systematically heard inner voices, taking them for voices of gods [43]. According to Jaynes, hearing voices by characters of Homer's 'Iliad' was not a literary metaphor but an accurate description of people's mind of that historical period. In this type of mind cognitive functions were divided between two parts of the brain: One part of the brain was 'speaking', and the other was 'listening'. People stopped hearing voices when they developed the ability of self-reflection; however, even today people with certain distortions of the brain functioning (e.g., schizophrenia) may hear voices, which they sometimes still attribute to gods.

In the context of EXON theory, Jaynes's hypothesis implies that the ancients were unable to keep OR and SOR apart and the RD mechanism was not yet formed. This hypothesis was subject to criticism for insufficiency of historical and neurological evidence [44]. From the EXON perspective, historically the RD mechanism must have appeared in people much earlier than 1000 BC, perhaps in the time of the Upper Palaeolithic; the reason is that without the RD the ancients would have constantly mistaken the mundane for the divine, which would make it hard for them to effectively function in the everyday life, both socially (e.g., communication during hunting or war) and biologically (e.g., coping with the chores of everyday life).

Conflation between ordinary and superordinary realities did indeed happen throughout history, but it happened in the form of superstitions rather than hallucinations. Thus, in the ancient Rome people kept small idols in their homes, which they treated as household protecting deities (the Lares), yet the people viewed the idols as phenomena *representing* gods, whereas gods themselves lived in the higher realm. Occasionally people did report seeing images or hearing voices from the realm of the supernatural (e.g., mythical characters, Christ or Virgin Mary), but they distinguished those visions from entities of the OR. The ancients were superstitious, but not delirious. The feeling of being under constant surveillance of Gods did not deprive the ancients from the ability of making free choices.

Nevertheless, Jaynes's hypothesis raised important questions: The division of reality into the realms of OR and SOR, and the difficulties that arise from the necessity to live in both of these realms at once.

8.8 Conclusion: The price for being conscious

Altogether, having emerged in the prehistoric times, the person's ability to live in the OR and SOR simultaneously fundamentally changed human psychology, by making human behaviour executively controlled and giving rise to the concepts of morality, freedom of action and personal responsibility. By looking in the outlandish mirror of the supernatural, people created art, symbolic language, and ultimately modern religion and science. *But the price paid for symbolic consciousness was high: Mental disorders, hallucinations, witchcraft, witch hunting, Holy Inquisition, spontaneous killing spree, suicidal terrorism, and religious radicalism.*

Thus far, we have been looking at the ways our Self invests existence into various entities in external and internal realities – perceived and imagined objects, thoughts and ideas, rational constructions and, ultimately, the division between OR and SOR. However, the ability of our Self to reflect upon its own existential status raises the question of the conditions that determine the Self's own HLEXON. In other words, under what conditions do we stop taking for granted that our Self is a miserable part of the universe and begin to realize that our Self is the necessary condition for the universe to exist? The next chapter addresses this question.

References

[1] Subbotsky E. (2017). Consciousness as a Look into the Supernatural. *SENTENTIA. European Journal of Humanities and Social Sciences*, 1, 55–74. https://nbpublish.com/library_read_article.php?id=21374

[2] Frazer, J.G. (1923). *The golden bough. A study in magic and religion*. Macmillan & Co. Ltd.

[3] Subbotsky, E. (2010). *Magic and the mind. Mechanisms, functions and development of magical thinking and behaviour*. Oxford University Press.

[4] Cole, M. & Subbotsky, E. (1993). The fate of stages past: Reflections on the heterogeneity of thinking from the perspective of cultural-historical psychology. *Schweizerische Zitschrift fur Psychologie*, 52, 103–113.

[5] Wertsch, J. V. (1933). *Voices of the mind. Sociocultural approach to mediated action*. Harvard University Press.

[6] Subbotsky, E. (2015). Impossible phenomena as mediators in cognitive functioning and education. *SENTENTIA. European Journal of Humanities and Social Sciences*, 4, 156–173. DOI: 10.7256/1339-3057.2015.4.17369 https://nbpublish.com/library_read_article.php?id=17369

[7] Shafran, R., Thordarson, M. A., & Rachman, S. (1996). Thought-action fusion in obsessive-compulsive disorder. *Journal of Anxiety Disorders*, 10, 379–391.

[8] https://en.wikipedia.org/wiki/Obsessive–compulsive_disorder

[9] Rozin, P., Millman, L., & Nemeroff, C. (1986). Operation of the laws of sympathetic magic in disgust and other domains. *Journal of Personality and Social Psychology*, 4, 703–712.

[10] Subbotsky, E. (2009). Can magical intervention affect subjective experiences? Adults's reactions to magical suggestion. British Journal of Psychology, 3, 517–537. DOI: 10.1348/000712608X368270

[11] http://en.wikipedia.org/wiki/Extremism#cite_note-ab-1

[12] Atran, S. (2003). Genesis of suicidal terrorism. *Science*, 2999, 1534–1539.

[13] Tragediya v Kazani obrastaet podrobnostyami (2021). https://www.kommersant.ru/doc/4803373

[14] Roth, A. (2018). Crimea college attack: student carries out mass shooting in Kerch. *The Guardian*. Retrieved from https://www.theguardian.com/world/2018/oct/17/crimea-college-rocked-by-deadly-bomb-blast-kerch

[15] Komsomolskaya Pravda, September 6, (2017). https://www.kp.ru/daily/26728.4/3754368/

[16] Toppo, G. (2009).10 years later, the real story behind Columbine. *USA TODAY*. https://usatoday30.usatoday.com/news/nation/2009-04-13-columbine-myths_N.htm

[17] Ansbacher, H. L., Ansbacher, R. R. (Eds) (1964). *The Individual Psychology of Alfred Adler: A Systematic Presentation in Selections from His Writings*. Harper Perennial.

[18] Dnevniki ubiitsy: zapiski kertchenskogo strelka ob'yasnili motivy napadeniya. *KMRU*, 2018. https://www.mk.ru/social/2018/11/15/dnevniki-ubiycy-zapiski-kerchenskogo-strelka-obyasnili-motivy-napadeniya.html
[19] Subbotsky, E. (2020). *The Bubble universe: Psychological perspectives on reality*. Palgrave.
[20] Bender, M. B., Feldman, M. & Sobin, A. J. (1968). Palinopsia. *Brain: A Journal of Neurology*, 91, 321–338.
[21] https://www.nhs.uk/conditions/charles-bonnet-syndrome/
[22] Sacks, O. (2013). *Hallucinations*. Vintage.
[23] Batson, C. D. (2009). These things called empathy: Eight related but distinct phenomena. In J. Decety & W. Ickes (Eds.), *The social neuroscience of empathy* (pp. 3–15). Cambridge: MIT Press.
[24] Huxley, A. (1954). *The doors of perception*. Chatto & Windus
[25] James, W. (2009). *The Varieties of Religious Experience: A Study In Human Nature*. CreateSpace Independent Publishing Platform.
[26] Pollan, M. (2018). *How to change your mind: The new science of psychedelics*. Penguin Books.
[27] Silva J. A. & Leong G. B. (1992). The Capgras syndrome in paranoid schizophrenia. *Psychopathology*, 25, 147–153. https://www.karger.com/Article/Pdf/284765
[28] Briere de Boismont, A. J. (1853). *On hallucinations: A history and explanation of apparitions, visions, dreams, ecstasy, magnetism, and somnambulism*. Lindsay and Blakiston.
[29] Tylor, E. (1920/1871). *Primitive culture*. J. P. Putnam's Sons.
[30] Lewis-Williams, J. D. & Dowson, T. A. (1988). Signs of all times: Entopic phenomena in Upper Palaeolithic art. *Current Anthropology*, 29, 201–245.
[31] Persinger, M. (1987). *Neuropsychological bases of god beliefs*. Praeger.
[32] Kandinskii, V. K. (2007). *O psevdogallyutsinatsiyakh*. Meditsinskaya Kniga. (First published in 1885), https://en.wikipedia.org/wiki/Victor_Kandinsky
[33] Lauveng, A. (2015). *Tomorrow I Have Always Been a Lion*. BAKhRAKh-M.
[34] Foucault, M. (2003). *The birth of the clinic*. Routledge.
[35] Zilboorg, G. & Henry, G. W. (1941). *A history of medical psychology*. W.W. Norton & Co.
[36] Michelet, J. (1998). *Satanism and witchcraft: The classic study of medieval superstition*. Kensington Publishing Corporation.
[37] Szasz, T. (1971). *The Manufacture of Madness: A Comparative Study of the Inquisition and the Mental Health Movement*. Routledge & Kegan Paul.
[38] https://en.wikipedia.org/wiki/Acts_of_Peter
[39] Miller, D. (2011). *Magiya – v pomoshch'. Kak zashchitit'sya ot magicheskikh i psikhicheskikh atak*. Sankt-Peterburg: Izdatel'skaya gruppa «Ves'»
[40] Subbotsky, E. (2014). The belief in magic in the age of science. *SAGE open*. https://journals.sagepub.com/doi/full/10.1177/2158244014521433
[41] https://en.wikipedia.org/wiki/The_Sleep_of_Reason_Produces_Monsters
[42] Harris, P. L., Brown, E., Marriot, C., Whittal, S., & Harmer, S. (1991). Monsters, ghosts and witches: Testing the limits of the fantasy–reality distinction in young children. *British Journal of Developmental Psychology*, 9, 105–123.
[43] Jaynes, J. (1976). *The origins of consciousness in the breakdown of the bicameral mind*. Houghton Mifflin.
[44] https://en.wikipedia.org/wiki/Bicameralism_(psychology)

9
EXISTENTIALIZING THE SELF

9.1 Can one's existence be a dream? Cognitive EXON on the Self

In the perspective of EXON theory, the antient philosophical principle of 'thought and being identity' splits in two versions. The *weak version* states that existence of the world is a necessary condition for existence of our Self, and the *strong version* asserts that the world of perceived objects gets its existence from our Self (see Chapters 1 and 2). Simply put, the weak version implies that our Self cannot exist without the world, and the strong version contains the opposite statement that the world cannot exist without our Self.

In order to find out whether a theoretically unsophisticated person can realize the weak and the strong versions of the 'thought and being identity' principle, two interviews were conducted with 95 Russian children aged 4, 5, 6, 7, 9,13 and 14 years [1].

Interview 1 was conducted in order to examine whether the children were able to reflect upon *the weak version* of the 'thought and being identity'. Along with some introductory questions, the interview contained the following key questions:

1. Can the following be the case that you are now asleep, and it seems to you in your dream that the objects are such as you see them at the moment, but when you wake up you will see that in reality, they are different: tables are made of soft cotton, the Sun has a square shape, and this room is a big bubble of glass?
2. Can you see in your dream a certain entity, such as a dragon, which in reality doesn't exist, or you can't?
3. Can this be the case that all these objects – the table, the Sun and the whole world – they are only in your dream as was that dragon, but in reality, they don't exist?

DOI: 10.4324/9781003219521-9

4. I'd like to propose an interesting game. Its name is 'The unusual dream'. In this game we agree that we are in a dream and all this – this Sun, this table, and this world - they are part of the dream, but in reality, they don't exist. Can we play such a game, or we can't?

Questions 1 and 2 were asked to tune the children's attention to the fact that perceived entities might be illusions and depend on our mind; the aim of these questions was to lead the children to the other two questions, which tested the children's ability to reflect upon the impossibility to think about the Self without the external world. If the children are able to catch this impossibility, then their HLEXON, albeit with the help of prompting, is able to make them realize that existence of the external world is a necessary condition for the existence of their Selves.

In response to the first two questions, most preschoolers and middle age schoolchildren refused to accept that familiar perceived objects could have different shapes, but most 11 to 14-year-old children, after some contemplation, agreed that they could. However, in response to Question 3, the overwhelming majority of children in all age groups denied that the world can be just a dream. Whereas most preschoolers were unable to give grounds for their negative answers, the rest of the children provided four types of arguments. Three of these types were *empirically grounded* and thus belonged to BLEXON. They were the *tautological argument* ("the world exists because all this is real and really exists"), the *appeal to the clear and distinct character of perceptions* ("the world exists because I can feel all this clearly", "There cars are passing by, and birds are flying, I could not see all this in a dream that clearly"), and the simple intuitive *observation* that a dream can't be so long. The fourth, and the most popular argument was *theoretical* and belonged to HLEXON: the children referred to the *impossibility of their own existence in a non-existing world* ("The world exists because we have to live somewhere", "If there were no Galaxies there would be no planets and I would not exist either", "This can't be the case, otherwise where would I be situated?", "I exist, and how would I be able to exist without this world?", "If it were the case, where would I wake up then?"). Characteristically, the 'proofs' provided by the experimenter to challenge the children's 'argument had no effect on the children. Here are two examples.

Lena S. (a girl, 11 years)
In the course of the interview, Lena acknowledged the possibility for the objects to have shapes different from what they normally appear to be, but when asked about the possibility for the external world not to exist she replied in the negative. The experimenter expands along the line:

E: Well, if objects can be different from what they seem to be, is it possible that there are no objects at all?

L: And where would I be asleep then? No, it is not possible that there are no objects at all.
E: But can you acknowledge at least a tiny probability that this is possible?
L: No, I cannot. Where would I be sleeping then?

Roma (a boy, 13 years)
During the interview, Roma agreed that there was some possibility for the objects and his own body to have different shapes, but he firmly rejected the possibility for the world not to exist.

R: I don't think this is possible because if there were nothing then I would have no dreams at all and there would be no myself either.
E: Do you think that there is yet a very small probability of this to be true?
R: No because…in order for me to exist without the world…no. There isn't a slightest probability of that.

On the same theoretical ground, about 30% of the total sample denied the possibility of the outer world nonexistence even in play. They argued that it would be impossible to play the game without the world because there would be no place where to play the game. Other children agreed that such a game can be played but they never forgot to mention that such a play would be "only a fantasy" and not a real thing.

Altogether, most 4-year-olds intuitively understood the weak version of the 'thought and being identity principle', but only 11-year-olds and older participants were able to provide a theoretical justification for the statement that existence of the world is a necessary condition for existence of their conscious Selves.

Interview 2 targeted the strong version of the 'thought and being identity principle'. This version contains two implications. The *first* is that *for our conscious Self it is impossible to doubt its own existence,* since doubting one's conscious Self means immersing one into the logical circle. As Descartes famously argued, the very act of doubting one's Self is a piece of subjective experience and therefore a part of our Self.

The second implication is that our Self is *an entity with the absolute existential status*, which means that *existence of our conscious Self is a necessary condition for existence of the world*. Indeed, assuming existence of the world without our conscious Self contains a logical contradiction, because the world consists of phenomena, which means that subjective experience is a necessary part of the world.

If the first implication is understood by a person, the person would *refuse to accept that his or her own conscious Self can be non-existent*. The second implication is a more mind-boggling one: A person who understands this implication should *acknowledge that with his or her mind being unconscious, there is no possibility to speak about the world*.

At the beginning of this interview, the children were asked directly whether they would allow for the possibility to put under doubt the fact of their personal existence. Understandably, none of the children agreed to doubt their own

128 Existentializing the Self

existence. This, however, might have been a simple empirical observation and left open the question of whether the children attributed their Selves with the *absolute* existential status. To examine whether the children's belief in their personal existence was not a simple intuitive observation (i.e., BLEXON) but could be supported by theoretical justification (HLEXON), the experimenter repeatedly and in different terms asked the children questions about whether it was possible to put their personal existence under doubt. The questions were as follows:

1. Please, tell me do you exist or don't you?
2. But can the following be the case that it only seems to you that you exist, but in reality, you don't exist?
3. Let us assume that you are asleep at the moment and it seems to you in your dream that you exist, that you are sitting here and answering my questions, but in reality, if you wake up, you will find that you don't exist. Can it be the case, or it can't?
4. And can it seem to you in your dream that you don't exist, or it can't?
5. You know, I invented an interesting game. In this game, we pretend that we are asleep and have a dream that we exist but in reality, if we wake up, we find that we don't exist. Can we play a game like that, or we can't? Why do you think so?
6. And when you are asleep without dreams, do you exist or not? Why do you think so?

The first question directed the children's attention to the trivial fact of their own existence. Questions 2 to 5 tested the understanding of the *first implication* of the strong version of the 'thought and being identity' principle: The impossibility for a conscious Self to doubt its own existence. Question 6 tested the understanding of the *second implication* of this principle: The conclusion that our Self (and, as an implication, our body that represents the outer world) disappear when our conscious Self temporarily shuts down when sleeping without dreams.

As expected, in their responses to Questions 1 to 5, the overwhelming majority of children strongly denied the possibility of putting their personal existence under doubt. There were four main types of children's justifications for their negative answers.

The most popular theoretical justification implicated Descartes' formula 'I am thinking, therefore, I exist'; it consisted of pointing out that *it was not possible for someone to be aware of something (e.g., to have a dream) and not to exist at the same time.* Justifications of this type appeared first in some 5-year-old children, although in a rather simple form ("I exist in this world. When I was in my mum's belly, I had no dreams", "If I didn't exist then there would be no dreams, no dream can emerge, and if I do exist then there is a dream"). Older children put this justification in a more complex form: "Yes, I exist, otherwise how could I be able to feel myself?", "If I didn't exist then I wouldn't be able to think or sleep", "If I didn't exist how would I be able to have the dream that I don't exist?", "If I didn't exist, I wouldn't be able to imagine that I exist", "If there is something that appears to be, then there must be somebody to whom this appears").

The rest of the children produced justifications based on their personal experience: Some referred to the clarity of their self-perceptions ("I exist because I am sitting here right now"), others appealed to adults' opinions ("Mam told me that if a person is on Earth then it is for life"), still others pointed out to the fact that such a long dream was impossible and, therefore, what they were seeing and feeling at the moment was not a dream but reality.

Nevertheless, a large number of children acknowledged the possibility of their Selves' nonexistence in the domains of dreams or play. At the same time, while saying that a person can see a dream in which he or she does not figure personally and play a game "as if it seems to us that we exist but in reality, we don't", the children never forgot to mention that these statements were only assumptions ('as though'). Obviously, the children could feel that answers to questions 4 and 5 implicated a subjects' presence in two domains of reality at one time: in the domain of OR (i.e., at the moment when the conversation was taking place) and in the domain of SOR (dreams and play). In the domain of SOR, in which logical control is relaxed or absent, situations are possible in which a subject can be unaware of his or her own activity ("Yes, I may not exist, because I can see a dream in which I am not acting but some other people are acting there", "Yes, you can play such a game but only...as a fantasy", "In play everything can happen but in reality this cannot happen", "You cannot play this game in reality, but you can in your imagination", "You can play this, but when you wake up - you exist"). In other words, while acknowledging that 'inside' a dream or a play they could not exist, the children were nevertheless sure that 'really and truly' they existed.

Paradoxically, even a larger number of children denied the possibility of personal nonexistence in their responses to Question 6 (sleeping without dreams). Here the possibility of doubting one's personal existence was rejected by the majority of children in all age groups. Most preschoolers provided no grounds for their answers, whereas most schoolchildren argued from the 3rd person position ("Yet I am asleep, therefore, I exist", "I still am, I exist, I am lying in my bed", "If I can be in my bed, therefore I exist" "I am, I am asleep, but I don't disappear anywhere", "I exist, I am lying in my bed seeing no dreams, but then I wake up and see something, right?", "I exist, because sometimes I wake up during the night, and if I wake up – I am, am I not?"). By providing this kind of argument, the children revealed their inability to imagine a subject who has no acting conscious states; instead, the children were imagining themselves staying next to themselves sleeping without dreams, and this prevented them from understanding that termination of the 'subject/object' division in the sleep without dreams implies a cessation of the subjects' body and the external world to which the body belongs.

Nevertheless, some of the older children did acknowledge that at the moment of sleeping without dreams they did not exist, but they accompanied these acknowledgements with comments that it was not 'really so' ("I don't exist but...in reality I do", "I do not exist during this state, but when I wake up, I come back to existence", "I do not exist for myself at that time, but for other people I do", "It would seem to me that there are no myself and there is darkness only, but when I wake up, I can touch my body and see that I exist", "I do not exist for myself, I somehow…go out of myself, but from the outside, if you have a look at me, I exist").

Replication study in Britain yielded similar results. Altogether, the overwhelming majority of children of all age groups in both cultures *understood the first implication* of the strong version of the 'thinking and being identity principle': They denied that they could not exist when they are conscious and most of them produced theoretical justifications similar to those given by Descartes. This supported the expectation that children invest their conscious Selves with the *absolute* existential status.

At the same time, most children *failed to understand the second implication*: They were unable to grasp the fact that the absence of conscious Self implies the absence of the world. Answering the key Question 6 on the existence when in the sleep without dreams, the children, directly or indirectly, took the 3rd person position, by judging about the unconscious themselves as a part of the objective world.

Put in terms of the EXON theory, the results of these interviews can be summarized as follows. On the level of BLEXON, even 4-year-old children can understand the weak version of the 'thought and being identity' principle, but only 11-year-olds could upgrade this understanding to the level of HLEXON. Four-year-old children could also grasp the first implication of the strong version of this principle, by investing their conscious Selves with the highest possible absolute existential status (see Table 2.2). On the level of HLEXON however, only some 5-year-olds and most older children can provide theoretical justification of why existence of their conscious Selves cannot be put under doubt. At the same time, the second implication of the strong version of the 'thought and being identity principle' proved to be inaccessible for children.

This means that the children HLEXON was able to make it clear for the children *the necessity of the existence of the outer world* and the *impossibility of their personal non-existence* while they were conscious (i.e., the famous 'cogito ergo sum' principle), yet it failed to illuminate to the children the fact that *the outer world attains its existence from their own conscious Selves*.

Put in a wider theoretical context, the failure of HLEXON to grasp the second implication of the strong version of the 'thought and being identity principle', which is likely to extend up to the adulthood, may be a main reason for the reductive thinking in psychology: The idea that the human mind can be derived from workings of perceived entities, such as neural networks of the brain (see [2] for more on reductive thinking in psychology).

In the context of the everyday life, the relationships between our Self and the external world can be assessed on EXON's emotional dimension . Let us consider the possibility that, under some circumstances, our Self's strong existential status on the EXON emotional dimension *can undergo further, more subtle variations*.

Originally, we defined emotional dimension of EXON as having only two values: Strong and weak (see Table 2.2). Now, let's assume that, depending on the intensity of the subject/object relations, our Self's existential status on EXON's emotional dimension can still vary on another (vertical) axis – the axis of the tension of being the Self. Taken on this axis, *the 'thought and being identity' principle stops being just a philosophical idea and acquires a psychological filling.*

9.2 The emotional tension of personal existence

Like a string of a musical instrument can be stretched out to different degrees, the experience of the relations between my own Self and the external world may be in one of the three states: the *state of normal tension*, the *state of hypotension* and the *state of hypertension*.

When the relation between our Self and the world is in the state of normal tension (*Normaself*), we hardly notice our Self. In the morning we wake up, have breakfast, do exercise and go to work. During the day our Self feels as if it is dissolved in current affairs. Like a transparent glass, our Self is invisible; it lets our sight through, and we see the world of external objects as if our Self did not exist at all. But there comes a time when the stress of the day subsides and we suddenly feel a kind of emptiness inside, as if the string that has been producing the sound of the desired tone suddenly eased. Usually, we call this state of our Self 'the state of boredom'. We feel that we are lacking something but don't know exactly what. At some point, we realize that what we are lacking is sensations – any sensations that let us feel the *resistance of the outer world*, and thus allow our Self to feel *its own presence* through overcoming this resistance. Let us call this kind of relations between the Self and the world the state of hypotension of the Self (*Hypoself*). When brought to the extreme, the Hypoself can plunge a person in depression and even lead to suicide. In an attempt to overcome this condition, some of us are looking for fun: We go to movies, play computer games, watch TV or read. Left unattended, Hypoself brings a strong feeling of discomfort. The Hypoself sufferer begins to feel that his or her existence is meaningless. In terms of the EXON theory, the Self's existential status on the EXON's emotional dimension is thinning out. In the previous chapter, we described the condition when the state of Hypoself develops as a result of disappointment in one's ability to control one's life. This downgrading of one's Self, which grows into the *inferiority complex*, can later change into the *superiority complex* and result in a crime or/and a subsequent suicide. The weakening of the existential status of the Self can also be observed in patients who lost their sight and both hands. "It was as if I was only reading about things, not seeing them... the things were farther and farther away" (this is a description of his state by an amputee, who had gone blind. He complained that when somebody greeted him he felt "as if there were nobody around") [3, p.136].

The state opposite to hypotension is the state of hypertension of the personal being *(Hyperself)*. A state like that we experience in the moments of social success, triumph or victory. We rejoice when we win a competition, successfully pass an important exam, or succeed in personal relationships with a loved one. In the state of Hyperself, we are acutely aware of our Self's importance in this world, of the strength of our Self, our ability to overcome the resistance of things and events. The condition of hypertension can be caused artificially, by stimulating the 'pleasure centres' in the brain by nicotine, alcohol or stronger drugs. As in the case of Hypoself, when brought to the limit the state of Hyperself can end tragically by a nervous breakdown, suicide or death from an overdose. Some psychologists use people's attraction toward the state of Hyperself for organizing communication and 'personal growth' groups. Sometimes, but not always, these training groups (or T-groups as they became known [4]) can indeed increase the tension of the participants' Selves; unfortunately, the T-groups open the possibility for the trainers to abuse the power given to them by the group for promoting their own inflated Selves [5].

But there are times when the normal state of our Self is challenged on a mass scale. This indeed happened during the recent mass epidemy – COVID-19 in the spring of 2020, and in the following waves of the pandemic in 2021.

9.3 Self-isolation as a challenge to the 'normal Self'

Psychologists of this century hardly allowed for the possibility of a psychological experiment of this magnitude. The COVID-19 pandemic created the condition under which hundreds of millions of people on Earth have to observe a regime of self-isolation. So, what actually is happening?

The forced Self-isolation is a complex influence on the psyche, which affects different layers of the people's Selves and switches on various compensatory mechanisms. Thus, the discomfort from the lack of our ability to travel could be partially removed by viewing videos and photos on our past travels. Discomfort from the lack of personal communication with friends could be eased if we communicate with friends online. The list of 'psychological compensations' could be extended. However, the effect of the self-isolation could permeate the deeper layers of our Self – the subconscious. There, in the subconscious, processes unfold that could only be understood via special psychological studies. One such study was the study on the effects of *sensory deprivation*.

Sensory deprivation (from the Latin 'deprivatio') is a partial or complete blockade of our senses, which prevents the passage of signals from the outside world to the brain. Usually, sensory deprivation takes place when a person is isolated in a confined space such as a spaceship or a coal mine. To explore sensory deprivation, American physician and psychologist John Lilly created a special sensory deprivation chamber – a tank, impervious to light and sound and half full of saltwater, density and temperature of which was equal to the density and temperature of the body [6]. Being in this chamber redirects the person's attention from the external world to his or her inner state and allows the person to feel processes going in his or her mind with special clarity.

Experiments revealed that, placed in the sensory deprivation chamber, a person initially experiences a state of psychological comfort and peace of mind. However, when the sensory deprivation continues, the person begins to fall into the state of anxiety, disorientation in time and space, the inability to concentrate and, ultimately, depression and hallucinatory visions. States like that are akin to post-traumatic stress disorder (PTSD), which can occur after a brain concussion or other super-strong negative psychological impact.

Similar states were also reported in prisoners after long periods of solitary confinement, who developed obsessive thoughts, delusions, agitation, and impulsive self-directed aggression [7].

But why does the short-term psychological comfort in the state of sensory deprivation quickly changes to the state of anxiety and depression? From the perspective of EXON theory, this is the consequence of getting into the extreme state of Hypoself caused by two psychological factors: (1) the shortage of perceptual signals that confirm the existence of the stable external world, and (2) depriving the person of the opportunity to actively influence the surrounding world. In the normal state of affairs, both of these factors provide the person's Self with the subconscious feedback from things-in-themselves. When this psychological thread thins out, the feeling appears that a person is suspended in space without the fulcrum of the opposing objective world. As a result, the person begins to doubt the very foundation of personal consciousness - the existence of his or her own Self (see Section 9.1 of this chapter). In terms of the EXON theory, the existential status of the person's Self is downgraded from the *absolute* to the *incomplete* one (see Table 2.2).

However, sensory deprivation is an extreme form of deprivation. There are other, softer types of deprivation, such as *socio-cognitive* deprivation. Under normal circumstances, our Self receives a constant feedback from social environment. For example, religious people seek support of their faith in co-believers, and for most people their belief in science, like the belief God, is based not on independent thinking but on the tacit support of their social environment. When in a psychological experiment educated adults were deprived of such 'tacit support', up to 50% of the participants in their behaviour dropped their previous belief that the laws of physics are unbreakable [8]. The uniqueness of the situation on our planet created by the COVID-19 pandemic is that an unusually large number of people were put in the state of the soft social-cognitive deprivation.

Indeed, in the normal way of life people daily come into direct personal contact with other people from whom they receive the 'tacit feedback'. This feedback includes several components:

- Proof that the world is stable and maintains its usual condition.
- Confirmation that I am a person named X and will continue to be the one.
- Confirmation that my mental condition is normal.
- Confirmation that my plans for the future are under my control.
- The opportunity to fill my consciousness with external activities: Movements in space and personal contacts with people.

These psychological factors distract people's attention from focusing on existential issues, such as the meaning of life and the inevitability of death. The regime of self-isolation partially deprives a person of such social recharge. Of course, movies about travelling and video conferencing online is an effective simulation that reduces the traumatic effect of isolation. But this simulation provides only partial compensation for psychological losses because the real travelling or real personal communication involves not only sight and hearing but also other sensory channels: The proprioceptive sensations coming from the parts of the body, the senses of balance, smell and touch. In addition, online interaction puts restriction on the remaining channels – hearing and vision: one can see the face of another person, or frames incoming into the camera lens, but is deprived of the opportunity to perceive and analyze the context. As illusory contours [9] vividly demonstrate, context is what largely determines our understanding of objects and events (see Figure 9.1). These psychological losses, together with social and economic factors, could lead to negative psychological effects, though not as dramatic as in the case of complete sensory deprivation. Among these negative consequences are most phenomena of Hypoself: boredom, depression, pessimistic thoughts about the future, and focusing on one's illnesses.

However, the paradox of self-isolation is that along with narrowing of the mind it can also widen it. Deprived of their usual duties and social functions, partially liberated from distractions and challenges of the everyday life, people are free to face their own Selves. There appeared thoughts about our place in this world. Usually, we reserve such thoughts for later or even try not to think them at all. But in the state of isolation, these nagging thoughts start crossing our minds. This

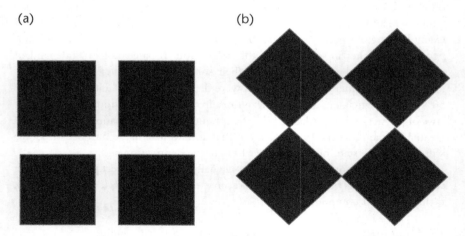

FIGURE 9.1 The role of context. We are seeing a white cross (a), but a slight change in the background converts the cross into a square (b) Four black squares situated in the corners of an imagined quadrangle create the illusory contour of a cross (left part of the picture), but when each square is rotated 45 degrees around its centre, the illusory cross turns into an illusory square (right part of the picture)

happens because, unlike animals who have their meaning of existence (survival and reproduction) hardwired in their instincts, humans have to invent such meaning themselves. As a result, being partially isolated from society people begin to think 'big thoughts' and ask themselves philosophical questions, such as "Why am I here? Am I a tiny fraction of the endless universe, or something more significant?"

Natural sciences assert that a person is a physical body on a small planet in the infinite ocean of space-time. If that is the case, then my life is a ripple on the surface of the ocean that will disappear without a trace. All I can do is to leave a small trail – my children and my contribution to culture – and even this trail will eventually be wiped out by the river of time. Like the efforts of the mythical Sisyphus, who had to endlessly push a boulder up a mountain, only for the boulder to roll down every time it neared the pinnacle, life is a hopeless and meaningless exercise [10].

But physical science itself is created by people, and it is human to err. What if physical science is wrong, and not a person is a fraction of the physical universe, but the universe is a fraction of the person? To some of us, this idea might look insane: The contrast between the vastness of the universe and the fragility of an individual person is so hypnotizingly great that it seems totally impossible to think of reversing this 'part versus whole' relationship. However, even the most persuasive perceptions could be wrong.

Indeed, after all, what is the world without the human mind, yours or mine? The world not observed by our Self does not exist. Of course, we can believe that the world existed before us and will continue after us, but it is faith, not knowledge. And because the world before and after us is the idea in our head, this idea, again, needs Us alive. As argued in Chapters 1 and 2, believing and knowing are two different modes of EXON. Knowledge we extract from perception, and faith we produce from ourselves. We don't have to make an effort in order to know that Archimedes' law works; all we need to do is to read about the law in a handbook and confirm it by simple experiments. But the belief in God or in the world without my Self requires an effort and sacrifice. The idea that the world will stay after my death is *a matter of belief*. In contrast, the image of the universe in my head is the experience that *I know for sure* because I can perceive people, trees, stars and galaxies. And if the world is a part of my consciousness, then other people are part of myself too. And I am responsible for this whole world and for all of the people.

These are the kind of thoughts that can cross our heads during self-isolation when the impact of society on our Self is partially weakened. Of course, in the heads of philosophers such thoughts happened before. But in the time of pandemic thoughts like that could come to any of us. And something has to be done with these thoughts – they have to either be suppressed or thought through down to the consequences. And if they are thought through, they might lead us to an important conclusion. But before we spell this conclusion out, we need to consider one more class of entities.

In this chapter, we have considered the entity on the top of the scale of existence – our Self. Now it is time to have a look at the bottom of this scale – the entities that 'don't really exist' – the *impossible entities*. Usually, we consider such entities as pure fantasies and invest them with the weak existential status (Table 2.2). Still, however weak, such entities are different from nothing. Let us consider what uses can be extracted from these seemingly useless entities.

References

[1] Subbotsky, E. (1996). *The child as a Cartesian thinker. Children's reasonings about metaphysical aspects of reality*. Psychology Press.
[2] Subbotsky, E. (2020). *The bubble universe. Psychological perspectives on reality*. Palgrave.
[3] Leontiev, A. N. (1977). *Dejatel'nost', soznanije, litchnost'* [Activity. Consciousness. Personality]. Politizdat.
[4] Bradford, L. P., Gibb, Benne, J. R., & Benne, K. D. (1964). *T-Group theory & laboratory method*. John Wiley & Sons.
[5] Yalom, I. D. & Lieberman, M. A. (1971). A Study of Encounter Group Casualties. *Archives of General Psychiatry*, 25, 16–30. 10.1001/archpsyc.1971.01750130018002 http://archpsyc.jamanetwork.com/article.aspx?articleid=490477
[6] Black, D. (1979). Lie down in darkness. *New York Magazine*, 12 (48): 60.
[7] Grassian, S. (2006). *Psychiatric Effects of Solitary Confinement*. New York University. https://openscholarship.wustl.edu/cgi/viewcontent.cgi?article=1362&context=law_journal_law_policy
[8] Subbotsky, E.V. (2001). Causal explanations of events by children and adults: Can alternative causal modes coexist in one mind? *British Journal of Developmental Psychology*, 19, 23–46.
[9] Kanizsa, G. (1955). Margini quasi-percettivi in campi con stimolazione omogenea. *Rivista di Psicologia*, 49, 7–30.
[10] Varava, V. (2020). *Sed'moi Den' Sizipha. Esse o Smysle Chelovecheskogo Suschestvovaniya*. Moscow: Rodina.

10
USES OF THE IMPOSSIBLE

10.1 Something from nothing: Practical functions of impossible entities

By definition, on cognitive EXON dimension, the *impossible entities (IMPE)* have a weak existential status; they exist as *imaginary entities in the mind*, or as *virtual re-presenting phenomena* that figure in pictures, cartoons, movies and computer games. The essential feature of IMPE is that they don't have perceived embodiments in the OR (see Table 2.2). On the emotional dimension of EXON, IMPE can be strong (e.g., a ghost) or weak (e.g., the impossible triangle). For example, a mermaid can be imagined or represented symbolically as a word or a picture, but it doesn't exist as a living creature supported by the proper RC. Most entities that we use for practical purposes (e.g., food, cloths, armament) are perceived entities, which by definition are possible entities (PE), whereas IMPE are predominantly employed in art and entertainment. But this doesn't mean that IMPE are useless for practice. The domain where IMPE can be used for practical purposes is the mind itself.

Indeed, the fact that IMPE are not anchored in the perceived world gives them the property of *flexibility*. Studies reviewed in Chapter 4 demonstrated that fantastical entities, unlike perceived and imagined physical objects, don't obey the OP demands. Whereas some fantastical entities, such as technical inventions of the distant future, can in fact be possible, IMPE is a version of fantastical entities that are impossible by definition. Being the IMPE means that such entities cannot exist or be created as the PE according to the known laws of nature. The IMPE's ability to change into other entities instantly and without effort makes them an effective tool for imagination. While being existentially inferior to PE, epistemologically IMPE have the advantage. Theoretical science operates with ideal objects (e.g., ideal gas or ideas steam engine), and the ideal objects belong to the class of IMPE and exist only in the imagination [1]. Nevertheless, these ideal objects can serve as an RC (ideal models) for perceived objects (e.g., real gas and real steam engine) and thus are indispensable in construction and engineering. This *modelling function* is the first important property of IMPE.

Another important function of IMPE is the *transcending function*. This function allows scientists to theoretically predict objects and processes that from a strictly scientific point of view are impossible in the observed physical universe. However, IMPE could find perceived embodiment in other universes or sections of the observed universe that are inaccessible for observation. One of the processes impossible in the observed physical universe is the process that denies physical causality. Nevertheless, in theoretical physics the idea circulates according to which at a certain level of the universe (e.g., at the point of gravitational singularity in the beginning of the observed universe, or inside the black holes) it is possible to think about structures that don't obey physical causality. In the beginning, such structures existed as typical IMPE, until scientists indeed discovered processes in which causality was denied [2], [3], [4], [5]. Another effect that contradicts the laws of the observed physical universe is the 'mind over matter and 'mind over mind' causality: The direct causal action of thinking over physical processes or over minds of other people. Nevertheless, in a number of strictly controlled experiments such effects have been registered [6][7][8][9]. Such experiments became possible due to the transcending function of IMPE – their ability to create a pool of theoretical possibilities beyond limitations of conventional science. Having been properly studied, such possibilities could turn into discoveries of perceived entities that contradict the known laws of nature [10].

Both modelling and transcending functions of IMPE belong to the department of HLEXON – the explicit employment of IMPE by scientists for creating new scientific concepts - RC. But there are also important functions which IMPE play on BLEXON, since interaction with IMPE can implicitly affect people's perception, thinking and memory. One of such implicit functions is *creativity promoting function*.

10.2 Impossible entities as promoters of creative imagination

Mediation is a key feature in functioning of the mind. Building a ship with bare hands (an unmediated action) is more difficult than building a ship with the assistance of tools (a mediated action), and communication by a gaze referencing (an unmediated action) is less precise than communication by language (a mediated action). Mediators, or 'psychological tools', vary from manual tools (such as a hammer) to semiotic artefacts (signs, symbols, texts, formulae, and languages) [11], [12], [13], [14], [15]. The ability of mediators to amplify perception, thinking and memory is so commonly known that it almost became a triviality. Less common, and of special interest for the present analysis, is the ability of mediators to enhance *creative imagination*.

A typical definition of creativity includes the ability to generate "novel behavior that meets a standard of quality and/or utility" [16, p. 308]. Creative imagination is able to freely move between alternative options and different versions of solving a certain task, with the aim of comparing between the alternatives and choosing the best one. Creativity is akin to *divergent thinking* - the ability to solve problems that have a variety of alternative solutions. Solving divergent thinking tasks (i.e., one can move from Point A to Point B by using a car, a train, a dragon or a magical carpet), requires the ability to instantly change one object for another, fantasize and not exclude bizarre and even 'mad' possibilities. Clearly, such ability is incompatible with the OP demands. Because IMPE are free from the OP demands and emotionally attractive at the same time, they might be an ideal tool for amplification of creative thinking through prompting and (or) association.

By definition IMPE are cognitively weak entities (see Table 2.2). The Penrose triangle, a centaur, and a wizard creating a castle by a magic spell are examples of IMPE. Being free from the OP demands, IMPE can be contrasted to images of their perceived opposites - the entities that conform to the OP demands (CSEWE). For instance, for the IMPE such as a mermaid the contrasting PE are images of a girl and a fish, and for the IMPE such as a table flying in mid-air by itself the contrasting PE is a image of table standing firm on the ground. When looking for effective cognitive tools to amplify creativity, one might ask the following question: *Is IMPE a more efficient amplifier for creative imagination than images of contrasting PE?*

Indeed, recent experiments indicated that reading clips from the Harry Potter series to participants activated different areas in the participants' brains depending on whether the clips included or didn't include IMPE [17]. Such experiments confirmed that, viewed in the retrospect, it had been a relevant question to ask, which of the two kinds of mediators – IMPE or contrasting PE – if framed within a film or a TV program, would affect human imagination to a greater extent [18]. Although both IMPE and contrasting PE, when framed in a picture or a film, exist as representing phenomena (see Chapter 2 for more on that), these two types of representing phenomena differ in terms of their sensitivity to the OP demands. Indeed, IMPE are representing phenomena that don't have matching prototypes in the perceived world, whereas movie images of contrasting PE are imagined physical objects that represent real perceived entities. As experiments reviewed in Chapter 4 have shown, imagined physical objects are viewed by people to be as permanent as their real perceived prototypes, whereas fantastical entities are treated as largely non-permanent.

Consequently, regarding the aforementioned question, two alternative hypotheses can be put forward. Hypothesis 1 suggests that images of contrasting PE are better amplifiers of creative imagination than IMPE, because the images of contrasting PE represent objects that are embedded in people's everyday experience and IMPE don't (*the PE/IMPE hypothesis*). For instance, in the everyday life we often see girls and fishes, whereas a mermaid is a representing phenomenon that can only be seen in pictures, movies or dreams. Alternatively, Hypothesis 2 contends that the amplifying power of IMPE should be greater than that of images of contrasting PE (*the IMPE/PE hypothesis*), because IMPE are free from gravitational attraction of the OP demands, and the images of contrasting PE are not.

The 'liberating' influence of IMPE on imagined perceived entities is likely to be particularly relevant in children. Indeed, as follows from Figures 4.3 and 4.4, children don't differentiate between fantastical and imagined physical objects in terms of their tendency to obey the OP demands; this makes one to expect that observing (or playing with) IMPE can directly affect the imagined physical entities. In contrast, adults are less likely to transfer the fluidity of IMPE into the domain of imagined physical objects, because in the adults' view fantastical entities, IMPE including, differ from imagined physical entities not in the degree but in kind.

In order to examine observation of which kind of entities – IMPE or images of contrasting PE – will better enhance creative imagination in children, Study 1 was conducted. In *Experiment 1* of this study, British children aged 4 and 6 years were divided into experimental and control groups [ibid]. Children of the *experimental groups* were shown film clips taken from the original movie 'Harry Potter and the Philosopher's Stone' that contained IMPE images, such as people riding broomsticks, animals talking with humans, and people becoming invisible (the IMPE film). In the *control groups*, children watched clips from the same movie, with the same characters doing similar but ordinary actions (the contrasting PE film). Independent experts rated the movies for such properties as the impossibility of phenomena, pace, emotional attractiveness and visual and sound effects. On all of these properties, except the impossibility of phenomena, the films were rated as approximately identical. Creativity was assessed on Torrance's 'Creativity in Action and Movement' test [19], and on the modified version of Karmiloff–Smith's 'Drawing the Impossible Entities' test [20]. Both inventories contained divergent thinking tasks. On some subtests of these inventories children were tested before exposure to the films, and on the remaining subtests they were tested after the exposure. Results indicated that after, but not before exposure to the films, children in the experimental groups scored significantly higher than controls on the majority of TCAM subtests (see Figure 10.1).

Similar differences were obtained on the Drawing the Impossible Entities test.

The aim of Experiment 2 of this study was to replicate the data of Experiment 1, with different groups of children aged 6 and 8 years, coming from a different county of England, and with a different experimenter. Another aim was to find out whether exposure to the IMPE film, along with facilitating children's creativity, will also make the children upgrade the IMPE's existential status. The procedure of this experiment was the same as in Experiment 1, except that, after exposure to the films, the children were also given a questionnaire, which tested their belief in that IMPE exist not only in their imagination, but also in reality [21]. As in Experiment 1, in Experiment 2, after but not before watching the films, children of the experimental groups exhibited significantly greater creativity scores than children of the control groups (Figure 10.2). However, there were no significant differences found between experimental and control groups on children's belief in IMPE's reality.

Uses of the impossible 141

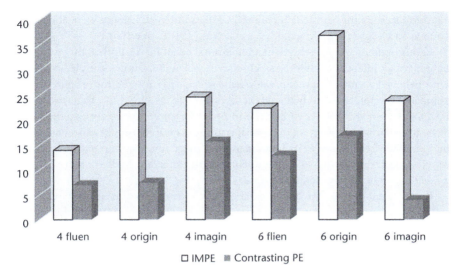

FIGURE 10.1 Mean summary scores on TCAM (fluency, originality and imagination) as a function of *Film* (IMPE versus Contrasting PE), and *Age* (4 and 6 years), in Experiment 1

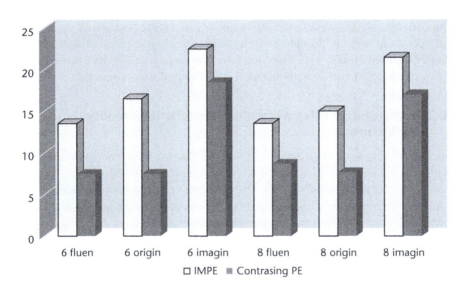

FIGURE 10.2 Mean summary scores on TCAM (fluency, originality and imagination) as a function of *Film* (IMPE versus Contrasting PE), and *Age* (6 and 8 years), in Experiment 2

Altogether, both experiments supported the IMPE/PE hypothesis: Exposing children to the film with IMPE facilitated their creativity to a significantly greater extent than exposing them to the film with images of contrasting PE. At the same time, watching the film with IMPE did not affect IMPE's existential status: After exposure to the film with IMPE children's beliefs in IMPE's reality were about the same as in children who watched the matching IMPE-free film.

Earlier studies demonstrated that children's belief in reality of the watched content may affect the children's subsequent behaviour. For example, children who believed a violent film clip was *a documentary* later reacted more aggressively compared to children who believed the film was a *fiction* [22], [23]. In terms of the EXON theory, this happened because in order for an entity we are experiencing to be invested with the strong existential status, the entity's 'ring of existence' must be complete (see Figure 6.4). Documentaries meet this requirement and fiction movies don't; that is why watching documentaries affected children's behaviour to a greater extent than watching fiction.

But if watching violent documentaries had a *destructive effect on children's social behaviour*, might it not be the case that watching films with IMPE could have *a similar effect on children's MOD*? As we know, the EXON tool that allows to verbally distinguish fantasy from reality - the MOD - appears in children at the age of 4 years (see Figure 3.1, grey bars). If exposing children to IMPE weakens the MOD, this might create an obstacle for the children's later attempts to absorb scientific knowledge [24], [25]. Indeed, with weakened or absent MOD children might transfer their early beliefs in magic into the realm of physical entities and events, thus extending their belief in magic and creationism into this realm. Alternatively, one might expect that exposure to IMPE, instead of confusing children about what is possible and impossible in the real physical world, will sharpen children's realization of the fantasy-reality distinction. In order to examine which of these alternative expectations is true, Study 2 was conducted.

10.3 Impossible entities as facilitators of fantasy/reality distinction

Study 2 examined whether *children's exposure to IMPE improves or hinders the children's MOD – the ability to distinguish between images of magical (the version of IMPE) and ordinary (the version of PE) entities*. To address this question, 6- and 9 - year old children from a primary school in England were encouraged to watch short films containing either IMPE or images of contrasting PE [26].

The same films were employed as in the previous study. In the *experimental groups* children were shown the film with IMPE, whereas the control group watched the film with images of contrasting PE. Before and after exposure to the films, the children were offered an interactive test on their ability to distinguish between PE and IMPE visual images, specially designed for this study. The images were photos of great paintings or their fragments. In the *test trial*, a child was presented a computer screen with a display that had a target picture on top and two test pictures at the bottom. The target pictures were either PE or IMPE images, and one of the test pictures was an IMPE as well. The right/left position of the IMPE test picture was randomized. The child was instructed to pick one of the pictures at the bottom that matched the target picture on top in regard to whether it was showing a possible or an impossible entity or event. There were 42 test trials altogether.

The result supported the IMPE/PE hypothesis: It showed that after exposure to the films, the children who had watched the IMPE film obtained significantly higher mean scores on correct distinctions between images of fantastical and ordinary entities than before the exposure; in contrast, the children who had watched the contrasting PE film didn't show significant changes in their scores of correct identifications of such images (Figure 10.3).

This result is in concordance with the idea that exposure to IMPE enhances children's MOD component in the EXON's implicit block (see Figure 8.1): It becomes easier to the children to perceptually distinguish between IMPE and PE images. This fact diminishes the concern that exposure to IMPE might inhibit children's absorption of scientific concepts; as long as scientific concepts are representations of PE, children's exposure to IMPE sharpens their realization of that scientific concepts are fundamentally different from their early intuitive concepts which included the belief in magic. Nevertheless, the fact that children's exposure to IMPE enhances MOD warrants an explanation.

One possible explanation could be the contrasting nature of human thinking. Indeed, seeing a picture of IMPE (e.g., a flying horse) could make children imagine the contrasting PE (e.g., a common horse and a bird) and thus reflect upon the difference between impossible and possible images and events, whereas seeing a

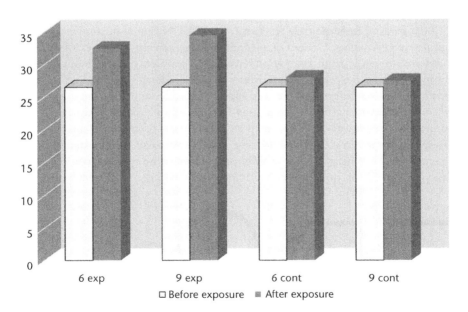

FIGURE 10.3 Mean number of correct identifications (out of 42) as a function of *Group* (Experimental vs Control) and *Time of testing* (Before vs After exposure to the films)

144 Uses of the impossible

picture of the contrasting PE couldn't. In other words, exposure to IMPE is a psychological challenge that sharpens *children's memory on the distinctive properties of IMPE* and thus improves their ability to discriminate between fantasy and reality.

But if exposure to IMPE could intensify memorizing, could such exposure also inhibit forgetting? This possibility was examined in Study 3.

10.4 Impossible entities as inhibitors of negative BLEXON

As we know, sooner or later, all that lives has to die, which means to stop existing. But mental entities die as well. They die when we forget them.

Indeed, in the perspective of EXON theory, for an entity to exist in my universe it has to be present in my mind. An entity that is not present in my mind doesn't exist for me. Of course, there can be a case when I forget something that I am well familiar with, like my telephone number or a name of a famous actor, but I know that with time the number or the name will surface back to my conscious mind. When such a case happens, we say that the entity existed in my subconscious. But what if the forgotten entity never comes back? Obviously, such an entity disappears completely from my personal universe. In other words, *the entity completely forgotten is the entity that ceased to exist.* And vice versa – the better we remember the entity, the higher the entity's existential status is. Simply put, while perceiving an entity for the first time and learning about the entity is the *positive part of BLEXON*, which brings the entity into existence, forgetting is the *BLEXON's negative part*, which decreases the entity's existential status, down to the level of complete non-existence (Figure 10.4).

Two types of forgetting are relevant to the EXON theory – *complete forgetting* and *temporary forgetting*. Under complete forgetting the entity disappears from the mind and therefore from the person's world; in contrast, under temporary forgetting we only lose a part of the entity's ring of existence (see Figure 6.1). For example, we can forget the person's appearance (phenomenon) but retain the person's name (mental image) and knowledge of the person's social role (RC). Sometimes the entity's remembered parts of the 'ring of existence' can help to restore the forgotten element of the ring; thus, if we haven't been thinking of a certain person for many years and forgot the person almost completely but suddenly see the person in the street, we might recall the person's face and even the

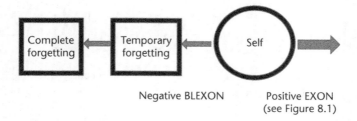

FIGURE 10.4 The structure of negative BLEXON

name. In psychology of perception, this effect is called *recognition*. Obviously, recognition occurs only if we forgot the entity temporarily, thus increasing the entity's existential status from WE (temporarily forgotten) to SE (recognized) (see Table 2.2).

Just like positive BEEXON can be *assisted* (see Chapters 4 and 5), so negative BLEXON can be *resisted*. Tools assisting positive BLEXON are *facilitators* of the entity's existential status (e.g., convert the idea of god from WE to SE). Conversely, tools resisting negative BLEXON are *inhibitors* that prevent the entity from losing its existential status. For example, a company may advertise its product as a possession of a popular movie character. In that case, the movie character, with whom the product is associated, serves as an inhibitor of negative BLEXON on that product, which increases the probability that the product will not be forgotten by the viewers or at least will be forgotten only temporarily. In light of the above, the question can be asked *which of the two types of entities – IMPE or images of contrasting PE – is a better inhibitor of the item's forgetting?*

Indeed, memory experts have long advocated that bizarre imagery facilitates learning through reduced interference ('bizarreness effect') [27], [28]. The IMPE are implausible and can therefore be qualified as bizarre. Studies have shown that placing commercial products within films can elicit successful recognition of the advertised products through cues and association [29], [30]. Commercial advertisements are often framed in the context of IMPE – animals talking human languages, flying dragons and other fantastical creatures. It can be assumed that *marketing companies frame their advertised products in the context of IMPE because they believe that association with IMPE inhibits the negative BLEXON and makes viewers better remember these products.*

To examine whether this belief is grounded, in Study 3 British adolescents and adults were individually shown films with IMPE and films with images of contrasting PE [31]. The IMPE film included advertising brands such as Levi, Pepsi Maxx and Mini Cooper, framed in the context of impossible phenomena (e.g., talking animals or inanimate objects coming to life), and the contrasting PE film showed clips with similar brands framed in the context of equally interesting and exiting but possible phenomena (e.g., architectural wonders or masterpieces of art and sport). The films were matched according to other dimensions, such as pace, action and emotional content. After watching the films, the participants were asked to recall the films' advertised products. They completed a general recall test and a recognition test. The recognition test included 18 brands, 9 of which had been shown in the film, and the other 9 were used as distractors.

Results revealed no difference on the *general recall test* between the IMPE and the contrasting PE films; however, on the *recognition test* significant differences were obtained. On *immediate recognition*, adolescents recognized a significantly larger number of brands from the IMPE film than from the contrasting PE film, but there was no such difference in adults (Figure 10.5).

However, on *delayed recognition* two weeks later, the reverse results were obtained: Adults, but not adolescents, showed the IMPE/PE effect (Figure 10.6).

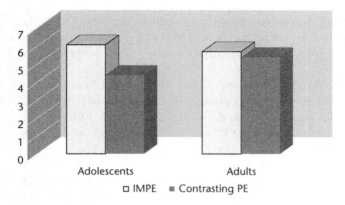

FIGURE 10.5 Mean number of correctly recognized brands on immediate testing, as a function of *Film* (IMPE vs Contrasting PE) and *Age* (Adolescents vs Adults)

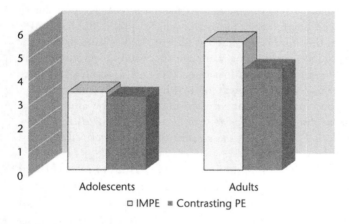

FIGURE 10.6 Mean number of correctly recognized brands on delayed testing, as a function of *Film* (IMPE vs Contrasting PE) and *Age* (Adolescents vs Adults)

Overall, the results indicated that framing brands into the context of IMPE does indeed make negative BLEXON on these brands significantly smaller compared with the negative BLEXON on brands included in the context of contrasting PE. However, this effect occurs only in the participants' *implicit memory* tested via recognition of brands.

10.5 Impossible entities and education: Conclusion

It is natural for humans to think through contrasting an object of our thinking to other objects. Whenever we think of a certain entity (e.g., about nice weather), we inevitably also think of entities, which make a contrast to the entity that is currently in the focus of our attention (e.g., about rainy and cold weather). Because the contrasting entities exist in our subconscious mind, we are usually not aware of the fact that we think through contrasts. Nevertheless, in terms of the EXON theory, thinking means constantly making a choice between contrasting entities, by scanning the alternatives on the EXON's cognitive and emotional dimensions, selecting one of them and leaving the rest in darkness of the subconscious.

Teachers sometimes take advantage of this feature of human thinking. For example, 'compare and contrast' is a popular strategy used in a classroom in order to make students to comprehensively ponder and analyze a topic. Psychologists who examined various forms of instruction at a classroom discovered that comparative analysis is superior to other forms of analyses and has the greatest effect on students' achievements [32], [33]. In children's literature, books that use contrast for education are in the hundreds [34], [35]. Using IMPE in a classroom is a case of teaching through contrasts, with the aim of helping children to reflect upon and analyze known laws of physics and other sciences.

Experiments showed that even 3-year-olds exhibited some realization that fantastic objects are different from perceived or imagined physical objects [36], [37]. Five-year-olds and older children are as good as adults at distinguishing between fantastic and perceived objects [38]. When children of this age watch cartoons or TV advertisements, they become sensitive to violations of physical laws. The author of this book once observed a 7-year-old boy who, when seeing a commercial in which washing machines were flying, commented "Washing machines cannot fly", and even a subsequent remark that the washing machines actually had small propellers attached to them could not reassure the child.

Viewed in terms of the EXON theory, most IMPE have two separate but related properties: (1) they are free from the OP demands, and (2) they belong to the domain of SOR and therefore present contrast to the perceived and imagined physical entities. It is these properties that make IMPE an efficient tool for manipulating both positive and negative BLEXON.

Studies reviewed in this chapter have shown that the IMPE's *ability to violate the OP demands* can be used for relaxing the rigidity of the mind via prompting and/or association, and thus facilitate divergent creativity in children (Study 1). Another IMPE's property – *to make a background to the contrasting PE* – was used for facilitating the children's ability to cognitively distinguish between images of fantastical and realistic objects (Study 2). Finally, the IMPE's *strong existential status on the EXON emotional dimension* makes them an effective inhibitor of forgetting when they are used in advertising commercial products (Study 3).

Using these special features of IMPE educationalists can discuss scientific problems with children in a manner more vivid and memorable than the manner provided by traditional teaching style. Ultimately, this line of research might lead towards constructing special 'alternative handbooks' on various subjects, in which events provocatively violate the laws of nature. Of course, the IMPE-based handbooks would not replace the traditional ones; rather, the former would make a useful supplement to the latter, helping students better reflect upon the laws of science and memorize these laws. As a matter of fact, this kind of 'handbooks' already exists, albeit not in a printed form. In some books, movies and computer games known properties of solid objects, light, gravity, animal and human psychology and biology are suspended. Lewis Carroll's 'Alice's Adventures in Wonderland' is a classic example, and J. K. Rowling's Harry Potter series is a more recent one. Thus, in the Harry Potter series, when Harry puts on a mantle that makes him invisible, the question can be asked whether he can see other people. If he can, then the bottoms of his eyes should absorb light and thus be visible to others; to be completely invisible, Harry has to be blind. When the Hogwarts School students are riding broomsticks, do they have weight, or are they weightless? If they have weight, how can they keep balance on a wooden stick without support when turning at sharp angles at a high speed? And if they are weightless, why do they sometimes fall from the broomsticks? When the python in the zoo communicates with Harry, can it understand what Harry says, or is it reading Harry's mind telepathically? Discussions like that can enrich and complement direct instructions on the laws of sciences.

To conclude, IMPE are useful tools for improving divergent creative thinking, perception and memory. IMPE owe their amplifying power to their freedom from limitations of the OP demands, their ability to make a contrasting background to perceptual objects that populate ordinary reality, and their emotional attraction.

References

[1] Kant, I. (2007). *Critique of pure reason*. Penguin Classics.
[2] Matson, J. (2012). Quantum teleportation achieved over record distances. *Nature News* https://www.nature.com/news/quantum-teleportation-achieved-over-record-distances-1.11163
[3] Francis, M. (2012). Quantum entanglement shows that reality can't be local. Ars Technica, https://arstechnica.com/science/2012/10/quantum-entanglement-shows-that-reality-cant-be-local/
[4] Bavaresco, J., Araujo, M., Brukner, C., & Quintino, M. T. (2019). Semi-device-independent certification of indefinite causal order. Cornell University. https://arxiv.org/abs/1903.10526.pdf
[5] Rubino, G., Rozema, L. A., Feix, A., Araujo, M., Zeuner, J. M., Procopio, L. M., Brukner, C., & Walther, P. (2016). Experimental Verification of an Indefinite Causal Order. Cornell University. https://arxiv.org/pdf/1608.01683.pdf
[6] Bem, D.J., & Honorton, C. (1994). Does Psi exist? Replicable evidence for an anomalous process of information transfer. Psychological Bulletin, 115, 4–18.
[7] Radin, D., & Nelson, R. (2000). Meta-analysis of mind-matter interaction experiments: 1959 to 2000. http://www.spiritualscientific.com/yahoo_site_admin/assets/docs/Review_of_Mind-Matter_Interaction_Articles_19592000_RNG_Articles, 12960830.
[8] Subbotsky, E. (2013). Sensing the future: Reversed causality or a non-standard observer effect? *SAGE open*, January-March, 6, 1–17. 10.2174/1874350101306010081.
[9] Subbotsky, E. & Ryan, A. (2009). Motivation and belief in the paranormal in a remote viewing task. *The Open Behavioral Science Journal*, 8, 1-7. http://www.lancaster.ac.uk/staff/subbotsk/Subbotsky & Ryan 1.pdf

[10] Subbotsky, E. (2018). *Science and magic in the modern world: Psychological perspectives on living with the supernatural*. Routledge Press.
[11] Vygotsky, L. S. (1978). *Mind in society: The development of higher psychological processes*. Harvard University Press.
[12] Bodrova, E. & Leong, D. (1996). *Tools of the mind: The Vygotskian approach to early childhood education*. Merill.
[13] Cole, M. (1996). *Cultural psychology: A once and future discipline*. Harvard University Press.
[14] Engestrom, Y. (2007). Enriching the theory of expansive learning: Lessons from journeys toward co-configuration. *Mind, Culture and Activity*, 14, 23–39.
[15] Frawley, W. (1997). *Vygotsky and cognitive science: Language and the unification of the social and computational mind*. Harvard University Press.
[16] Eisenberger, R., Haskins, F., & Gambleton, P. (1999). Promised reward and creativity: Effects of prior experience. *Journal of Experimental Social Psychology*, 35, 308–325.
[17] Hsu, C. T., Jacobs, A. M., Altmann, U., & Conrad, M. (2015). The magical activation of left amygdala when reading Harry Potter: An fMRI study on how descriptions of supra-natural events entertain and enchant. *PloS ONE*, 10(2):e0118179. 10.1371/
[18] Subbotsky, E., Hysted, C., & Jones, N. (2010). Watching films with magical content facilitates creativity in children. *Perceptual and Motor Skills*, 111, 261–277. https://pubmed.ncbi.nlm.nih.gov/21058605/
[19] Torrance, E. P. (1981). *Thinking creatively in action and movement*. Scholastic Testing Service, Inc.
[20] Karmiloff-Smith, A. (1989). Constraints on representational change: Evidence from children's drawings. *Cognition*, 34, 57–83.
[21] Bolton, D., Dearsley, P., Madronal-Luque, R., & Baron-Cohen, S. (2002). Magical thinking in childhood and adolescence: Development and relation to obsessive compulsion. *British Journal of Developmental Psychology*, 20, 479–494.
[22] Atkin, C. (1983) Effects of realistic TV violence vs. fictional violence on aggression. *Journalism Quarterly*, 60, 615–621.
[23] Comstock, G., & Scharrer, E. (2006). Media and pop culture. In W. Damon & R. M. Lerner (Senes Eds.) and K. A. Reninger & I. Sigel (Vol.Eds.), *Handbook of child psychology* (Vol.4, 6th ed.), Wiley, pp. 817–863.
[24] Bloom, P. & Weisberg, D. S. (2007). Childhood origins of adult resistance to science. *Science*, 316(5827), 996–997.
[25] Shtulman, A. (2017). *Scienceblind: Why Our Intuitive Theories About the World Are So Often Wrong*. Basic Books.
[26] Subbotsky, E. & Slater, E. (2011). Children's discrimination of fantastic vs realistic visual displays after watching a film with magical content. *Perceptual and Motor Skills*, 112, 603–609. https://www.researchgate.net/publication/51214016_Children's_Discrimination_of_Fantastic_VS_Realistic_Visual_Displays_after_Watching_a_Film_with_Magical_Content
[27] Wollen, K. A., Weber, A., & Lowry, D. H. (1972). Bizarreness versus interaction of mental images as determinants of learning. *Cognitive Psychology*, 3(3), 518–523.
[28] Einstein, G. O., McDaniel, M. A., Lackey, S. (1989). Bizarre imagery, interference, and distinctiveness. *Journal of Experimental Psychology: Learning, Memory, and Cognition*, 15, 137–146.
[29] Babin, L. A., & Garder, S. T. (1996). Viewers' recognition of brands placed within a film. *International Journal of Advertising*, 15, 140–151.

[30] Gupta, P. B., & Lord, K. R., 1998. Product placement in movies: The effect of prominence and mode on audience recall. *Journal of Current Issues and Research in Advertising*, 20, 47–59.

[31] Subbotsky, E. & Matthews, J. (2011). Magical thinking and memory: Distinctiveness effect for TV commercials with magical content. *Psychological Reports*, 109, 1–11. https://journals.sagepub.com/doi/abs/10.2466/04.11.28.PR0.109.5.369-379?journalCode=prxa

[32] Marzano, R. J. (2007). *The art of science and teaching*. ASCD Publ.

[33] Marzano, R. J., Marzano, J. S., & Pickering, D. J. (2003). *Classroom management that works. Research based strategies for every teacher*. ASCD Publ.

[34] Briggs, R. (2012). *Fungus the Bogeyman*. Penguin Books.

[35] Dahl, R. (1980). *The twits*. Puffin Books.

[36] Harris, P. L., Brown, E., Marriott, C., Whittall, S. & Harmer, S. (1991). Monsters, ghosts and witches: Testing the limits of the fantasy-reality distinction in young children. *British Journal of Developmental Psychology*, 9, 105–123.

[37] Wellman, H. M., & Estes, D. (1986). Early understanding of mental entities: A re-examination of childhood realism. *Child Development*, 57, 910–923.

[38] Sharon, T. & Wooley, J. D. (2004). Do monsters dream? Young children's understanding of the fantasy/reality distinction. *British Journal of Developmental Psychology*, 22, 293–310.

11
CROSSING THE EDGE: SUMMARY

11.1 Facing the void

We are confidently walking the solid path of knowledge, but this path suddenly ends. Having approached the edge, we cautiously and fearfully peep down into the precipice that opened beneath our feet. But something is pushing us from behind. Gradually, we realize that leaving the path and stepping into the void ahead is unavoidable. The only option for us is to grow wings and fly. Faith is our wings.

We began this book by asking the questions: What does it mean to exist? If we are in the state of general anaesthetics, do we exist or don't we? Does the world exist or it vanishes? Usually we say yes, because, after recovering a conscious state of mind we can usually remember being ourselves before losing consciousness and see the world as it had been before . But what happens when we die? Certainly, logically speaking, our mind ceases to exist, taking all the memories with it. Still, we can think about the universe before our mind emerged and after it disappeared. But how can we do this, without us being there? Obviously we can't, which means we are still there, at least in our imagination. This brings us to a rather controversial conclusion that our mind can never cease to exist as long as the universe exists, and the other way round. In other words, talking about before and after our own existence is a game of sorts. The only thing we can sensibly talk about is existence within the scope of our working mind. Paradoxically, when in the primordial earth the first form of life emerged, we must already be there, with our full consciousness. The trick is that we have to be in two points of time simultaneously: Now, at the moment when we are talking of the Earth before life, and (in our imagination) in the time we are talking about, billions of years ago. But the situation looks paradoxical only if we forget that it is impossible to talk about existence without the opposition between object and subject. In philosophy, this opposition is called 'thought and being identity'.

DOI: 10.4324/9781003219521-11

"But what about things that have no consciousness? – a reader might ask. – Sure, most things in the world are inanimate yet they do exist, don't they?" Yes, they do, but their existential status is different from that of the person who is aware of his or her existence. As argued in Chapter 2, there are two ways the thing X could exist: Authentic and derivative. Authentic existence is when an entity is aware of itself (in this case we say the X exists for itself), and derivative is when somebody else is aware of X (in this case X exists for other conscious creatures). The authentic existence of my Self has the highest existential status, and derivative is spread along the scale between strong, incomplete and weak existential statuses (see Table 2.2). Bearing this in mind, we can talk about history before our conscious existence and even before the emergence of life without explicitly mentioning that we are tacitly present there. In reality, whenever I talk about the history of my family, nation, humankind and life, or about people and the world after my death, I extend my mind back and forth beyond my personal existence, thus inflating existence into the past and the future.

11.2 Existence, faith and psychology

To summarize, from the perspective of EXON theory, existence is a fundamentally psychological concept. This concept cannot be logically defined, since any logical definition will have to link existence with other and more general concepts, thus plunging the definition into a logical circle. For example, asking the question whether existence is a property of an individual and "are there individuals that lack it?" [1] relates existence to such concepts as 'individuals' and 'property', which, in order to be spoken about, have to already exist. Since it is impossible to avoid the circle, we have to accept that existence is a primary intuition of being my own Self and having a conscious experience: perceiving something or thinking about something. As Rene Descartes famously maintained, this primary conscious experience is impossible to define; all that existence needs is a name. This means that existence is something that my own Self puts into things-in-themselves. Existence can only be opposed to Nothing, which is a false opposition, since Nothing as an opposition to existence also exists [2]. As a consequence of this, psychologically we can sensibly talk only about degrees of existence, with Nothing having the smallest possible degree on EXON's cognitive dimension.

A special form of inflating things with existence is faith. Unlike objects of perception and knowledge, which in order to be experienced require things-in-themselves, faith comes from within our Self. Although faith too needs an object to be pumped with existence, this object doesn't have to have a link to things-in-themselves and can be produced by the imagination. The aim of this book was to summarize studies that examined psychological structure of this fundamental process - investing things with existence through faith. Throughout this book, we called this process Existentialization (EXON).

While being fundamental, EXON nevertheless can be psychologically described. Chapter by chapter, we distinguished and analyzed levels (basic versus high), dimensions (cognitive versus emotional) and components of EXON, such as MOD, MTD, IPD, BOP, BONP, BOP/DM and RD (see Figure 8.1). We argued that although these components to some extent overlap with each other, they nevertheless are different facets of EXON, which can be operationalized and studied empirically. The results of these studies showed that the components appear at different times in the course of individual development. The studies also gave the ground to assume, that these components emerged at different stages of the historical development of consciousness. The reviewed experiments revealed how EXON invests with existence perceived and imagined entities, entities that are or are not personally significant, possible and impossible entities. We described and analysed entities with the highest (Self, God) and the lowest (impossible entities) existential statuses, and how EXON, through faith, can upgrade and downgrade the entities' existential statuses. Finally, the studies suggest that knowledge about psychological structure of EXON can be used not only for the explanation of how our mind works but also for the purposes of control over perception, thinking and memory.

11.3 Who might benefit from this knowledge

Philosophers and psychologists are the first who come to mind. Philosophers, because their most abstract notions, when traced to their sources, bump into a simple psychological question – do I exist? [3]. And psychologists, because they might help to answer this question [4]. Natural scientists need this knowledge as well, because, from time to time, they stumble upon phenomena whose existence is questionable, such as alternative universes, quantum entanglement and dark matter [5]. And of course, knowledge about EXON is needed by educationalists as they have to explain to students the basic differences between true and false, natural and the supernatural, and these differences are rooted in the notion of existence [6]. It would also be unfair to exclude artists from the list: After all, what is more fragile and culturally relative than our sense of beauty, and the judgement of whether this particular piece of art is or isn't beautiful hangs on the mechanisms of EXON. Art is a major source of generating impossible images, which can be employed as EXON tools for amplification of creative thinking, perception and memory [7]. Psychotherapists can employ components of EXON, such as the IPD and the RD, in order to explain and treat psychological problems. Psychiatrists, when making a judgement of whether a patient is healthy or displays symptoms of obsessive-compulsive disorder, thought action fusion or hallucinatory behaviour, might need knowledge of how the MOD and the RD work. Specialists in law enforcement and juridical system might use knowledge about the RD mechanism in order to better understand phenomena such as suicidal terrorism and spontaneous killing spree.

Of particular interest knowledge about EXON can be to those who professionally deal with the domain of faith: priests, theologians and specialists on the history of religions. Professionals in that domain are looking into the heart of the most delicate, deeply personal and rationally unexplainable process: The birth of the idea of the invisible entity – god – in the person's mind, which the person, using nothing more than the recourses of his or her own mind, upgrades to the status of a really existing entity.

Last, but not least, the knowledge of EXON might benefit professionals who specialize in manipulation with human minds, as well as those whose aim is to prevent such manipulations. Magicians make their living by entertaining people through faking existence. Coaches and psychotherapists aim at helping people to change and upgrade their images and beliefs about themselves. Political leaders, commercial advertisers, practicing witches and founders of controversial religious cults pursue more practical objectives: To make people embrace goals that are suggested to them as goals of their own. Whereas some of such manipulations may benefit both sides, others may force people to accept goals that go against their best interests. People use EXON in order to establish and correct interpersonal and international relations through love rituals, politeness and diplomacy.

Finally, every person might be interested in learning more about psychological mechanisms of how his or her mind and beliefs work.

References

[1] Nelson, M. (2020). Existence. Stanford Encyclopedia of Philosophy. Retrieved from https://plato.stanford.edu/entries/existence/#Con

[2] New Scientist (2013). *Nothing: From absolute zero to cosmic oblivion, amasing insights into Nothingness*. Profile Books.

[3] Descartes, R. (2010). *Meditations on first philosophy*. Watchmaker pub.

[4] Subbotskii, E. V. (1991). Existence as a Psychological Problem: Object Permanence in Adults and Preschool Children. *International Journal of Behavioral Development*, 14, 67–82. DOI: 10.1177/016502549101400104.

[5] Subbotsky, E. (2017). Miracles in law: Magical underpinning of physical universe. *SENTENTIA. European Journal of Humanities and Social Sciences*, 4, 22–40. DOI: 10.25136/1339-3057.2017.4.20949.

[6] Subbotsky, E. (2014). Magical thinking: From Piaget to advertising. *Psychology Review*, 2014, 19, 4, 10–13. https://www.researchgate.net/publication/261134149_Magical_thinking_From_Piaget_to_advertising

[7] Subbotsky, E. (2018). Art as a window into the supernatural. *SENTENTIA. European Journal of Humanities and Social Sciences*, 1, 21–35. 10.25136/1339-3057.2018.1.20774.

[8] Subbotsky, E. (2016). Religion and the belief in the supernatural SENTENTIA. European Journal of Humanities and Social Sciences, 4, 24–43. 10.7256/1339-3057.2016.4.21498.

FAITH AS AN EFFORT OF WILL: EPILOGUE

I was brought up as an atheist in the atheistic society of the former Soviet Union. And so were my relatives and friends. It was a great surprise for me when, soon after 'perestroika', many of my acquaintances joined the orthodox church. This made me think. Before that, I thought that I and my friends spiritually are 'on the same wave'; after that, I realized that it was not the case. For some of the people I knew the idea of God, which till now has been an abstract notion, suddenly became full of existential power, but for myself it stayed as abstract as it always was. I began thinking of what this wonderful and enigmatic phenomenon of human psychology – faith – is. Why does faith appear so suddenly, and where do people get strength to become believers in something that is not supported by their sensual experience?

It has long been noticed by writers and philosophers that faith is a phenomenon which includes two components: a subject and an object. Any entity I can think of – god, soul, miracle, atom and electron – can become an object of faith. We can begin to believe not only in the existence of conceptual entities, but in the statement (e.g., 'this closed box has pencils in it', or 'dogs hate cats') or in the imagined future event (e.g., that I can become a millionaire or that the world will come to its end in a couple of years). Still, one psychological question remained unanswered: What does faith add to an entity, which turns the entity from being a part of my imagination into being 'the real thing'?

Pondering this question, I came to the conclusion that cognitively faith adds nothing: The entity as a part of a person's imagination and the entity that the person believes in are cognitively the same. What faith adds to the entity is the entity's meaning in the person's life. The entity (e.g., god) that has been an abstract image or notion sitting somewhere in the person's mind periphery suddenly becomes important and changes the person's life: The person undergoes the rite of baptism, begins to go to church, pray and follow the rules of this particular religious

DOI: 10.4324/9781003219521-101

confession. In other words, the person begins making sacrifices – big and small – in order to maintain his or her faith in God. And so it goes about any object of faith.

It is also evident that the effort of faith varies in power: A person can have a strong faith in something, while other people's faith in the same thing can be weaker or absent altogether. For instance, at the moment I am writing these lines, the contagious disease – Coronavirus 19 – is raging in the world. But various people invest the invisible virus with the varying degree of faith. Some take it seriously: They rarely leave their flats, wear gloves and face coverings, order food to be delivered to their doors, and hurry to be vaccinated. Others give the disease a moderate degree of faith: They prefer to go shopping themselves while protecting themselves by wearing masks and gloves. Still others don't believe in the disease altogether and consider the pandemic to be some kind of conspiracy arranged by government elites in order to control the people's minds. As a result, any object of faith can be ascribed a special 'existential status'.

The weakest existential status an object can have is to exist only in our mind, without any 'input of faith' (e.g., a fantastical image or an abstract notion), and even this status can expire, like it happens with memories we have about the content of our night dream that lasts in our memory for a fleeting moment and is immediately forgotten. An entity that we used to perceive but do not perceive now (e.g., our late relatives of a car left in another city) has a stronger influx of faith than the entity we have never perceived in flesh (e.g., a mermaid). This entity has an incomplete existential status. A strong existential status the entity has that we are experiencing now (e.g., a toothache or an apple we are eating). Finally, our own reflecting Self, which is impossible to doubt, has a strongest – absolute – existential status; to the entity like that faith makes the strongest contribution.

Gradually, I began to think that ascribing existence to ordinary entities and faith in the superordinary ones are kin but not identical processes. Indeed, believing that a computer in front of me 'really exists' and believing in God are not the same experiences. The belief in the reality of the computer is supported by my perception, whereas the belief in God isn't. On this ground, it makes sense to distinguish between these processes, calling a more general of them 'existentialization' (EXON), and leaving the term 'faith' for a more specific one.

Indeed, as a general concept, EXON covers a range of subordinate processes. We can invest an entity with existence because we are seeing or hearing the entity (EXON via perceptual experience), because our logical thinking makes us believe that the entity is true (EXON via logical thinking), or simply because a person who we trust says so (EXON based on trust). Finally, we can invest an entity with existence simply because we want to. When we feel a need for something (e.g., to overcome the state of boredom or depression), we invest existence into the idea of watching a comedy and pay dear prices for a ticket to a movie theatre. Unlike EXON based on perception, thinking or suggestion (forced EXON), this kind of EXON (authentic EXON) is based on an autonomous effort of will. Using our authentic EXON, we can upgrade an abstract idea to the status of a real entity; at the same time, a person with disturbed perception or with a mental condition can inflate with existence an image that spontaneously surfaced from the subconscious, thus producing a hallucination.

One more property of EXON is that it is reversible. We can upgrade the entity on its existential status or stop investing the entity with existential power. For example, *a person* who we knew only superficially may suddenly become our best friend, or *god* from the abstract idea can turn into the God – a creator of the universe and our guardian in life (positive EXON). It can also happen that an old friend of ours may disappoint us and thus diminish his or her existential status on EXON's emotional dimension. Similarly, a scientific concept that people believed in for about a century (e.g., 'luminiferous ether' in physics) one day can become existentially empty and moved to the damping point of history. Finally, along with the acquisition of new knowledge and information, we have to free storage in our active memory by forgetting things (negative EXON).

In the light of these distinctions, faith becomes the emotionally powered authentic positive EXON – inflating the existential status of an imagined entity via the autonomous effort of will.

We begin our journey through life with the naïve notion that we are nothing but a small temporary speck on the body of endless and timeless universe. For most of us it takes life to realize that it is our own Self that makes the universe exist. Frightened by the scale of this responsibility, we invented gods. But the irony of things is that in order to lift the idea of god up to the status of the God we believe in, we have to rely on the magical ability of our Self to manufacture existence - EXON.

Some thinkers ask why a person is needed on Earth? Isn't the humanity a kind of mould, a parasite, sucking the juices of the primordial mother Earth, and would nature not be healed if humans disappeared? To such thinkers, I would like to remind the old philosophical dilemma: 'Does a tree that falls in a dense forest make a crackle, given the condition that at that moment there is no one nearby who would hear this crack?' Note that if we say that it does, we are already mentally present next to the tree and violate the condition. Without people, even with their terrible vices, there would be no Earth or the Universe for that matter. Through the human observers, through their consciousness, eyes and ears, the Universe changes from the state of Nothing to the state of Being. Mother Earth needs a human being like our body needs a heart.

The universe will disappear not when it comes to its gravitational collapse in billions of years from now; it will stop existing when the last surviving human individual expires on a radioactive dump into which we can turn the Earth (not recommended). One can even say that each of us is that last surviving person. With the person gone, the whole universe will follow into the oblivion; without an observer, the Universe is 'less than Nothing', because even the Nothing needs a person to think about it.

"And how about other people? – you might say. – After my demise, don't they remain to observe the Universe?" But remember the tale of the trees falling in a dense forest in the absence of any observer; other people are like those trees, and you are the observer. With you being no longer there, who will see the bodies and hear the voices of other people?

We have to realise, that each and every one of us, from the richest and mightiest to the poorest and weakest, have a crucial role in this universe. Like the Titan Atlas of Greek mythology, whose role was to support the sky on his shoulders, each of us – literally – is the holder of the Universe. It is your personal universe that holds the physical universe inside itself, not the other way round. Through faith, but also through simple perception, a person brings the Universe, including the humanity, into actual Being. Isn't the awareness of having the role of such cosmic magnitude enough for each of us to fill our lives with higher meaning?

INDEX

'a-priori' forms 22
Achilles 74, 86
Adler, Alfred 112
Alexander the Great 112
almighty being 76
Almighty Wizard 32, 76, 77, 78, 79, 80, 81, 82, 83, 84, 85
alternative handbooks 147
Alzheimer disease 117
Anselm of Canterbury 75
Archimedes 28
Archimedes' law 5, 135
argument from intelligent design 75

Being 6, 9, 10, 30, 76, 139, 157, 158
belief; see in God
belief in object permanence
BOP 7, 8, 9, 31, 35, 54
Big Bang 21, 22, 73, 85
bizarre imagery 145
black hole 115
BLEXON (basic level of existentialization) 9, 31, 32, 33, 35, 36, 37, 38, 39, 43, 44, 47, 48, 49, 50, 51, 53, 55, 57, 58, 59, 60, 61, 64, 66, 67, 68, 69, 70, 73, 82, 97, 99, 101, 102, 118, 126, 128, 130, 138, 144, 145, 146, 147
BONP (belief in object non-permanence) 9, 35, 36, 37, 38, 39, 40, 42, 43, 45, 47, 48, 49, 50, 51, 58, 82, 91, 93, 96, 102, 153
BOP defence mechanism (BOP/DM) 8, 96
brain 86, 96, 110, 111, 113, 115, 116, 117, 118, 121, 122, 130, 132, 133
Bubble universe 113

Capgrass syndrome 118

Carroll, Lewis 148
Cartesian maxim 4
causality 115
Chandler, Michael J. 54
Charles Bonnet syndrome (CBS) 113
Cherenkov radiation 29
Christianity 72, 120
Chumak, Allan 94
cloud chamber see bubble chamber
cognitive biases 75
cognitive dimension: of EXON 25, 26, 27, 31, 49, 55, 56, 61, 63, 69, 70, 74, 89
communication 6, 104, 120, 122, 132, 134, 138
computer 15
contagion: magical 107
contingent entity 22
cosmological argument 75
creative imagination 6
creative thinking 51, 107, 139, 148, 153
creativity 93, 95, 138, 139, 140, 141, 147, 149
critical thinking 32, 54, 89, 105, 108, 114, 117, 119
CSESE (cognitively strong emotionally strong entities) 9, 70, 85, 111, 112, 113, 117
CSEWE (cognitively strong emotionally weak entities) 9, 62, 63, 69
CWESE (cognitively weak emotionally strong entities) 9, 62, 63, 64, 69, 70, 85, 111, 112, 113, 117

dark energy 21, 30
dark matter 21
Dennett, Daniel C. 96
Descartes 74, 76, 86, 127, 128, 130, 152

Descartes, Rene 20, 21
Ding an sich (thing-in-itself) 5
divergent creativity 147
divergent thinking 93, 95, 139, 140
Dostoevsky, Fyodor 112
Dushamp, Marcel 15

Earth 22, 29, 129, 132, 151, 157
education 10, 146, 147
EEG 18, 27
EEG of the brain 18
Einstein Albert 1
electromagnetic waves 115
emotional dimension, of EXON 25, 26, 27, 31, 50, 55, 56, 62, 63, 69, 91, 131, 137, 147, 157
entity 6, 8, 9, 12, 17, 20, 21, 22, 23, 24, 25, 27, 30, 32, 36, 38, 39, 44, 45, 49, 50, 51, 54, 55, 59, 60, 62, 63, 64, 70, 72, 73, 75, 77, 79, 80, 82, 84, 85, 89, 90, 91, 93, 101, 106, 109, 111, 113, 118, 125, 127, 135, 142, 144, 145, 146, 152, 154, 155, 156, 157
entopics 119
Escher, Maurice 27
Existence 1, 6, 9, 10, 11, 35, 86, 88, 90, 152, 154
existence workshop 9, 38
existential status 8, 9, 11, 20, 21, 22, 23, 24, 25, 26, 27, 29, 30, 36, 38, 39, 42, 50, 55, 56, 59, 62, 63, 66, 67, 69, 70, 73, 75, 76, 78, 79, 80, 81, 83, 84, 85, 89, 90, 91, 94, 111, 113, 117, 123, 126, 127, 128, 130, 131, 133, 135, 137, 140, 141, 142, 144, 145, 147, 152, 156, 157; of objects 8, 12, 20, 25, 26, 30, 32, 36, 56, 61, 63, 64, 69, 96, 152
existentialist philosophers 6
EXON (existentialization) 5, 6, 7, 8, 9, 11, 12, 13, 14, 15, 21, 22, 23, 25, 26, 27, 29, 30, 31, 32, 36, 39, 43, 49, 50, 54, 55, 56, 61, 63, 65, 66, 69, 70, 74, 75, 77, 79, 80, 81, 84, 88, 89, 90, 91, 95, 96, 102, 104, 105, 106, 109, 110, 111, 113, 116, 117, 122, 125, 130, 131, 133, 135, 137, 142, 143, 144, 147, 152, 153, 154, 156, 157; assisted 55; perverted 80, 81; unassisted 55, 79, 80
EXON mechanism 106
EXON perspective 109, 122
EXON theory 11, 21, 29, 31, 39, 43, 50, 54, 74, 75, 80, 88, 89, 90, 109, 110, 111, 113, 117, 122, 125, 130, 131, 133, 142, 144, 147, 152

externality 14
EXUP (existential upgrade) 9, 23, 24, 25, 27, 64, 65, 66, 70, 81, 84, 85, 90, 91, 109, 111

faith 2, 3, 4, 7, 8, 22, 23, 25, 27, 32, 70, 72, 85, 93, 110, 120, 133, 135, 152, 153, 155, 156, 157, 158
fantastical entities 6, 21, 26, 53, 56, 57, 59, 60, 61, 62, 63, 69, 70, 84, 104, 105, 121, 137, 140
fantasy-reality distinction 70, 142, 150
forgetting: complete *vs.* temporary 144
Foucault, Michel 120, 124
Fowler, James W. 7
Freud, Sigmund 6

God 3, 8, 4, 6, 11, 21, 22, 23, 24, 25, 26, 27, 70, 72, 73, 74, 75, 76, 78, 80, 83, 84, 85, 86, 87, 93, 110, 112, 119, 120, 124, 133, 135, 145, 154, 155, 156, 157
God's existence 3, 24, 78, 80, 84
Goethe, Johann Wolfgang 108
Goya, Francisco 121

hallucinations 20, 33, 113, 114, 116, 119, 124, 157
hallucinatory phenomena 15
hallucinogenic drugs 118
Harry Potter series 148
hearing 115
Higg's boson 29
HLEXON (high level of existentialization) 9, 32, 36, 50, 51, 70, 73, 74, 75, 76, 77, 78, 80, 83, 84, 85, 89, 97, 114, 115, 117, 118, 119, 121, 123, 126, 128, 130, 138
hoarding disorder 28
Holy Inquisition 120
Homer 73, 122
Hyperself 131
hypnosis 27
Hypoself 131, 132, 133, 134

ideal objects 137
identity 12, 118; *see also* general properties
IE: sentities with incomplete existential status 6, 9, 82, 90
illusion 11, 15, 20, 27, 88, 89, 94, 113
illusory phenomena 15
imaginary objects 53
imaginary physical entities 53, 105
imaginary/perceived distinguisher (IPD) 8, 105
imagination 1, 2, 3, 6, 15, 21, 23, 36, 56,

59, 76, 77, 79, 82, 84, 89, 107, 115, 129, 137, 138, 139, 140, 151, 152, 155; creative 139
imagined physical objects 6, 53, 54, 56, 57, 58, 59, 61, 62, 104, 137, 140, 147
IMPE (impossible entities) 6, 9, 22, 25, 53, 135, 137, 138, 139, 140, 141, 142, 143, 144, 145, 146, 147, 148
improbable events 42
inclusion 12, 119; *see* general properties
individual 14
individual mind 6, 7
inferiority complex 112, 131
infinity 18, 73, 74
inhibitors 145
intermodality 14, 15, 32, 57, 90, 114
intersubjectivity 14, 32, 57, 90, 114, 117
IPD (imagined/perceived distinguisher) 8, 9, 57, 105, 153

James, William 124
Jaynes, Julian 121
Jones, Jim 94

Kandinsky, Victor 119, 120, 124
Kant, Immanuel 12, 22, 116, 148
Karmiloff–Smith, Annette 140
Kashpirovsky, Anatoly 94
Kierkegaard 6
Kinsbourne, M. 96
knowledge 3, 7, 15, 17, 20, 21, 24, 27, 56, 74, 75, 76, 89, 93, 104, 105, 115, 116, 120, 135, 142, 144, 151, 152, 153, 154, 157
Koresh, David 94

Lalonde, Christopher E. 54
Lauveng, Arnhild 120, 124
law of energy conservation 17
laws, of science 4, 13, 50, 52, 88, 107, 108, 110, 111, 120, 123, 133, 138, 147, 148
Lilly, John 132
locality 12, 119; *see* general properties
luminiferous aether 30

magic 7, 8, 9, 31, 36, 38, 39, 40, 42, 43, 44, 45, 46, 48, 50, 51, 52, 55, 57, 58, 60, 61, 62, 64, 65, 66, 68, 69, 70, 71, 73, 88, 89, 90, 91, 92, 93, 94, 95, 104, 106, 107, 108, 120, 121, 123, 139; real 43; true 43
magical behaviour 107
magical manipulations 31
magical participation 107, 118

magical suggestion 51, 61, 63, 64, 65, 66, 68, 70, 91, 93, 95, 120
magical system 106
magical thinking 52, 95, 107, 149
magic\ordinary distinguisher (MOD) 7, 8, 38
magic\trick distinguisher (MTD) 7, 8
Mann, Thomas 108
mass/energy equivalence 20
matter 3, 13, 21, 27, 29, 30, 33, 34, 43, 45, 54, 71, 73, 82, 107, 135, 148, 153, 157
May, Rollo 6
meaning of life 6, 134
memory 2, 3, 5, 6, 7, 20, 21, 27, 31, 34, 35, 53, 89, 93, 95, 96, 97, 99, 100, 101, 102, 116, 117, 138, 144, 145, 146, 148, 149, 153, 156, 157
mental eye 115, 116 17, 18, 20, 22, 27, 29, 32, 82, 89, 90, 116, 144
Michotte, Albert 36
mind 2, 3, 4, 5, 6, 7, 8, 11, 12, 13, 14, 15, 17, 20, 21, 22, 23, 24, 25, 27, 28, 29, 31, 32, 35, 38, 39, 45, 51, 52, 53, 55, 71, 73, 74, 75, 76, 77, 78, 79, 81, 84, 85, 86, 89, 90, 92, 93, 95, 99, 105, 107, 108, 110, 111, 112, 113, 114, 117, 118, 119, 121, 122, 123, 126, 127, 130, 132, 134, 135, 136, 137, 138, 144, 147, 148, 149, 151, 152, 153, 154, 155, 156; subjective experience 12, 115, 116
Minotaur 74
miracle 8, 37, 42, 89, 155
MOD (magic/ordinary distinguisher) 7, 8, 9, 38, 39, 40, 44, 45, 49, 104, 142, 143, 153
modes, of presentation 17, 20, 21, 23, 30, 32, 52, 86, 89, 90, 91, 135, 136
morality 75, 105, 122
MTD (magic/trick distinguisher) 7, 8, 9, 44, 46, 49, 57, 104, 153
Multiple Drafts Model 96
mystery 115

Napoleon 112
needs 116
neurons 115
night dreams 14, 108
Normaself 131
Nothing 11, 152, 157
Nothingness 9
NPE (non-permanent entity) 9, 31, 36, 37, 38, 39, 42

Index

obsessive-compulsive disorder (OCD) 108, 123
ontological argument 75, 76, 77, 78, 79, 80, 81, 82, 83, 84, 85
OP (object permanence) 9, 35, 36, 38, 39, 40, 43, 45, 48, 49, 50, 53, 54, 55, 56, 57, 61, 70, 82, 88, 89, 96, 97, 98, 101, 102, 104, 114, 137, 139, 140, 147, 148
OR (ordinary reality) 9, 31, 36, 37, 38, 44, 59, 61, 62, 90, 96, 102, 104, 105, 107, 109, 110, 111, 118, 120, 121, 122, 123, 129, 137
ordinary perceived objects 37, 48, 56, 57
ordinary suggestion 68

Palaeolithic cave art 119
palinopsia 113
Parkinson's disease 118
PE (perceived entity) 9, 36, 137, 139, 140, 141, 142, 143, 144, 145, 146, 147
perception 3, 4, 5, 6, 7, 8, 10, 15, 23, 25, 33, 35, 54, 89, 93, 95, 96, 99, 115, 116, 117, 119, 135, 138, 145, 148, 152, 153, 156, 158
perceptual illusions 27, 89, 113, 115
perfect entity 22, 84
permanence 9, 12, 14, 15, 30, 31, 34, 35, 36, 39, 52, 53, 54, 55, 58, 59, 61, 69, 71, 82, 87, 90, 96, 102, 104, 114, 118; see general properties
perpetual motion 17, 21
person, average 14, 118
phenomena 12, 13, 15, 116; magical 43; subjective experiences 8, 12, 13, 14, 15, 17, 18, 20, 21, 22, 23, 24, 28, 29, 30, 31, 32, 33, 34, 36, 37, 38, 43, 52, 54, 63, 73, 74, 85, 89, 94, 95, 102, 106, 113, 114, 115, 116, 117, 118, 119, 120, 122, 123, 124, 127, 134, 137, 140, 145, 153
phenomenon 12, 13, 14, 15, 17, 20, 22, 24, 27, 29, 32, 35, 36, 38, 43, 45, 48, 56, 82, 88, 89, 90, 93, 94, 110, 113, 114, 115, 118, 139, 144, 155
physical eye; see mental eye
physical laws 7, 30, 147
physical matter 116
physical mechanism; see magical system
physics 1, 3, 12, 28, 29, 33, 34, 88, 106, 107, 133, 138, 147, 157
Piaget, Jean 7, 10, 34, 35, 36, 38, 51, 71
PME (permanent entity) 9, 31, 36, 37, 38, 39, 42, 43, 45
PNE (personally not-significant entity) 9, 26, 51, 55, 56, 64

PNIME (personally not-significant imaginary entity) 9, 63, 64, 65, 66, 69, 70
Pollan, Michael 124
possible worlds 21
post-traumatic stress disorder (PTSD) 133
presenting phenomena 14
PSE (personally significant entity) 9, 26, 51, 55, 57, 64, 91, 109
PSIME (personally significant imaginary entity) 8, 9, 57, 62, 63, 64, 65, 66, 67, 69, 70, 84, 85, 93, 111, 120, 121
psychological tools 6, 138
psychology 6, 7, 8, 21, 33, 35, 71, 88, 89, 90, 106, 107, 108, 119, 122, 123, 124, 130, 145, 148, 149, 152, 155
Putin, Vladimir 94

qualia 12
quantum computers 74
quantum entanglement 21, 29, 153

Raskolnikov, Rodion 112
RC (rational construction) 9, 15, 17, 18, 20, 21, 22, 27, 29, 32, 56, 63, 89, 90, 91, 93, 113, 114, 115, 116, 117, 137, 138, 144
RD (realities distinguisher) 8, 9, 104, 105, 106, 107, 108, 109, 110, 111, 112, 113, 114, 115, 117, 118, 119, 120, 121, 122, 153
reality 1, 2, 3, 5, 6, 7, 8, 9, 11, 20, 23, 26, 31, 35, 36, 37, 42, 43, 53, 56, 61, 63, 70, 71, 73, 75, 77, 78, 86, 88, 91, 94, 95, 96, 97, 102, 104, 105, 107, 108, 110, 111, 117, 121, 122, 124, 125, 126, 128, 129, 136, 140, 142, 144, 148, 150, 156; types of 10, 15
recognition 145, 146, 149; immediate *vs.* delayed 145
religion 6, 8, 63, 71, 85, 87, 119, 120, 122
religious belief 7
religious extremism 110
religious radicalism 122
representation 14
representing phenomena 14, 15
ring of existence 90, 91, 142, 144
Rogers, Carl 6
Rowling, J.K. 148

Sacks, Oliver 33, 114, 115, 118, 124
Sartre, J.P. 6
scepticism 4, 73
Schneider, Kirk 6

science 1, 4, 5, 7, 8, 10, 17, 21, 28, 33, 34, 63, 71, 72, 73, 74, 85, 86, 87, 95, 105, 107, 110, 120, 121, 122, 124, 133, 135, 137, 138, 148, 149
science generated objects 20, 29
scientific concepts 15, 138, 143
scientific truths 4
SE (strong entity) 9, 78, 82, 83, 89, 90, 91, 145
Self 4, 5, 6, 8, 11, 12, 13, 14, 15, 17, 20, 21, 22, 23, 24, 25, 26, 28, 29, 30, 32, 33, 36, 54, 55, 70, 74, 84, 85, 96, 106, 109, 112, 113, 114, 116, 118, 122, 125, 126, 127, 128, 130, 131, 132, 133, 135, 152, 156, 157
self-awareness 6
Self-created entities 14, 15, 17
Self-created phenomena 14, 118
Self-related phenomena 15
sensations 3, 7, 31, 117, 131, 134
sensory deprivation 132, 133, 134
sensory deprivation chamber 132
simulating phenomena 15
Sisyphus 135
social suggestion 63
socio-cognitive deprivation 133
SOR (superordinary reality) 9, 31, 36, 37, 61, 62, 66, 102, 104, 105, 107, 109, 110, 111, 114, 115, 120, 121, 122, 123, 129, 147
space 115
Spong, John Shelby 72
spontaneous killing spree 110, 113, 122, 153
Stage magic 88, 89
Standard model 29
state of superposition 30
statuses of existence 20
subconscious 5, 89, 94, 97, 99, 108, 115, 132, 133, 144, 147, 157
subjective experiences 12, 15, 31, 95
suggestion: ordinary 63, 64, 65, 67; social 7, 8, 27, 31, 51, 55, 57, 59, 62, 65, 66, 67, 68, 69, 70, 71, 72, 73, 75, 76, 82, 84, 85, 90, 91, 93, 108, 109, 111, 123, 156
suggestive influence 64, 84
SUI (state of upgraded impossible) 9, 92, 93, 94, 95
suicidal terrorism 110, 122, 123, 153
superiority complex 112, 131

supernatural entities 26, 63, 85
supernatural event 42, 89
superordinary entity 70, 82
superordinary events 38, 42, 43, 48, 102, 107
supreme being 76
surrealistic painting 117
symbols 14
sympathy: magical 106, 107

tension of being the Self 131
Tertullian (155-240 AD) 3
theory of relativity 30
thing-in-itself 12
things-in-themselves 12, 13, 14, 116, 119, 133, 152
thought and being identity 125, 127, 128, 130, 151
time 12, 116
Torrance, E.P. 140
transcendental entities 23
transcendental objects 23
trick 7, 8, 9, 37, 39, 42, 43, 44, 45, 46, 48, 49, 54, 55, 57, 58, 64, 88, 89, 90, 91, 92, 93, 95, 97, 104, 119, 151
true magic 88, 90, 91, 93
truth 11, 25, 27

unidentified flying objects 18, 21
universe 33, 136, 157, 158
Upper Palaeolithic 105, 122

virtual culture 93
vision 115
visual cortex 115, 116
volition 5, 6
voluntary movement 18, 21, 27

Warhol, Andy 15
WE (weak entity) 9, 78, 82, 83, 89, 90, 91, 93, 145
Weinberg, Steven 29
witchcraft 67, 120, 122
wizard 42, 43, 76, 77, 79, 81, 82, 89, 139

Yalom, Irvin D. 6
Yeltsin, Boris 94

Zeno paradoxes 74